# PREFACE

SEVERAL circumstances have combined to retard the publication of these reminiscences of the epoch-making events which have opened a new chapter in Balkan history. Delay in such cases has its advantages. If some vivid impressions are lost, we are, on the other hand, able to correct too hastily drawn conclusions and to appreciate moves on the diplomatic chess-board which were, at the time, incomprehensible.

Many excellent and instructive books have been written on the Thracian campaign. Others have arrived to describe the experiences of war correspondents with one or other of the rival armies. I propose, however, to work along somewhat different lines. Stationed in the capital city of Macedonia, I was able to watch the rise and fall of Young Turkey, the temporary burial of the blood-stained Christian hatchets, the collapse of Ottoman civil and military power, the triumphal progress of the Greek, Servian and Bulgarian armies in Macedonia, the breakdown of the Balkan Alliance and the subsequent war between the quondam allies.

All these passing events I have sought to weave into a story. I have, as far as possible, avoided dry

v

military and historical detail, and though the soldier will find much that is instructive, and the historian much that is valuable in the succeeding pages, my object has primarily been to interest the "man in the street," and to bring him into closer touch with the fascinating tale of Macedonian strife.

If, with the facts before me, I have had occasion to somewhat severely criticise the Bulgarians, I beg them remember that they have so long feasted upon praise and flattery, that they must not complain if I have found it necessary to suggest that their actions have not always been in keeping with what one had been led to expect from Christian conquerors. To render justice is often to condemn, and if, as I believe, my statements cannot be disproved, then I submit that my criticism has been both fair and merited.

The Turks, too, must realise that the motive of this book has necessitated my pointing out their failures and not their virtues. The Constitutionalists did many good things, but these were not instrumental in bringing about the Balkan War. "The evil that men do lives after them; the good is oft interred with their bones." Many of us have reason to regret the departure of old and dear Turkish friends, and our regret will—if I mistake not—be shared by many among the Christian populations of Thrace and Macedonia who will henceforth live under alien rule.

Greeks and Servians will find little that is unpleasant in my criticisms. That result is again due

# THE BALKAN COCKPIT

## THE POLITICAL AND MILITARY STORY OF THE BALKAN WARS IN MACEDONIA

BY

### W. H. CRAWFURD PRICE

WITH AUTOGRAPHED PHOTOGRAPHS AND MANY ILLUSTRATIONS BY H.R.H. PRINCE NICHOLAS OF GREECE AND THE AUTHOR, AND SPECIALLY DRAWN MAPS OF THE MILITARY OPERATIONS.

to themselves rather than to any desire on my part to mete out more sympathetic treatment. Neither were faultless. Both had to deal with an enormous and unexpected extension of territory, and "war is hell." But, on the whole, they carried through their difficult task with highly commendable ability and humanity, and their conduct inevitably stands out in sharp contrast to that of their neighbours.

My acknowledgments are due to my journal for the use of extracts from my dispatches.

C. P.

[NOTE.—*The author had no opportunity of correcting the proofs of this book, as he was at the war while it was being printed.*]

# CONTENTS

ix

# CONTENTS

# LIST OF ILLUSTRATIONS

# THE BALKAN COCKPIT

## CHAPTER I

### THE CONSTITUTIONAL REGIME IN TURKEY

THOUGH the "Star and Crescent" had floated for centuries over the Government offices, though fez-crowned governors meted out Oriental justice in the Turkish tongue, and though, in town and country, the evidences of power denoted the supreme place held by the Moslems, it must not be supposed that the subject races of Macedonia ever considered these other than the signs of a temporary occupation, or that they failed to ceaselessly work, pray, and agitate for the day when, to their certain belief, the Turk should be sent back to Asia. Nor is it possible to dissociate these ideas of territorial expansion from the critical situation which continued to exist in the Orient until the Balkan War sealed the fate of Mohammedan power in Europe. The Christian races hated the Turk, who, knowing this, not only strove to safeguard his position, but further sought to impress upon his neighbours a due appreciation of his predominant force. The attitude of Bulgaria and Greece to Turkey was irrevocably bound up with the relations of their co-religionists to their governors within the Ottoman Empire itself.

When, in November, 1908, the first delegates to the new Ottoman Parliament arrived at Constantinople, Constitutionalism ran riot. I heard Moslem deputies speak of the glorious events that had ushered in an era of equality for all the myriad races of the Empire. I saw turbaned Turkish Hodjas, smock-frocked Greek and Bulgarian priests, and gabadined Jewish Rabbis unitedly heading triumphal processions, the while the air was rent with shouts of " Brotherhood."

Two years later one could have safely said that whatever conscientious endeavour the Turks may have put forth to act up to their fraternal promises, their efforts had been singularly unsuccessful. It may be held that their actions were misinterpreted; it may be advanced that, do what they might, the Mohammedans could never have convinced their fellow-citizens of the honesty of their intentions; but the fact remains that ere twenty-four fleeting months had passed, inter-religious strife was more acute, and the mutual mistrust of Moslem and Christian was, if anything, greater than before the Constitution. There was evident an entire lack of confidence which even the Turks no longer attempted to conceal. During the summer of 1910, in explaining the Government's point of view to me, the unseen head of the Young Turkish Party informed me that they wanted the Christians to look upon them as a " Paternal Government." The vital importance of the admission doubtless escaped him, but I was forcibly impressed by the difference

A RETROSPECT.
King Peter at Salonika during the Turkish Regime

between a "Paternal Government" and the "Brotherhood" of which I had heard so much two years previously.

Yet a further departure from the paths of Constitutionalism was indicated in the statement made to me about the same time by a highly placed official that "Macedonia has always been held by force, and we too must hold it by force." Young Turkish policy had already confirmed this attitude, and the Christian races had received abundant proofs that the Mussulmans intended to be recognised as masters in their own country.

I have always held that Europe was in a very large measure responsible for the deplorable travesty of Constitutional Government offered by the Committee of Union and Progress. The slave elevated to power becomes often the worst of tyrants; the youth pushed into position beyond his years anon develops an overbearing manner; the uneducated, sufficiently flattered, startle mankind by their arrogance. As with individuals, so with communities. The mere organisation of a bloodless revolution did not transform an intelligent telegraph clerk into a wise Minister of the Interior, or an eloquent schoolmaster into a sagacious Minister of Finance, any more than the course of history was changed by the mere act of overthrowing a despot and setting up parliamentary government in his stead. The Young Turks lacked experience, and it is little wonder that they lost their heads. The fault lay not so much with them as with the Europe which flatteringly hailed them as twentieth-century reformers, dubbed them "Gladstones," "Bismarcks,"

"Napoleons," and the like, and gave over unreservedly a mighty, complex empire into their
inexperienced hands.    With a criminal disregard
for the lessons of recent history, European statesmen
put on rose-coloured spectacles, reclined on diplomatic divans, and saw little save prospective valuable
commercial concessions in the smoke which curled
from the Ottoman " hubble-bubble."

Enthusiasm got the better of judgment.    The
unconditional acceptance of the new order of things
by the Powers, the fatal surrender of International
control in Macedonia and the increased power
vested in an untried Constitution, were no less
unfortunate for the Young Turks than for the
populations which they were so suddenly called upon
to govern.   If, while welcoming the step in advance
taken by Turkish democracy, and while manifesting
a paternal interest in the development of Constitutional Government, the Powers had not only maintained but temporarily strengthened their control
over the gendarmery and the financial administration
of Macedonia, the story might have had a different
ending.   The gendarmery, following the withdrawal
of executive control from its foreign officers just as
it was developing into a useful, crime-preventing
body, went rapidly to pieces until little was left of
it save the uniform.   The benefits of the financial
control were, in a large measure, preserved only by
the transference of the International Commissioners
to the Turkish Ministry of Finance.   In short, at
this stage, Europe should have insisted upon the
appointment of Advisors with executive authority to
aid the young, inexperienced Ottomans to carry on

the administration of the country in a constitutional manner. The Turks should have been given clearly to understand that they were on their trial and that their new government was accepted on approval only.

Instead of this, chauvinism was allowed to get the upper hand. The young Orientals, with a thin veneer of Parisian mondainity or Berlin militarism, were puffed up until their heads swelled to bursting point, and we heard little save talk of the abolition of the Capitulations, the Turkification of the Christian races and the progressive recapture of all the lands over which the "Star and Crescent" had once floated. I well remember, in the fall of 1908, travelling to Constantinople in company with a young officer, who described to me how Greece, Bulgaria, Servia, Egypt, Tunis and Morocco were soon to become once again part of the Ottoman Empire.

"And Spain," I queried, "are you not going to retake the old Moorish kingdom?"

"Yavash, yavash" (meaning in this sense "little by little"), he answered. "We cannot do it all at once."

It cannot be gainsaid that the Christian Macedonians while, as has already been stated, clinging to their Utopia of emancipation, at first accepted the promises of the Young Turks at their face value. The spectacle of rival "komitadji" leaders hugging one another in the streets of Salonika was absurdly picturesque, but it manifested the desire of the Macedonians to live at peace with one another and with the Constitutionalists. They thought that

" Liberty, Fraternity, and Equality " really meant
" Liberty, Fraternity, and Equality." They discovered their mistake long before it dawned upon
a trusting Europe.  The elections proved the first
awakening.  While I sympathised with the Young
Turks in their determination to keep the power in
their own hands in the first representative Chamber,
the Christian view of Mussulman ideas of " Equality "
received a rude shock when it found districts divided
up in a wholly illogical manner and the elections
scientifically farmed in order to ensure the return
of a majority of Mohammedan deputies.

# CHAPTER II

## THE NURSERY OF DISCONTENT

UNIVERSAL MILITARY SERVICE.—The first really great blunder of the Young Turks, however, was the enlistment of Christians in the army. The Government's position was a somewhat difficult one. There was, in some directions, a demand on the part of the Christians to enjoy what they were pleased to call, for some unaccountable reason, "the right of serving their country." Many leading Young Turks, on the other hand, offered a determined opposition to the movement. Some distrusted the Christians; others feared the obvious unpopularity of the scheme. My own opinion, often expressed to the Committee leaders, was that the change was inadvisable on account of its radical nature, and I favoured the fixing of a time limit which would have delayed the application of universal service to the non-Mussulmans until the next generation, schooled in the new-born idea of civil brotherhood, had reached an age at which it could be called upon to bear arms. The no-compromise party gained the day, however, and the Constitution was subjected to its first real strain, as a result of which its vitality was considerably weakened.

7

Little attention need be paid to stories of alleged ill-treatment of the non-Mussulman recruits (though the reports current at the time were by no means unfounded), but the Christian enjoys a somewhat higher standard of living than the Moslem, and the conditions under which masses of men are herded together in the Turkish army are frankly unattractive. Further, the average Mussulman soldier is so docile a creature that the sudden appearance of a stubborn Bulgar or an argumentative Greek in the ranks must have sorely tried the patience of many an old-fashioned Ottoman officer. Generally speaking, however, Turkish military men proved themselves much more tolerant than the civil officials, and it was not unfitting that the subsequent opposition to Young Turkism should have had its origin in the army.

But the conscription of non-Mussulmans was attended by consequences more immediately serious than the mere fomentation of discontent. Rather than join the Ottoman colours, thousands of young Christians—the very flower of Macedonia manhood —left factory, or field, or flock, and fled, the more honest of them to other climes, the rest to the mountains, there to augment the bands of political "komitadji," or highway robbers, with which the country-side was already infested. For a land already suffering acutely from a shortage of labour, the emigration of able-bodied youths was the more serious development. It still further diminished the yield of a magnificent agricultural country which, although under-populated, was nevertheless incapable of accomplishing the primitive task of feeding itself. It meant a heavy addition to the already large percentage of uncultivated land; it brought in its train increased poverty, and prepared the *terrain* for that revolutionary propaganda which so very quickly followed.

It might have been expected that the gravity of this result of their lack of foresight would have been sufficiently obvious to have warranted the application of immediate remedial measures by the Young Turks. Strange as it may appear, however, the movement gave intense satisfaction to the more powerful and chauvinistic wing of the party. Dr Nazim Bey informed me with great enthusiasm that 1200 young Greeks had quitted the Island of Lemnos alone in order to escape service in the Ottoman army, and wagged his head, wisdom-wise, when he added that this exodus would be a benefit to the Empire.

" Why ? "

" Well, because they will be replaced by Mussulmans from Bosnia ! "

Those self-same Bosnians whom a Turkish Valli of Salonika had some few days previously characterised as "dirty and lazy." Empire-building, according to the most powerful wire-puller in the Committee of Union and Progress, consisted in the driving out of bodies of young, strong, intelligent natives, and the substitution in their stead of lazy, dirty, feeble, dull-witted aliens, incapable even of speaking the language of their adopted country.

THE BOSNIAN IMMIGRATION.—The normal unfolding of our story has brought us to the Bosnian

Immigration Scheme which, while it exercised but little influence upon the march of events, is instructive in that it gives us an additional insight into Young Turk methods. It therefore warrants a passing attention. The importation of the Bosnian " Mohadjirs " was a serious attempt on the part of the chauvinist section of the Committee to " settle " the Macedonian question. The argument was, in brief, as follows :

In Macedonia to-day there are more Christians than Mussulmans. If we can increase the Mohammedan population until the followers of the prophet are in the majority, the infidels will be overpowered, and the " question " will automatically disappear. This method of reasoning was somewhat original, hardly statesmanlike, and frankly unconstitutional. But it triumphed without encountering serious opposition, and then began the immigration of the dregs of Bosnia. I call them " dregs " advisedly, because no Bosnian worth anything in his own country would have dreamt of emigrating to Macedonia, even after he had listened to the enticing word-picture of Koranic bliss drawn for him by the silver-tongued emissaries of the Committee.

Many thousands of the lower order of Bosnian Mussulmans were, however, induced to pack up their rugs and coffee pots and come over into Turkey. For the furtherance of this propaganda enormous sums of money were expended from the private funds of the Committee, and the Government, while too poor to hand over a whittled-down pittance for the support of the widows and orphans of the Adana massacres, yet felt itself sufficiently

GREEK TOBACCO GROWERS IN MACEDONIA.

MACEDONIAN VALACH PEASANTS.

rich to vote fortunes in aid of this new patriotic adventure. The " Mohadjirs" themselves, when they arrived, were dumped down often with a total disregard for their own needs or those of the district which received them, and an attempt was made to keep them alive by doles of money wholly insufficient for even their meagre requirements. Once enticed to Macedonia, no adequate arrangements were made either for their present or future well-being, with the natural consequence that numbers of the immigrants subsequently returned to Bosnia at the expense of the Austrian Government. Many of those who remained found it necessary to steal to live, and some of them, caught in the act of stealing, degenerated to murder. I have already sufficiently enumerated their qualities to make it clear that they were anything but desirable citizens, and it is not unfitting that a large proportion of them should have been numbered among the refugees who, at a later date, fled before the Bulgarian advance, and that they should thereafter have been kept alive for months by funds subscribed for that purpose by the charitable public of Europe. The observant passer-by in Salonika might frequently, during the period following the Turkish war, have seen an Austrian Lloyd liner anchored off the Austrian Consulate General, and had he troubled to ask, he would have learned that those boat-loads of destitute humanity whom he saw being rowed off to the steamer were the last of Dr Nazim Bey's " Mohadjirs" going back to their native Bosnia.

THE DISARMAMENT.—The disarmament of the Macedonian population in 1910 had preceded some

of the phases of the constitutional regime which we
have already considered, but it exercised so paramount an influence upon subsequent events and was
so essentially the genesis of the Balkan League,
that it demands special consideration at our
hands.

It cannot be denied that, in principle, the disarmament of the Macedonian peasantry was a most
necessary measure.  When the Young Turks took
up the reins of government they inherited a terrorised
country in which every peasant was a walking
arsenal.  Men, armed by the Revolutionary Committees, went their way with their " Mannlicher "
or " Gras " slung over their backs, and bands of
murderous ruffians infested the mountains, seeking
every opportunity for slaughter and pillage.  Peaceful inhabitants lived under a reign of terror, and,
on many occasions, when journeying in the interior,
have I passed along a blood-stained defile where a
group of unfortunate peasants had met their death
from bandits' bullets fired from the heights above.
As a measure to establish security of life in the
country, the disarmament was therefore an admirable conception.

While the Turkish Government should be credited
with an honest desire to suppress banditism and outrage, it is undeniable that they were infinitely more
concerned by the presence in Macedonia of a mass
of armed Christian peasantry who were terrorised by
their revolutionary leaders.  The Porte determined
to neutralise these possible auxiliaries in the event
of a war with Bulgaria or Greece, and therefore
prosecuted the disarmament more vigorously than

would have been the case had its sole concern been the establishment of a greater measure of public security.

The Greeks gave little trouble. There was some obstinate resistance at Naoussa—an aforetime Greek revolutionary centre where very harsh measures were resorted to by the authorities—but, in general, the Hellenes delivered up their arms and went back to their farms doubtless rejoicing in the prospect of a more peaceful existence.

The disarmament of the Bulgarians, however, offered a much more serious problem. While the Greeks dreamt little of conquest, and very largely contented themselves with the measures necessary for the preservation of their own Hellenic colonies, the Bulgars were playing for bigger stakes. Bad Turkish government was to be made worse, European intervention was to be provoked, Macedonian autonomy was to be established, and the autonomous state was subsequently to be effectually Bulgarised so that, upon the expected decomposition of the Ottoman Empire, the autonomy would be forthwith incorporated in the Bulgarian kingdom. Consequently their organisation, directed from Sofia, was more perfect and obstinate. Bands had again been organised in the interior, others had crossed the frontier from Bulgaria, and even the redoubtable ruffian, Sandansky—that specialist in Macedonian murder—had once more taken to the mountains with his companions. Moreover, the Bulgarian "komitadji" leaders had carried on a most prosperous business in forcing the peasantry to buy rifles at prices vastly in excess of the market value. Look-

ing at the matter from a personal standpoint they
saw not only a possible check to their ideas of
territorial expansion, but the cessation of a profitable
gun-running enterprise.    The unfortunate Bulgar
peasants therefore found themselves between two
fires.    On the one hand, their own revolutionary
leaders threatened them with summary massacre if
they yielded their weapons, and, on the other hand,
the Turkish authorities rewarded obstinate resistance
to surrender with a particularly severe beating.
Proofs are not lacking that the Turks went to severe
lengths—some of their victims were undoubtedly
beaten to death—but the harrowing stories of brutal
cruelty that were issued from Bulgarian sources
should not have been unreservedly accepted.    The
Turk is consistently held up as the personification
of human devilry, but it is questionable whether the
punishment meted out by Turkish gendarmes ever
matched the savagery of the Bulgarian " voivodes."
Within two hours of Salonika, a Bulgarian priest,
who had counselled his flock to surrender their arms,
was found brutally murdered.    On his breast was
pinned a letter which promised a similar fate to any
others who might be tempted to comply with the
demand of the authorities.    Again, near Uskub,
four Bulgars who were found guilty of recommend-
ing voluntary disarmament to their friends and
families were marched into a forest and well-nigh
hacked to pieces.    Had Turkish gendarmes committed these and similar deeds the world would have
rung with tales of their infamy.

Where the Government showed its hand and
rendered the entire campaign unjustifiable was in

its failure to methodically disarm the Moslems. It is impossible for one to speak for the whole of Macedonia, but where I was able to investigate, I found that in some cases the Mohammedans had been disarmed and publicly beaten; in others they had not only been left in possession of their guns, but the rifles taken from Christians had actually been served out to Moslem villages and to the Moslem immigrants from Bosnia and Hertzogovina.

Although the authorities collected a considerable number of firearms—mostly obsolete—they succeeded in convincing the Christian population that all hope of constitutional treatment must forthwith be abandoned. The Young Turks thereby forged a weapon for their own destruction, more potent than the hidden rifles of Christian Ottomans.

THE GROWTH OF ANARCHY.—In the meantime, further difficulties confronted those genuine reformers who possessed any influence with the Committee. Chief among these was the necessity of maintaining in harness the administrative *personnel* of the old regime. The Young Turks were driven to the hazardous experiment of putting new wine into old bottles. While they had found it possible to form a Ministry by availing themselves of the services of some prominent deserters from the Hamidian ranks and, for the rest, by fitting a number of square pegs into round holes, they were compelled to maintain in office the provincial governors of despotic days. For the old Turkish " Mutessarif" could not change his skin, nor the " Kaimakam " his spots. On the other hand, these men, actuated by a sense of self-preservation, joined the ranks of the Committee, and then helped to build up a secret bureaucracy which laid the foundation of many of the ills from which Turkey-in-Europe subsequently suffered. The Committee had displaced the Caliphat as the power in the land. Its provincial branches speedily became the real rulers of the country and its protégés enjoyed a complete immunity from the law.

THE COMMITTEE BANDS.—When the Christians began to show signs that the Turkification of Macedonia was not to be accomplished without opposition, drastic measures were applied with the object of coercing the population into its acceptance. It would perhaps be an exaggeration to say that the purpose of the Committee was to remove from the sphere of earthly politics all Christians who refused to bend the knee to the Mohammedan Baal. There were, nevertheless, grounds for suggesting that the Committee of Union and Progress was shepherding a movement which had for its purpose the extermination not only of the old Christian nationalist leaders, but of those also who seemed to have been marked out as possible chiefs of the opposition to Ottoman chauvinism. At one time there existed in the vilayet of Salonika alone no less than seven bands, all Turks, and all carrying on their murderous work with a tolerance on the part of the authorities which amounted to direct encouragement.

THE TYRANNY OF THE LOCAL COMMITTEES.—The Government, as a Government, completely lost control of Macedonia, with the consequence that constitutional rights became non-existent. Justice was unknown, the peasantry were killed off like flies, and oppression was practised on every hand. I credit the cabinet with an honest desire to put an end to this disorder, but the unfortunate truth is that they were but a hopelessly incompetent collection of ministers endeavouring to administer a country with a tribe of indifferent and fanatical governors who, for the most part, recognised no authority save that of the local Committee of Union and Progress.

Truly, the last state of the Macedonian house was worse than the first. Hamid had been a tyrant, avaricious and cruel, but there was only one of him. In his place there were set up two hundred Hamids in the shape of the local Young Turk Committees who ruled the people with an absolutism, a cruelty and an injustice which would have been worthy of the great despot himself. The hated restraint of Hilmi Pacha's inspection, the supervision of the European Commissioners, and the foreign gendarmery officers, were gone. The Turkish officials understood that the Constitution meant government by the Turks and for the Turks. With the fall of Hamid they preconceived the disappearance of authority, except in so far as they themselves chose to exercise it. They could never quite grasp the idea that a Christian is the equal of a Mussulman. Their history, life and mentality opposed the very idea of equality, with the result that when a Turk murdered a Christian, the chances were that the assassin went unpunished. If, in the first days of the Constitution, a hue and cry had been raised after every murderer, were he Moslem or Christian, the probabilities are that crime could have been kept

B

within normal limits; but once it was shown that the Mussulman could shoot and steal with impunity, it is small wonder that assassination and robbery increased with alarming rapidity.

One of the most disgraceful pages of the history of murder in Macedonia is that concerning Langazar —a district situated a matter of two hours from Salonika—where, during the month of October, 1911, alone, there were no less than twenty-seven assassinations by unknown murderers. Here Greek after Greek fell victim to knife or bullet, until a list had been built up sufficient to condemn any Government to capital punishment. At one time four Turkish bands were known to be roaming the region. The motive of this wholesale slaughter could not well have been other than political, for the corpses were, for the most part, found by the roadside, free from any evidence of attempted robbery. None of the murderers was discovered, and so notable became the scandal that, following a triple assassination, the Governor-General of Salonika—a subsequent Young Turk Minister of Justice—went down to make a personal investigation. As a result, he came to the astonishing conclusion that the assassination of the Greeks had been carried out by organised Greek bands with the object of discrediting the Turkish administration in the eyes of Europe! A Parliamentary Commission which subsequently visited Langazar found, however, that the outrages had been committed chiefly by Turkish bands; that, though no arrests had been made, men upon whom the gravest suspicion rested were perambulating freely in the streets; and that the authorities had been

A BULGAR-MACEDONIAN SCHOOL AT POZAR.

ALBANIAN VOLUNTEERS.

.

guilty of negligence in failing to lay hands upon the murderers. And Langazar was but a notable example of the condition of the rest of Macedonia. Can it be wondered at then that discontent was rife, and that the weary, persecuted Christian peasant sighed for the days of Abdul Hamid?

# CHAPTER III

## THE BEGINNING OF THE END

THE SPREAD OF ANARCHY.—1911 was a bad year for the Young Turks. The war with Italy was draining the national exchequer and exciting the Balkan States; anarchy had laid hold of Macedonia; the general situation in the province had become untenable. There was an entire absence of security for life and property; pillage and murder were rife, and the authorities proved incapable of controlling the lawlessness which sprang up on every hand. Within a stone's throw of Salonika the rural population was so terrorised that at sunset each family barricaded itself within its own house. Cattle were left untended, fields went uncultivated, and business visits to market were suspended until bodies of twenty to twenty-five peasants were ready to make the journey *en masse*.

The Government's eleventh hour quack remedy for this appalling condition of the country was the dispatch of flying companies of gendarmes, who passed from village to village, exhorting the Mussulman and Christian populations to live in peace and concord. But no attempt was made to grapple with the root of the evil, with the result that the Committee of Union and Progress succeeded in accomplishing the seemingly impossible. It united Greek and Bulgar, these aforetime irreconcilable enemies whose natural hatred the one for the other had been sedulously fanned by Hamid. Thus were sown the seeds of the Balkan League. True, the Young Turks did make an effort to use the Valach propaganda as a weapon with which to oppress the Greeks and thereby prevent a *rapprochement* between those closely allied races, but the attempt was crude both in its conception and application. Some Greeks were beaten to death, others were threatened with a similar fate, and the danger of putting a stick into the hands of a barbarian even if his character happens to be hidden underneath a gendarmery uniform, was clearly demonstrated.

BULGARIAN ACTIVITY.—The citation of events in strictly chronological order is impossible if the reader is to obtain a concise idea of the importance of each of the divers movements which had for their result the downfall of Young Turkism, and it must be borne in mind that throughout practically the whole of the period with which this chapter deals the Bulgarians were seeking, by means of their revolutionary organisation, to render life in Macedonia more intolerable than even the Turks had succeeded in making it, with the unique object of encouraging European intervention. It must be admitted that some demonstration had become necessary in order to awaken the Government to a sense of its responsibility. Banditism and " Bombism " steadily increased during the year 1911 until, in the month of November, the old Bulgarian Revolutionary

Committee issued a memorandum which was forwarded to the representatives of the Great Powers and which foreshadowed a recommencement of its activities. Despite the strengthening of the frontier guards, hostile bands crossed from Bulgaria in large numbers. Three bomb outrages on the railway and a mosque wrecked by a dynamite explosion, followed by a massacre, provided an effective commencement, and there was every evidence to show that the organisers were acting according to a well-arranged programme. Despite constant patrolling, the discovery of bombs on the railway line was of daily occurrence, and outrages were planned and executed with more or less success.

It gives an instructive insight into the determination which characterised this Bulgarian propaganda to observe that the avowed object of the outrages was to incite the Turks to a massacre of Christians and thus to provoke European intervention. The responsibility for the Istib and Kotchana massacres lay not with the Ottoman authorities but with the Bulgarian organisation which deliberately planned them, and the cruel sacrifice of Moslem and Christian life thus occasioned robbed the cause of much of the sympathy it would otherwise have enjoyed. Though the situation was chronically abnormal in Macedonia, much additional suffering was caused by the methods adopted by the Revolutionary Committee to enforce its programme upon the peasantry, and some of the most revolting crimes of the period were perpetrated by Bulgarian bands against their own kith and kin who refused to lend their support to the new propaganda.

DISAFFECTION IN THE ARMY.—It had, nevertheless, become plainly evident that the policy of the Young Turks had most dismally failed. The attempts at Turkification had been disastrous, and it is questionable whether it would not at that time have been too late to inaugurate a scheme of federal government. In any case, however, the Committee of Union and Progress was disinclined to admit any such proposition. They probably realised that every Christian race in Turkey was intellectually superior to them, and that, given an equal chance all round, the Turk would soon become little better than a hireling. For this reason they turned their attention with redoubled energy to the creation of a strong, all-powerful army, and practically admitted that all the fervent talk of " Liberty, Fraternity, and Equality " had been nothing more than a gigantic oratorial sandbag hurled in the eyes of a gullible Europe.

But, unfortunately for the Salonika clique, the army, upon which they ever counted for their existence, was already divided against itself. True, the officers at Salonika remained loyal to the Committee. Following his quarrel with the Young Turks, the late Mahmoud Chefket Pacha had appointed two anti-Committee generals, Hassan Tahsin Pacha and Enver Pacha, as Commandants of the 5th Army Corps and the Salonika Division respectively; but when, in order to preserve his position as the Minister of War, the future Grand Vizier was forced to come to heel, these two officers were replaced by junior generals known to be fervent partisans of the party then in power.

Further afield, however, the rot had set in, and

the defection from the ranks of the Committee became as noticeable in military as in civil circles. The most trustworthy evidence of the then existing frame of mind can be obtained from the tenor of a communication forwarded at the end of 1911 to the Grand Vizier and the President of the Chamber by the corps of officers stationed as far apart as Yanina, Monastir and Scutari respectively. The fact that the document from these three isolated points was drawn up in more or less identical terms, suggests that the anti-Committee movement in the army had already been carefully organised. It read as follows:

" For some time we have been carefully watching your *marche-a-faux-pas*, and notice that, despite your oath, you fail to fulfil your promises. Of late the representatives of the nation have occupied themselves solely with their personal quarrels and are thereby conducting the Empire to decay and ruin. If you do not put a stop to this strife between ' interested ' persons, we warn you that at the end of the year, we, the undersigned *officers* of the army, will proceed to Constantinople and settle our account with you personally."

Very little attention was paid to this warning. Perhaps it was that the executive of the Committee was too busy with the quarrels in its own camp. These were of a remarkable nature, and developed with extraordinary vigour, particularly at Monastir, where the party split up into two sections, each of which possessed its own organisation and ran its own newspaper. Even the visits of Enver Bey and other idolised patriots failed to bring the rivals to reason. However, after several partisans had been murdered the difficulties were smoothed over, but not before the system as a whole had been sapped of much of its vitality.

THE ENTENTE LIBERALE.—Prior to this development of dissention in the army and in the ranks of the Committee itself, thoughtful Turks had begun to think. It had become evident to many that if the Empire was to be saved from disruption some effort must be made to crush the Young Turk despotism. On all hands influential Mussulmans began to withdraw their support, and the masses were no longer at the beck and call of their former masters. Thus, largely owing to the initiative of Sadik Bey, a party designated the "Entente Liberale" was formed. The object of the new party was to gather together under one banner all the discontented elements in the Empire, and it produced a programme designed to satisfy Young Turks and Old Turks, Greeks and Bulgars, Kurds and Armenians, and, in fact, to reconcile the irreconcilable. It had as many planks as there were parties, and promised everybody everything. As a programme for an Opposition it was perhaps ideal, but it could never have been put into execution by a Government. It served a useful and necessary purpose, however, in providing a standard around which discontented Turks, Greeks, Bulgars, Armenians and the rest could rally, and, like all party programmes, was capable of amendment.

The "Entente Liberale" found the future Christian section of its party ready made. The political inexperience and successive mistakes of the Young Turks had, as we have already observed, thrown Greeks and Bulgars into one another's arms, and the Greek members of the Ottoman Chamber took in hand the elaboration of a programme establishing in a clear and precise manner the means of restoring peace in Turkey, and assuring the existence of the divers nationalities. This programme was immediately accepted by all the Christian peoples of the Empire, and a permanent Committee was formed on which were represented the Greek and Armenian Patriarchs, the Bulgarian Exarch, the Serbs, the Armenians and the Arab Christians. In May, 1911, all these sections delivered notes, couched in identical terms, to the Sublime Porte demanding the acceptance of their common programme. This programme was, at a later date, adopted by the " Entente Liberale " party, to which the majority of the Mussulman population, disgusted by Young Turk methods and failures, had by this time adhered.

THE SECOND ELECTIONS.—Preparations were at once begun with the object of defeating the Committee at the general elections which were now within sight. Provincial clubs were founded under the presidency of Turkish " intellectuals," and the support of the Moslem priesthood was very largely secured. The executive apportioned the number of seats which were to be allotted to each section of the party and thereby removed the possibility of future friction on that account. Since the division of seats as between Greeks and Bulgarians is a factor of considerable importance in the discussion of the differences between allies which arose as a result of the subsequent overwhelming defeat of the Osmanli, the agreement then arrived at is worthy of our attention. The document exchanged between the Greek and Bulgarian deputies of the first Ottoman Chamber and signed, on the one hand by the representatives of the Greek members and the Counsellors of the Patriarchate, and on the other by the representatives of the Bulgarian members and the Counsellors of the Bulgarian Exarchate, allotted five seats to the Bulgarians in Macedonia and only one in Thrace. The Greeks, by reason of their numerical superiority, received eight seats in Macedonia and seven in Thrace. We omit the three Greek seats in Constantinople and the four in Epirus as they bear no relation to future discussion between the two races. It would seem established, therefore, that in the year 1911 the Bulgars did credit the Hellenes with a considerable superiority in point of population both in Macedonia and in Thrace.

On the eve of the elections for the second Ottoman Chamber the Young Turks were quite aware that their position was precarious and they accordingly made up their minds, by fair means or foul, to maintain if not to increase their supremacy. There was early evidence of a determination on their part to use the power which possession of the administration placed in their hands to hinder, menace and intimidate all opposition. The Turkish electoral system lending itself to easy manipulation, bunches of Christian villages were split up and severally attached to outlying districts where a Turkish majority was to be found. The Vallis, Mutessarifs, Caimakams and Commandants of gendarmery—all nominees of the Committee—were called upon to use their influence in favour of the party to which they owed their positions. The secrecy of the ballot went unrespected, and despite the official alliance of the Ulema with the " Entente Liberale," the Mussulman vote was split to the advantage of the Committee. At the polling booths the presence of large numbers of police and army officers served to strike an initial fear into the hearts of the voters, ballot papers were numbered in order that the votes could afterwards be controlled, agents of the Committee tossed bundles of ready-filled voting papers into the boxes, and every description of pressure was applied to ensure the election of the Young Turk candidates. The result of these manœuvres was the return of a Union and Progress Government to office by a huge majority, but the Christian population had at length understood the determination of the Moslems to keep the power in their own hands and had become convinced that the watchword of the young champions of Constitutionalism was " Turkey for the Turks."

# CHAPTER IV

## " VERS LA GUERRE "

THE LAST ALBANIAN RISING.—Nowhere were the methods which the Young Turks had adopted to secure a majority in the new Parliament more resented than in Albania, and the elections were barely finished when the murmur of general discontent rolled over the northern hills like the thunder of mighty cannon. Hadji Adil Bey, the new Minister of the Interior, was sent through the province on a tour of inspection, and the enthusiastic receptions (made to order) received by his commission and the fervent telegrams of loyalty forwarded to the Grand Vizier, apparently blinded the Government to the real state of the country. Early in May, 1912, however, the embers of revolution began to glow; troops were rushed north, while the rebels threatened to loot the depots of arms which had been provided with the object of arming the Mussulmans in the event of war or a rising on the part of the Christian tribes.

The revolution spread with startling rapidity, and the Government responded with promises of reform and the dispatch of an adequate punitive force. The Albanians sneered at the one and defied the other. After a cleverly worked political intrigue had led to

a refusal on the part of some of the troops to fire
on their Moslem brothers, and orders to attack Issa
Boletinatz had gone unexecuted, an *entente* was
established between the rebels and the army at
Djacova, from whence threatening telegrams were
forwarded to the Sultan in the name of the civil and
military populations.

Though these communications never reached the
Caliph, they were not altogether ineffective, for
the Government now consented to the dispatch of a
parliamentary commission to investigate the alleged
grievances, and an armistice was agreed to by the
rebels. A few days later (July, 1912), Said Pacha's
Committee Government resigned office, and Kiamil
Pacha and the Old Turks found themselves called
upon again to take charge of the destinies of the
Empire.

The first act of the elder statesmen was to issue a
proclamation by the Sultan to the Albanians, in which
the shedding of blood between *frères fidèles* was
prohibited when questions involving the existence
of the Empire were not at stake. The hillmen
were accordingly beseeched not to provoke punitive
action by the army, and were promised a Cabinet
composed of practical, impartial statesmen who
would be imperially charged to act justly towards the
Albanian reclamations. Having drawn first blood,
however, the rebels, whose leaders were now determined to crush the Committee of Union and Progress,
indicated their intention of continuing their agitation
until the dissolution of the Young Turk Parliament
had become effective. They decided, further, to
convoke an Albanian National Assembly at Pristina,

where 1200 Albanians seized the telegraph office
and station (22nd July), and threatened to destroy
the railway line if any attempts were made to send
up military reinforcements.

In the meantime, the new Ministry had issued a
long manifesto to the Albanians, which opened with
a flattering reference to the estimable qualities of that
race, and indicated the peaceful tendencies of the
Government by declaring that henceforth the use
of armed force against the Albanians on any pretext was categorically forbidden. They attempted a
compromise on the dissolution of Parliament by an
assurance that an inquiry would be made into the
circumstances of the elections, and that any deputies
who owed their election to the undue influence of
the Committee would be unseated. The Albanians,
however, while they telegraphed their thanks to the
Sultan and assured His Majesty of their confidence
in the new Cabinet, showed every disposition to drive
home their initial victory. Although they faithfully
observed the armistice, their control over Albania
was complete, and with the exception of the Mutes-
sariflik of Ipek, all Government positions were in
their hands. Hassan Bey prohibited the dispatch
of cipher telegrams over the wires, and forbade the
Imperial troops to advance northward.

At this time (26th July) the Catholic tribes of
the North—the Mirdites and Malissori—came into
prominence. They rightly considered themselves
excluded from the Sultan's proclamations, which
had undiplomatically referred to *frères fidèles*, and
they accordingly broke the armistice, and severe
fighting occurred in the districts of Mat and Selemié.

This fact is worthy of note, for even at that date the Montenegrins were abnormally active, and the hostile action of the Catholic Albanians was undoubtedly due to their instigation.

On 30th July, the Albanian Medjliss, assembled at Pristina, demanded the dissolution of the Chamber within forty-eight hours. Failing compliance, they threatened to march on Uskub. In the early days of August, the Cabinet capitulated on the main question, and the Albanians returned to their homes, while the chiefs remained at Pristina in order to draw up a scheme of reforms.

The Albanian leaders quickly formulated their demands, ten of which were immediately accepted by the Cabinet of elder statesmen. These concessions were received with mixed satisfaction by the chiefs, and Uskub was, in consequence, invaded by thousands of rebels who, in their own fashion, proceeded to enjoy the fruits of victory. The Government was consequently compelled to make an imposing military demonstration, following which the rebel camp began to melt away.

Yet the insurgents by no means accepted the promises of the Sultan in the spirit of childlike confidence in the Caliph that had been expected of them. They were in no mood to be fooled again, or even to await the natural evolution of Cabinet concessions. Desiring arms, these simple highlanders looted the military depots and stole a matter of sixty thousand rifles; objecting to the continued incarceration of their friends, they forced prison doors and liberated them; discontented with certain Government officials, they drove them from their posts; demanding compensation for damages suffered during the military operations, they fixed their own price and threatened to seize State funds unless they got it; wishing for luxuries they had no means to purchase, they looted towns; clamouring for education, they burned down new Committee schools—and they further demonstrated their sense of playful humour by stealing flocks of sheep and selling them back to their rightful owners at seven-and-sixpence per head. It was only when Islam was called upon to face other and more critical developments on its frontiers that the Albanian revolution dissolved under the rays of a Moslem sun, superheated by the fires of religious fanaticism.

Just as the milk and water policy of the new Government in Albania had led to an aggravation of the situation there, so in Macedonia matters had gone from bad to worse. It would be difficult to adequately describe the condition of absolute chaos which then prevailed, but it is safe to say that anything corresponding to effective administration had ceased to exist. Individual outrage and assassination were rampant, the while strong bands roamed the province north, south, east and west—menacing, killing and pillaging with apparent impunity. All this may have been and probably was the aftermath of the misguided policy of the Young Turks; but it was clearly evident that the situation was out of hand and that the new Government felt itself, for one reason or another, incapable of exercising that authority which should have been its first attribute.

The Bulgarian revolutionary propaganda had

c

recommenced with renewed vigour, and Macedonia had sunk into a deplorable state of lawlessness. Deliberate attempts to again provoke massacres of Christians by Mussulmans by means of dynamite outrages had been successful at Kotchana and unsuccessful at Doiran, while daily attacks on the railway line rendered travel unsafe, and created an untenable situation which called for immediate remedy of one kind or another.

Simultaneously with this outbreak of internal anarchy, frontier incidents between Turkish and Bulgarian troops became appallingly frequent, and were often attended with considerable loss of life. Fighting on the Montenegrin borders likewise became a matter of daily history, and the excesses to which the Servian Ottomans were subjected by the Turkish irregulars and Albanians, infuriated public opinion in Servia, and led to reprisals.

By the end of September, 1912, the Macedonia barometer was pointing to very stormy weather, and the Turkish Government was fully convinced that there were breakers ahead. The Macedonian garrisons were still further reinforced, and, on 20th September, twenty wagons of war material for the account of the Servian Government, which had been transhipped at Salonika, were arrested at the frontier. Three days later a further eighty wagons suffered a similar fate, and Belgrade was formally notified that the material would be retained until the Porte received satisfactory assurances of the pacific intentions of the Servian Government.

It had been evident for some little time that Bulgaria, Servia, and Montenegro were in bellicose mood. Now, however, came the news that Greece, whose hostile intentions had been hitherto unsuspected, was actively preparing for war. The Turks, for their part, signalled their appreciation of the circumstances by mobilising the Drama, Serres, Istib and Uskub Reserve divisions, thus putting an additional 30,000 men under arms.

But while the Committee of Union and Progress had been resorting to universal military service, disarmament, Bosnian immigration, boycott and general oppression, as a means of bringing about the Turkification of all Ottomans in the Empire, negotiations had been proceeding between Athens, Belgrade, Cettinge and Sofia, which were soon to sound the death-knell of the power of the Osmanli in Europe.

The history of negotiations having for their object a combination of the liberated Balkan States against Turkey goes back to the close of the Russo-Turkish war of 1877.[1]  On that occasion, however, they were singularly short lived, for, following the Bulgarian revolt in Eastern Roumelia of 1885, Greece and Servia demanded compensation, and the scheme was forthwith relegated to the archives. Six years later the idea was received by Tricoupis, one

[1] For much of the information concerning the discussions between the Balkan States, resulting in the formation of the Balkan League, the author wishes to acknowledge his indebtedness to the Chief Correspondent of the *Times* in the Balkan Peninsula, whose able articles on the subject were read with world-wide interest upon their publication. It is unfortunate that Mr Bourchier's modesty has prevented him from throwing more light upon the highly important part which he himself played in the negotiations.

of Greece's greatest statesmen, who took advantage of a temporary freedom from cares of office to expound his proposals in the Servian and Bulgarian capitals. His suggestions were welcomed in Belgrade, and his reception in Sofia was so favourable that he was led to disclose his plans to Stambouloff. It is reported that, at the famous interview between the two statesmen, Stambouloff, who had betrayed the Greek scheme to the Porte, concealed the Turkish Ambassador behind curtains in the audience room in order that His Mohammedan Excellency might become thoroughly conversant with the Greek proposals. Whether this version of the episode be correct or not, the circumstances and its results certainly cast a shadow of suspicion on Bulgarian loyalty. The Bulgarian Church—churches are organs of political propaganda in the Balkans— had been re-established in 1870, and, as it was immediately pronounced schismatic by the Greek Patriarch, the struggle which for so many years effectually prevented any reconciliation between these two Christian races, and which was destined to stain the soil of Macedonia red with the blood of victims of religious hate, set in in earnest. The Turks rewarded Stambouloff for his treachery by the granting of several new Bulgarian bishoprics—or agencies for the propagation of Bulgarism—and it may therefore be inferred that, if the accusations against Stambouloff are unfounded, he was singularly favoured in being able to obtain so great a concession without supplying any *quid pro quo*.

With the exception of a further Greek attempt to obtain Bulgarian assistance during the disastrous

Greco-Turkish war of 1897, when Bulgaria again elected to favour Turkey and again received a grant of bishoprics as her reward, the untoward result which followed the initiative of Tricoupis stifled Balkan alliance proposals for twenty years, and as late as 1909, when the writer, then *en voyage* in Macedonia, ventured to suggest the formation of a Christian block against the Crescent as the only means of obtaining decent conditions of existence, he was not only assured by the Greeks that they dared not risk further negotiations with Bulgaria, but was regarded with suspicion as a possible agent of the Bulgarian Government.

With the advent to power of Mr Venezelos, came a Greek statesman unaffected by the story of past negotiations, and, contemporaneously with the *entente* between the Christian deputies in the Ottoman Parliament, the Greek and Armenian Patriarchs and the Bulgarian Exarch, he determined to invoke the pacific co-operation of the Bulgarian Government to second the efforts of the Christian block at Constantinople, and to further the attempt to reconcile the Christian elements in Macedonia. Mr Venezelos was not without hopes that an *entente* would speedily develop into an alliance, and in April, 1911, he unofficially proposed a Greco-Bulgarian *entente* for common action in the defence of Christian privileges in Macedonia, and an eventual defensive alliance against an attack by Turkey on either of the contracting parties.

No reply was forthcoming from Bulgaria, and for some months there were no further *pourparlers* between Athens and Sofia. In the meantime, however, Mr Hartwig, the energetic Russian Minister at Belgrade, had been persistently working to bring about a Serbo-Bulgarian reconciliation. Russia's object was, of course, to create a hostile Slav combination as a foil to Austrian activity in the Balkans, and it was Austria whom Servia then, as now, regarded as her hereditary enemy. With the Porte King Peter had no quarrel. In fact, following the rupture of Austro-Servian commercial relations in 1906, the Serbs became dependent upon Turkey for their economic existence, and they were in consequence desirous of cultivating the most friendly relations with the Moslem State. The only inducement for them to enter the projected Slav combination lay in the prospect of regaining the old Servian kingdom and the extension of their frontiers to the Adriatic.

In the spring of 1911, probably again as a result of Russian pressure, negotiations were resumed between Servian and Bulgarian diplomats, and upon the outbreak of the Turco-Italian war in September, 1911, the Servians came forward with definite proposals for an *entente*—proposals which resulted in the signature of an alliance between the two states on 13th March, 1912. The underlying idea in the Servian mind is clearly indicated by the fact that the military convention attached to the treaty called upon Bulgaria to send an army of 200,000 men to aid Servia in the event of Austrian intervention, whereas Servia bound herself to provide 100,000 to support Bulgaria against Turkey. Further, as Bulgaria favoured the creation of a Macedonian autonomy (which she hoped ultimately to annex) Servia insisted upon its definite division into spheres of influence. The terms of the military convention were repeatedly amended, and only those decided upon prior to mobilisation are of contemporary interest.

Shortly before the actual signature of the treaty with Servia, and when we may assume that negotiations to that end were already far advanced, Mr Bourchier left Sofia for Athens, the bearer of a message from Mr Gueshoff to Mr Venezelos, inviting the Greek Premier to open official negotiations. Mr Venezelos lost no time in acceding to the request, and *pourparlers* were commenced through Mr Pannas, the able diplomat who then represented Greece at Sofia. By mid-April, 1912, an agreement was reached, and on 29th May Mr Gueshoff and Mr Pannas signed the Greco-Bulgarian alliance. The two states bound themselves to aid each other if attacked either in its territory or by a systematic violation of its rights, and to use their influence with their kindred populations to contribute sincerely to the peaceful existence of the elements constituting the population of the Ottoman Empire. The treaty was to remain in force for three years, and the contracting parties agreed to avoid any description of aggression or provocative treatment with regard to Turkey, and to endeavour to induce their kindred populations in the Empire to dwell in peace with their Moslem fellow subjects.

Montenegro had always been ready to enter any combination directed against Turkey, and though her formal entry into the League was not definite until the signature of a Serbo-Montenegrin alliance in September, 1912, her adhesion to the project had been practically assured from February of the same year.

Thus was completed the chain of alliances which constituted the Balkan League, and with Turkey weakened by the revolts in Albania and in the Yemen, and handcuffed by the war with Italy, which not only sapped her vitality but prevented the transport of troops from Asia Minor to the European provinces, the Balkan statesmen determined to defy Europe and strike for freedom.

During the second half of September, 1912, there existed an unofficial state of war on the Bulgarian and Montenegrin frontiers, and numerous engagements occurred in which the losses were of a serious nature. In Macedonia the Bulgars, through the medium of bombs and bands, were spreading terror far and wide. Servia was quiet, but known to be in league with Bulgaria. From Greece, however, there came only reports of military movements and partial mobilisation, which were not inconsistent with the unsettled political conditions prevailing generally in the peninsula. It was, therefore, not unnatural that the comparatively pacific attitude of the Greek Government should have misled Turkish statesmen, and that the Porte, now convinced of the hostile intentions of her northern neighbours, should have attempted to buy out the Hellenes. According to a statement made to me about this time by a Turkish diplomat, Turkey would have been willing to cede the Island of Crete, and to agree to a revision of the frontier in the Mecovo districts as the price of Greece's neutrality. Certain it is that the Porte addressed a telegram to Athens inviting the Greek Government to open negotiations at Constantinople.

.   .   .   .   .   .   .

The advice of the mobilisation was received by the Consuls-General of the Balkan States at Salonika on 1st October, 1913. In European circles there was a pardonable disposition to consider that at the last moment the Powers would step in to avoid war, but the Servian representative was under no such delusion. That same day saw Mr Baloukditch busily packing his effects, confident that his recall was but a matter of hours. The dark cloud upon the horizon was the expectation that the Turkish Government would not dare to retreat before a bellicose demonstration on the part of its neighbours. As to the Turks themselves, they accepted the news with commendable sang-froid and declared themselves ready to respond to the call to arms, quietly confident in their ability to defend their country against all invaders. The mobilisation of the Turkish army naturally followed close upon that of its rivals, and large supplies of ammunition and stores were hurried into Macedonia from Constantinople.

While fruitless negotiations were in progress between Turkey and the Balkan States, the tide of Moslem patriotism rose rapidly. The Albanians forgot their grievances and asked only that weapons should be served out to them to repel the invading hosts. The hillmen were, in effect, so confident of their strength that they assured the Government of their ability to defeat the combined Montenegrin and Servian armies without the aid of Imperial troops. It would at this date have been impossible for the

Porte to have avoided war, and the scenes of enthusiasm which accompanied the reading of the Sultan's Firman exhorting his subjects to rally to the defence of their country faithfully reflected the martial spirit which permeated the entire Moslem population.

When, therefore, during the first week in October, the news arrived that the Montenegrins had crossed the frontier and destroyed the Ottoman blockhouses, the Government accepted the challenge and ordered their commandants to defend their charges to the best of their ability.

Meantime, the Turkish mobilisation had proceeded according to a programme drawn up by the German officers during the preceding winter, and it is worthy of note that so thorough was this organisation that until the completion of the movement not a single train reached its projected destination more than five minutes late. Immediately, however, the Turkish General Staff was left to its own resources, the whole scheme went to pieces.

# CHAPTER V

WHICH IS EXPLANATORY.—For over thirty years diplomacy had cherished the shibboleth that the final liquidation of the Turkish Empire in Europe would be necessarily accompanied by a European war. It is, therefore, indeed curious that the Powers did so little during that period to avert the crisis they so greatly feared. True, they time and again bolstered up Abdul Hamid; they shut their eyes to his blood-stained system of misgovernment; they condoned his organised massacres of defenceless Christians; they plotted and intrigued for supremacy at the Sublime Porte. But beyond a few half-hearted attempts at reform, which national rivalry never permitted to outgrow the purely academic stage, they had failed to carry into execution the powers accorded them in 1878 to give to Macedonia a just and equitable administrative system. They had been content to scrape on the fiddles of international jealousy while Macedonian Rome was burning. Ever and anon, when catastrophe loomed large, the tattered and torn Treaty of Berlin was trotted out and an ineffectual attempt made to dam the rushing waters of Ottoman dismemberment; but for all the benefit it conferred upon the down-trodden Christian populations, the famous Article 23 might never have been drafted.

And so when, in September, 1912, it became evident that the patience of the suffering Macedonians was again exhausted and pitcher No. 23 was once more sent to the well for a new draft of the soothing waters of promise and procrastination, it broke. For thirty-four years the Powers had shirked their responsibility until the Balkan States themselves, subordinating their interracial quarrels to the menace of a common enemy, determined to make good the delinquencies of their self-elected protectors.

The Powers were at length awakened from their coma and, choosing Austria-Hungary and Russia as their mouthpieces, they delivered on 25th September, 1912, the following threatening epistle to the now allied Balkan States:

"The Governments of Austria-Hungary and Russia declare to the —— Government:

"1. That the Powers energetically disapprove of all measures calculated to bring about a breach of the peace.

"2. That, by virtue of Article 23 of the Treaty of Berlin, they will undertake, in the interest of the populations, the realisation of reforms in the administration of Turkey-in-Europe, it being understood that these reforms will not in any way diminish the sovereignty of His Imperial Majesty the Sultan, or imperil the integrity of the Ottoman Empire; this declaration, however, reserves to the Powers the liberty to proceed to the collective and subsequent study of the reforms.

"3. That if war nevertheless breaks out between

the Balkan States and the Ottoman Empire, they will not admit, at the close of the conflict, any modification of the territorial *status quo* in Turkey-in-Europe.

"The Powers will collectively take the steps rendered necessary by the preceding declaration at the Sublime Porte.

"AIDE MÉMOIRE.—The Powers having decided by their united efforts to obtain reforms in the spirit of Article 23 of the Treaty of Berlin, and taking into consideration the fact that the Porte has the intention of agreeing to the unanimous desire of the Powers, the Russian Government considers that, at this moment, any action of the Balkan States tending to aggravate the situation and to jeopardise the maintenance of peace, would be in the highest degree imprudent. It is beyond doubt that the Balkan States will, at the cost of heavy sacrifices, be unable to obtain, in favour of the Christian populations, greater concessions than those which the Powers expect to obtain from the Porte.

"The Imperial Russian Government in consequence hopes that the ——— Government will permit the Powers to complete the work they have commenced under the most favourable auspices."

To this imposing document the allies, convinced that the psychological moment had arrived for decisive action, severally replied on 13th October:

"The ——— Government, having taken note of the declaration of the six Great Powers presented

to it by the Governments of Austria-Hungary
and Russia, and having communicated with the
Governments of the other Balkan States, expresses
its gratitude for the interest shown by the six Great
Powers in favour of the populations of Turkey-in-
Europe, and for their promises to undertake the
realisation of reforms in the administration in virtue
of Article 23 of the Treaty of Berlin. The
Governments of the Balkan States, however, consider that, after so many promises of reforms have
been so often and so solemnly given by Turkey,
it would be cruel not to endeavour to obtain, in
favour of the Christian populations of the Ottoman
Empire, reforms of a more radical and definite
nature, which would really ameliorate their miserable condition if applied sincerely and in their
integrity. It is for this reason that they have
thought it their duty to address themselves directly
to the Government of His Majesty, the Sultan, in
indicating to him the principles upon which the
reforms which are to be introduced shall be based,
and the guarantees which it will be necessary to
give to ensure their sincere application. They are
further convinced that if the Imperial Government
desires to accept these proposals, order and tranquillity will be re-established in the provinces of
the Empire, and that a durable peace will be
assured between Turkey and the Balkan States,
who have hitherto too often suffered from the
arbitrary and provocative attitude adopted by the
Sublime Porte towards them."

Simultaneously with this dignified response to the

Great Powers, the Ottoman Ministers in Athens, Belgrade, and Sofia were handed the following ultimatum:

" The undersigned Minister of Foreign Affairs has the honour to request His Excellency, the Ottoman Minister, to communicate to the Imperial Ottoman Government the following communication and the note thereto annexed:

" ' Despite the note delivered by the Governments of Austria-Hungary and Russia on behalf of the six Great Powers to the Balkan States—a note by which they promise to undertake the realisation of reforms in the administration of Turkey-in-Europe—the Governments of Bulgaria, Greece, and Servia nevertheless consider it necessary to address themselves directly to the Imperial Government of His Majesty the Sultan, in order to declare that only reforms of a radical nature, applied sincerely and in their integrity, can really ameliorate the miserable condition of the Christian populations of the vilayets of the Empire, guarantee order and tranquillity in Turkey-in-Europe, and assure a solid peace between the Ottoman Empire and the Balkan States, towards whom the Sublime Porte has, without justification, too often adopted an arbitrary and provocative attitude. The Governments of Bulgaria, Greece, and Servia, while regretting that the Government of Montenegro is unable, owing to recent events, to join in this demand, invite the Porte to immediately proceed, in collaboration with the Great Powers and the Balkan States, to elaborate and apply to

Turkey-in-Europe the reforms provided for by Article 23 of the Treaty of Berlin, founding same on the principles of ethnical autonomy (administrative autonomy; Belgian or Swiss governors-general; elected provincial assemblies; gendarmery; free instruction; militia); and in confiding the application thereof to a Conseil Supérieur, composed of Christians and Mussulmans in equal number, under the surveillance of the ambassadors of the Great Powers and the Ministers of the four Balkan States. They hope that Turkey will be able to declare that she accepts this demand, that she will undertake to put the reforms contained in the present note and its annex into execution within a period of six months, and that she will, as proof of her consent, withdraw the decree of mobilisation of her army. Annex:

" ' 1. Confirmation of the ethnical autonomy of the nationalities of the Empire with all its consequences.

" ' 2. Proportional representation in the Ottoman Parliament for each nationality.

" ' 3. Admission of Christians to all public posts in the provinces inhabited by the Christians.

" ' 4. Recognition of the equality of Christian schools of all grades with Mussulman schools.

" ' 5. Engagement by the Sublime Porte to under no consideration endeavour to modify the ethnological character of the provinces of the Ottoman Empire, or to thereto transplant Mussulman populations.

" ' 6. Regional recruiting of Christians for military service with Christian cadres,

"'7. Reorganisation of the gendarmery in Turkey-in-Europe, vilayet by vilayet, under the effective command of Swiss or Belgian organisers.

"'8. Nomination in the vilayets inhabited by Christians, of Swiss or Belgian Valis (governors) agreeable to the Powers and assisted by councils-general elected by the electoral districts.

"'9. Institution at the Grand Vizirat of a Superior Council composed of Christians and Mussulmans in equal number, to supervise the application of these reforms. The ambassadors of the Great Powers and the Ministers of the four Balkan States at Constantinople to supervise the work of this council.'"

A refusal on the part of the Turks was, of course, awaited with confidence. In any other case, the ultimatum would doubtless have included still more stringent and less acceptable conditions. Bulgaria, though she had been compelled to forego her demand for Macedonian autonomy as a result of the opposition of Servia, Greece, and Montenegro, to neither of whom the proposition appealed, doubtless hoped to carry her point as the result of a more or less successful conflict.

Servia was possessed of a determination born of two vital considerations. She was bent on establishing her political supremacy in old Servia, and on cutting her way through to the Adriatic. The fulfilment of these dreams had been threatened by the carte blanche given to the Albanians. When the hillmen overran Uskub (the ancient capital of the Servian Empire) the Porte was warned that Servia

D

could not remain a disinterested spectator, and a decision was immediately come to at Belgrade that the moment for action had arrived.

Montenegro was, as usual, in quest of fertile plains. Greece hoped at least to obtain possession of Crete, and secure better treatment for the Hellenes in Macedonia, whatever might be the result of the struggle. The idea of doubling their territory at the expense of Turkey in Europe had occurred to none of the allies.

Abdul Hamid, had he ever permitted the Balkan States to draw together, which is extemely unlikely, would doubtless now have accepted their programme of reforms, confident in his ability to create future disaccord between them, and to once again exploit their natural antipathy for one another to the benefit of the Mussulmans. Such a development would have been a calamity for the allies, but the existing hatred between Old and Young Turks fortunately protected them against any such interference with their carefully laid plans.

The Turks, as it subsequently transpired, were not altogether correctly informed as to the strength or intentions of their enemies. They credited the Greeks with the ability to put an army of about 80,000 men in the field, the greater part of which force it was estimated would concentrate at Larissa, and march north via Elassona; it was expected that a smaller force would attack the frontier at Mechovo, and endeavour to reach Yanina. The Epirote fortress was considered safe in the hands of the local garrison, aided by Albanian volunteers, while in view of the fact that all the points of strategic importance on the frontier were in Ottoman hands, Hassan Tahsin Pacha, with a force which originally numbered but 30,000 men (it was subsequently heavily reinforced) was presumed to be sufficiently strong not to actually defeat the Hellenes, but to retard their advance. His mission was to oppose the Greeks, and, if defeated, to retire, fighting the while a series of rear-guard actions, thus delaying his opponents until the Serbs and Bulgars had been defeated in Macedonia, when sufficient reinforcements were to be drafted south to enable him to crush his enemy and march on Athens.

The Montenegrins were likewise held cheaply, the Ottoman General Staff considering that the Scutari and frontier garrisons, aided by Essad Pacha's Tirana Redif division, then *en route* northward, and the Albanian volunteers, would be able to encompass their defeat without difficulty.

It was towards the north and north-east that the Turks turned their eyes. Anticipating a Bulgarian invasion down the valley of the Struma River, through the Kresna Pass, they concentrated a division of about 25,000 men under Ali Nadir Pacha, south of Kresna. The Servian army was expected to divide into two parts: a comparatively weak right wing descending south towards Prichtina, which the Albanians were to hold in check; a main column following the railway or the Morava Valley towards Uskub. The Turkish plan further calculated that a strong Bulgarian army would march down the road from Kuestendil, and attempt to effect a junction with the Servian forces to the north of the Plain of Ovtchépolé. They therefore concentrated in the northern valley of the Vardar River, the flower of the Turkish army in Macedonia, which had been heavily reinforced by the addition of picked divisions from Asia Minor. This force, which counted over 100,000 bayonets, was placed the supreme command of that experienced general and excellent gentleman, Zeki Pacha, and included the 6th (Monastir) Army Corps under Djavid Pacha, the 7th (Uskub) Army Corps under Fethi Pacha, a mobile corps of two divisions of the 5th (Salonika) Army Corps under Kara Said Pacha, together with Sulieman Faik Pacha's independent cavalry division, and some 25,000 to 30,000 Albanian volunteers.

This concentration is important in view of the generally accepted theory that the first Balkan War was won and lost exclusively upon the Plains of Thrace. According to information supplied at the time, however, the Turks were by no means assured of their ability to more than hold their own in Thrace. On the other hand, their plan (and I write now after reference to notes made after an interview with an officer of the Turkish Staff on 17th October, 1912), was that Zeki Pacha should attempt to get between the Servian army advancing down the Morava Valley, and the presumed Bulgarian force marching south-west from Kuestendil, and forthwith crush the Serbs, turn against and defeat the Bulgars, and fight his way to Sofia with all possible speed. Ali Nadir Pacha, in the Struma Valley, was not to attempt to march up the Kresna Pass, but, if successful in defeating or turning the Bulgarians—who would presumably be opposed to him—was to follow the route from Pechevo to the Bulgarian frontier, and effect a junction with Zeki Pacha on the Sofia road. The effect of this strategy, had it been successfully carried out, would have been to threaten Sofia and recall the Thracian army to the defence of the capital, or, if the Bulgarians had decided to sacrifice Sofia, they would have found their troops in Thrace between two fires, and their speedy annihilation imminent. Had the Turks known that the force on the Kuestendil road was in reality part of the Servian army, and included but one Bulgarian division, their plan would thereby have appeared to them all the more feasible.

The issue hung upon Zeki Pacha's ability to put this strategy into execution, and had he, as he hoped, defeated the Serbs at Koumanovo, the whole course of events in Thrace would probably have been altered. Koumanovo was, therefore, the decisive battle of the campaign, and it was the great Servian victory of that name which, more than any other engagement (and, of course, the successes of the allies were interdependent the one on the other), rendered the Balkan States masters of Macedonia.

It will have already become obvious that the Turkish General Staff at Salonika—presided over by Ali Riza Pacha, generalissimo of the western armies—had made several miscalculations concerning the forces opposed to them. It has been noted that the Turks had mistaken the second Servian army (in which was included one Bulgarian division) which was marching south from Kuestendil, for an exclusively Bulgarian force, and they remained under this misconception until after the battle of Koumanovo. They further estimated the Greeks at 80,000, whereas the Hellenes actually mobilised an army of 120,000 men. This numerical superiority of the Greeks was early recognised, with the result that Hassan Tahsin Pacha was systematically reinforced by new arrivals from Asia Minor.

While the Turkish soldiers were full of enthusiasm and their officers as replete with confidence, it was obvious from the very commencement of the concentration that the movements of the Ottoman troops were to be seriously handicapped by an inefficient army service, and an inadequate commissariat. To those of us who professed some anxiety as to how the armies were to be fed, and who pointed out that in the face of a poor harvest the 400 wagons of Servian grain which had been seized by the authorities would only very partially solve the difficulty, the reply was given that the troops would live on the country. There was, likewise, a shortage of winter clothing, and thousands of the men left for the front in the pelting rain with no more cover than that provided by their light summer uniforms. To the absence of footwear no one gave serious consideration, for it was always understood that on the outbreak of war the Turkish soldier would fling away his boots and take to the hide coverings known as charouks, to which he is accustomed.

The Ottoman army, as a staff officer pointed out to me with pride, was provided with all the latest scientific apparatus of modern warfare. They had aeroplanes, field telegraphs and telephones, wireless, steel pontoons, and the very best that Krupp could provide in the way of artillery. These accessories were, in themselves, excellent, subject to the Turks knowing how to employ them; but, as events were so quickly to demonstrate, the Moslem, while he would probably prove as good a soldier as ever under the conditions which in past centuries covered him with martial glory, has been utterly unable to assimilate the teachings of modern science as applied to the art of human slaughter, or to understand the impossibility of revitualising a modern army by the primitive process of stealing corn by the wayside. Whether the field telephones were ever used I know not, but the Turkish attempts, as I saw them, at range-finding and fuse-timing were lamentable; the wireless broke down within a few hours and was never repaired, while the aeroplanes only flew (driven by French mechanics engaged at princely salaries) when the Greeks were already at the gates of Salonika. As to the commissariat, not the least among the causes of the Turkish debâcle was the attempt to make men face shrapnel and cold steel on empty stomachs.

We have, in this account of the war in Macedonia, to deal almost exclusively with the actions of the Servian and Greek armies. Upon them fell the burden of the fighting. Montenegrin activities were mainly concentrated upon an attempt to capture the fortress of Scutari, while the Bulgarians, in three columns, hastened towards Salonika, encountering, thanks to the Greek and Servian victories, but little greater resistance than might be offered to the passage of an army by a few active bands of "komitadji." Their expedition was clothed rather with a political than a military atmosphere, and they wasted on that hurried rush to Salonika, to which we shall find it necessary to refer in a subsequent chapter, troops which might well have enabled them to drive home their victories in Thrace had they been turned eastward instead of southward after the collapse of the Ottoman resistance.

THE SERVIAN CONCENTRATION.—The Servian mobilisation, decreed on 30th September, commenced on 3rd October; six days later all the troops were mobilised and began their concentration. A further delay of only four days found the field transport ready to move. Four separate armies and an independent brigade was formed, and were disposed as follow:

*The First Army* (125,000 men).—Under the command of the Crown Prince Alexander, composed of five divisions and an independent cavalry division, entered Turkish territory from Vrania and proceeded along the Morava Valley.

*The Second Army.*—Under the command of General Stephanovitch, composed of one Servian and one Bulgarian division, descended by the road from Kuestendil.

*The Third Army.*—Four divisions under the command of General Yankovitch crossed the frontier at Prépovast.

*The Fourth Army.*—Composed of mixed troops, was divided into two independent columns.

Briefly put, the Servian forces totalled 258,000, plus fifteen regiments of the 3rd Ban (territorials, or home guards), equal to an additional 75,000 men. The plan of campaign called upon the first and second armies to march south towards Uskub and

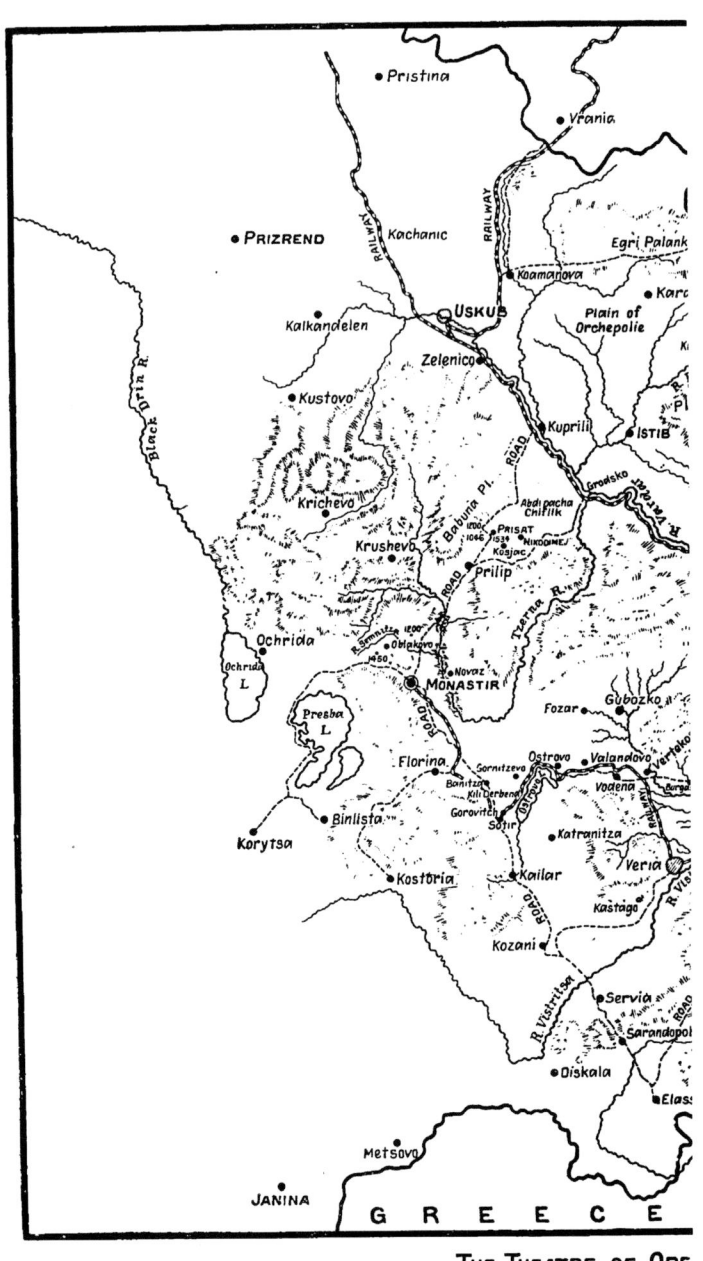

THE THEATRE OF OPE

ONS IN MACEDONIA.

eventually join the third army, whose mission was to descend to the same destination via Prichtina and the Katchanic Pass. The fourth army was detailed off to clear the Turks out of the Sanjack and proceed thence to the assistance of Montenegro.

THE GREEK CONCENTRATION.—The Greek mobilisation, decreed on 30th September, was completed in twelve days. The army consisted of eight divisions, seven of which were concentrated in Thessally under the command of the Crown Prince, and the remaining division in Epirus. Although the estimate of the General Staff placed their probable force at 85,000 to 90,000 men, so potent was the wave of patriotism which engulfed Hellas that, as we have already stated, the twelfth day of mobilisation saw their numbers swollen to 120,000 men. This figure included a Greek-American contingent of 30,000 who arrived already equipped at the expense of their co-religionists in the States.

The Greek plan of campaign requires but little explanation. The object of the Duke of Sparta's command was to engage and defeat Hassan Tahsin Pacha and then march northward. The duty of the division in Epirus was to attack, and, if possible, defeat the Turks on the western side and proceed to the siege of Yanina.

# CHAPTER VI

## THE BATTLE OF SARANDAPORON

IT had been decided that war against Turkey should be declared on 18th October. On 17th October there were two interesting developments. Ali Riza Pacha issued orders to his commandants to attack the Servian and Bulgarian lines, and the Duke of Sparta moved six Greek divisions up to the foot of the mountain frontier which separates Greece from Turkey. One division (VII) was left as reserve at Tirana. Hassan Tahsin Pacha received no orders to attack the Hellenic army. Isolated at Dishkata, he probably ignored the fact that a term had at length been set to Turkish evasion and procrastination, and was leisurely engaged in collecting the scattered forces which were to rally to his aid. The Porte, even at this date, still hoped to buy Greece out of the League, and, while leaving the door open for diplomatic negotiation at Constantinople, was indisposed to precipitate events on the southern frontier. This error of judgment, while it could scarcely have effected the ultimate result, placed the Turkish forces in Southern Macedonia at a further disadvantage, and Hassan Tahsin, apprised of the arrival of the Greek army on the frontier, was

obliged to give up the idea of profiting by the
strategic advantages he there possessed, and forced
to retire sufficiently far to the north as to permit
of his joining forces with the reinforcements then
*en route*, and to fortify himself in as favourable a
position as possible. By his unexpected advance
on 17th October, however, the Duke of Sparta had
got ahead of his enemy, and by dint of his rapid
and continuous forward movement, he never really
permitted the Turks to pull themselves together.
Reinforcements, as they arrived, joined hands with
men already beaten and discouraged, and the morale
of officers and men alike had suffered a blow from
which it never actually recovered.

When, therefore, at 6 a.m. on 18th October the
Greek army in four columns crossed the frontier,
the Turks garrisoned in the block-houses fired a
few volleys and promptly retired to the hills over-
looking the Plain of Elassona. Here the Greeks
were successfully delayed for several hours. Two
Hellenic divisions were ordered to execute a frontal
attack, and a skirmish of some importance continued
until the Ottomans, observing two regiments of
Evzones (Light Infantry) in the act of flanking their
left, bolted in a northerly direction.

The Turkish commander, realising that he had
lost the first round, wisely decided to retire right
back on Sarandaporon, where he could reasonably
expect to be allowed sufficient time to entrench
himself, and where, moreover, he was sure to
encounter the reinforcements then marching to his
aid from Salonika. Sarandaporon constitutes a
formidable natural stronghold and is, practically

speaking, the southern gate of Macedonia. It is considered by military experts to be well-nigh impregnable. Here the main road from Elassona to the town of Servia crosses an extensive plain until it reaches the mouth of the pass, from whence a mountain wall runs off on either side in a south-easterly and south-westerly direction. Entering the pass, the road winds through a long narrow gorge, flanked east and west by precipitous and inaccessible mountains, and resembling in some of its aspects the famous Pass of Kresna, to which we shall have occasion to refer more than once in this narrative. In the light of previous experience of Balkan warfare, a comparatively small force in possession of the heights at the entrance should have been able to successfully defy the onslaughts of a vastly superior army from the plain beneath. It was, therefore, but natural that Hassan Tahsin Pacha should hasten to entrench himself in this formidable stronghold and determine to there stay the advance of his enemy.

On 22nd October, 1912, the Greeks arrived on the plain to find the Turkish army in strong position on the heights commanding the entrance to the pass (see position marked A and B on sketch map). The Crown Prince then developed his attack, and the Turks found themselves faced by three Greek divisions, a fourth being held in reserve behind their centre, while two battalions of Evzones moved round on their extreme right. The difficulties of the Greeks were, however, increased in a marked degree by the impossibility of sending forward the artillery with the divisions to which it

THE GREEK ARMY—AN OUTPOST ACTION.

THE GREEK ARMY—IN THE TRENCHES.

respectively belonged, for the long stretch of plain leading up to the Turkish positions was, as Hassan Tahsin well knew, broken by deep gorges and ravines which rendered the transport of field batteries impracticable. The Hellenes were, therefore, compelled to mass their guns and send them along the main road in the wake of their centre. The infantry, particularly of the Greek right, was accordingly unsupported by its artillery and was exposed unprotected to the fire of the Turkish batteries for over three hours. This circumstance necessitated a premature development of the unities composing the Greek right, which were compelled to adopt battle formation in order to pass over the ridges of the undulating and ever-rising hills which led up to the Ottoman lines.

At midday, the first of the Greek batteries unmasked, and being steadily reinforced and advanced, their fire became very effective, the Turkish guns being eventually enveloped in a haze of bursting shrapnel. The Turks, naturally conscious of the superiority of their position, stood their ground bravely and poured down a continuous hail of lead and shrapnel upon their advancing enemy. Then the Greeks were seen to waver. For the great mass of Hellenes it was their first experience under fire, and it is small wonder that the men, deafened by the roar of the batteries behind them, should have gazed at the hostile guns above as they belched forth death and destruction, and have felt a distinct disinclination to advance farther into the inferno. The Turks gained confidence, and the issue was still in doubt when the General commanding the Greek III Division, accompanied by his staff, rode into the foremost lines, and shouting, " *Embros, paithia, Embros!* " (On, boys, on!) put renewed courage into the hearts of his men, and led them to victory. The cry of " *Embros* " was universally taken up and was clearly heard in the Turkish camp. The fight continued with increasing vigour, but towards 4 p.m. the fire of the Krupp batteries began to weaken, only, an hour and a half later, when daylight was yet on the wane, to recommence with renewed energy. The effect was to inspire the Greeks with doubt and indecision. As the rapidly bursting shells lit up the darkening battle-field with spasmodic flashes, it was obvious that the effort had become desultory and undirected. What meant this useless wastage of ammunition? Was it mere bravado, was it a crude demonstration of confidence, or was it a last, reckless precursor of retreat? None knew.

When darkness at length fell, the fire of the Turkish guns gradually ceased, and the Greeks prepared to pass the night in their positions. I have endeavoured to cull some idea of the state of mind of the Hellenes as they lay tossed on that pitiless sea of uncertainty. That the Turks had been effectively shaken was held to be beyond doubt, for the Greeks had crept up to within a few hundred yards of their lines, but they had fought stubbornly, and there were no available means of deciding whether they would retire under cover of darkness or again offer battle in the morning. The horror of that night at Sarandaporon can well be imagined. Tired, weary troops who for six days had pressed forward in pursuit of their retreating quarry and had now, through the long hours, stormed up the rising slopes midst a murderous hail from the heights above, while their comrades dropped by their sides, some dead, some rent by shot or shell, to lie there groaning with the agony of shattered limbs, or gasping out prayers as their life's blood oozed out on to the brown earth. And then the suspense of it all! Not to know whether morning's dawn was to bring the surety of life for another day, or whether that deafening roar would begin anew and cut down hundreds more as they sped on towards the guns that must be silenced. And then the cold, pitiless rain poured down, and black, fearsome clouds shut out the feeble starlight and caused stretcher-bearers to stay their task of carrying off the wounded; and the dead and dying lay all around, and on every side the air was rent with cries and groans and curses. Can the reader enter into the heart of that little Greek " piou piou," who a few days since had been weighing out flour or measuring out oil in his village store, as he lay there cold, hungered and wet in the midst of death and despair and thought of the wife and children he had left behind and whom he might cease even to think of to-morrow if—if the Turks were still up there! That these men bore the burden of patriotism willingly made it none the less heavy, nor did it render war any the less hellish. The Greek army, from Commander-in-Chief to drummer boy, would have given much to know, on that bitter, dismal evening, that Hassan Tahsin Pacha had indeed commenced to evacuate Sarandaporon.

When the main Greek force moved forward against Sarandaporon in the early morning of 22nd October, the IV Division, bereft of its field artillery and composed of nine infantry battalions and three mountain batteries (in all about 12,000 men), was ordered to follow a bridle path which runs over the mountains well to the west of the main road, which it joins again at the northern extremity of the pass near the little village of Rahovo. Hassan Tahsin Pacha must not be too harshly judged if he failed to provide against such an emergency, for the strategy was new to Balkan warfare and the Greek staff were even themselves in doubt as to its practicability.

The climatic conditions were of the most trying description, fog, rain and cold rendering the going difficult and hazardous. Throughout the whole day, without a halt, the division marched up and down the twenty miles of stony pathways in single file, and towards 7 p.m. reached Rahovo, where outposts were placed at the exit of the pass and upon the surrounding hill-tops. The fates were kind to the worn-out warriors, and the night passed without incident. In the grey dawn of the morning, however, a Turkish force of uncertain strength was observed to be marching south from Servia. An engagement of an hour's duration ensued, ending in the retreat of the Ottomans, and peace reigned once more until, at 7 a.m., the outposts reported that a column of considerable importance was approaching from the south. The winding road and the presence of a dense fog delayed the action of the Greek general, but immediately all doubt as to the identity of the enemy was removed, he ordered his three mountain batteries to open fire. The unfortunate Turks, disheartened by their defeat at Sarandaporon and weary with their day-long battle and night-long march, were taken unawares in a ravine which offered no possibility of defence. Terror-stricken and demoralised, they broke into frenzied rout. The infantry bolted in all directions, while the gunners cut the traces, and, mounting their teams, galloped for their lives. They left the whole of Hassan Tahsin Pacha's artillery—twenty-four field guns with a full complement of ammunition wagons—together with all their transport, in one long bedraggled line, stretching a mile and a half along the pass.

There is but little to add to the experiences of the Greek army whom we left before Sarandaporon the previous evening. As the windy, wet morning of 23rd October broke, anxious eyes were turned towards the Turkish positions, but on the hills, enveloped as they were in rain clouds, nothing could be seen. Then the pickets of the advance guard, having pushed their way right up to the enemy's trenches, found them empty, and with joyous hearts the men of the VI Division rushed into the pass in pursuit of their beaten prey. Behind them the medical corps took up the burden; the wounded were carried to a field hospital established at a deserted Turkish farm, and from thence evacuated in motor ambulances to Elassona.

The IV Division, which had so brilliantly executed the flanking movement on the Greek left, entered Servia on 23rd October, two hours behind

E

the retreating Turks who, despite their panic, had found time to wreak their vengeance upon the unfortunate Christian population, sixty members of which were mercilessly butchered in the streets of the town.  It has always been impossible for those of us who appreciate many characteristics of the Turks, to understand why they do these things and destroy that sympathy which would otherwise so willingly be theirs.  The massacre in Servia was so unnecessary, so uncalled for, and so likely to have occasioned reprisals on the Moslem civilians left behind.  As it was, though little blame could have been attached to the Hellenes had they exacted a life for a life, no excesses were recorded, and the following morning the Crown Prince Constantine entered at the head of his army, which was now accorded a well-earned rest.  Here we will leave them while we regard the great events which had almost simultaneously transpired farther north.

# CHAPTER VII

## THE BATTLE OF KOUMANOVO

THE reader will remember that Zeki Pacha, with his Vardar army, had received orders to offer battle to the Servian army, following which, if unsuccessful, he was to defeat the presumed Bulgarian force descending from Kuestendil and to march forthwith on Sofia. This impending encounter was consistently referred to by the officers of Ali Riza Pacha's General Staff in Salonika, as the " Great Battle " which was to decide the campaign, and we awaited the issue with almost as great a confidence as did the Turks themselves.

Farther west the Servians had drawn first blood. When their third army crossed the frontier the Turkish troops, together with their Albanian allies, retired to an advantageous position north of Pristina, where, after a bloody combat of six hours' duration, they were hopelessly defeated. Pristina itself fell into Servian hands with but little delay. Subsequently, they occupied Ferizovitch without resistance and advanced to the attack of the famous Katchanic Pass, which bars the road to Uskub. The fighting in Albania, if it served no other purpose, had successfully demonstrated that the Albanians were of very little value in modern warfare. Their aversion to cannon was well known to all who had followed the course of the punitive expedition sent against them by the Young Turks, but their present failure must have been disconcerting to the Ottoman staff, since considerable importance had been set upon the assistance which these irregular warriors would be able to render to the army. Ali Riza Pacha, at least, made no attempt to hide his disgust at their lamentable display, and he dispatched to Issa Boletinatz a telegram, the contents of which were communicated to me at the time, and which may be translated as follows:

"Although you have stolen 63,000 rifles from our depots, you have done nothing—we have lost Pristina. This is a disgrace for the army and the nation. Your promises have proved valueless. You are useless for warfare, but at least you might form bands and harass the enemy!"

Some considerable resistance could doubtless have been offered to the Servians at Katchanic had Fethi Pacha been able to carry out his intention to send up reinforcements, but the Uskub Commander was faced with developments nearer home which preoccupied his attention. The Serbs were also, however, on the eve of a surprise. They anticipated that the Turkish resistance would be offered on the Plain of Ovtchépolé, or even farther south. Their prognostications would have been correct had not so much precious time been wasted in *pourparlers*. Had war been declared a week earlier even the Turks would have been fearful of defeat, but by

17th October they had begun to advance northward from their first concentration camp at Kuprili (Veles), inspired by the consciousness of impending victory. I found it difficult to resist the many pressing invitations which I received to join that "Happy march to Sofia," but the necessity of controlling the facts relating to the operations over the entire Macedonian field detained me in Salonika until we lost touch with the vanquished Vardar army and I was able to go out and join the Turkish forces opposed to the Greeks.

So Zeki Pacha had gone north to deliver his great strategic battle, and he was in position north of Koumanovo, and ready to assume the offensive, when, during the afternoon of 22nd October, the Servian approach was reported and desultory firing commenced. A heavy fog hung like a pall over the battle-ground, and neither side was able to estimate the strength of its opponents. Zeki Pacha had, however, sufficiently unmasked his enemy, and following his prearranged plan, on the following morning engaged the Servians over their entire front, throwing his chief strength against the left of their three columns in a determined attempt to drive them back on to the centre and break the line. The Turks found themselves superior in artillery, for bad roads had hindered the approach of the Servian guns, and the Servian infantry was therefore called upon to bear the brunt of the attack Not content with this superiority, the Ottoman centre was also ordered to attack the Servian left, and the mobile division of Kara Said Pacha was told off to move north from Istib and threaten their flank.

Throughout the day fighting of a very fierce and determined nature continued. The Turks delivered attack upon attack in their effort to turn their enemy, whose position was rendered the more critical by the absence of reinforcements. Incessant rain and the transport of troops and impedimenta had turned the track into one long morass, and the much-needed reinforcements came not. Steadily, but irresistibly, the Osmanli advanced; the Serbs slowly retired with ever-thinning ranks until, organised opposition being no longer possible, the men continued an individual resistance. It was shortly after noon, and the battle had gone badly for Servia, when, in the nick of time, the indispensable reinforcements arrived, and, entering into the fight with vigour and determination, they rained lead upon the ever-approaching Turks. So the struggle continued until, in the fading light of day, the Moslems made a supreme effort. Rushing towards the Servian lines, heedless of the murderous fire which met their forward movement, they faltered not until, with the two races now face to face, it came the turn of cold steel. With bayonets fixed, all that were left of the Serbs hurled themselves upon the Osmanli and drove them steadily back towards their positions. I doubt not that the superior physique of the Servian peasant counted for much in that final assault, but as a last rally of a force inferior in numbers and decimated by day-long combat, it was a magnificent, supreme effort.

Simultaneously, fighting of a much less strenuous and indecisive character had been proceeding in other parts of the field; but on the whole the

AFTER KOUMANOVO.

The Auto "snapped" unawares while photographing congested streets.

fortunes of war had gone to the Turks, and Zeki Pacha's dispatches, while admitting enormous losses, were of a most confident nature. His staff had, in fact, little doubt that their first mission had been accomplished and that the junction between the Servian and presumed Bulgarian forces had been practically prevented.

Bright eyes and glad hearts greeted me the following morning when I paid my accustomed visit to Ali Riza Pacha's headquarters in Salonika. Staid staff officers gave themselves up to merry jest, and there was more than the usual allowance of coffee and cigarettes, for the great battle had been won; their imagination already saw the domes of Sofia's churches standing out against the horizon, and the Bulgarians were at last to be punished for the wrongs they had wrought in Macedonia. As the news spread through the town with lightning rapidity, Jews and Moslems joined in general rejoicing at the success of Ottoman arms. It is well that the future is veiled from our gaze. At least that kind provision of Providence permitted the disciples of Allah in our Ægean seaport one short hour of triumph—the last they were to enjoy for many a day. That night, while all Salonika babbled of the glorious victory, I remained in the quietness of my own home. I liked not to mingle with the throng and breathe the atmosphere of martial triumph lest I might perhaps throw an unconscious shadow over their happiness. For I already knew that Zeki Pacha had been beaten and that his great army was nothing but a beaten, panic-stricken mob flying on the wing of terror before its Christian conquerors.

A sad, downcast Ottoman, one who had shared the Pacha's friendship with me in happier days, had communicated to me the text of the telegram by which the Turkish Commander-in-Chief had announced his defeat. This is what he said:

"I have already advised you that the great battle yesterday lasted until 5.30 to 6.30 p.m. (the telegram gave the always questionable Turkish hour). The 7th Army Corps lost heavily. In order to allow the 7th Corps to retire, I ordered Djavid Pacha to create a diversion on the Servian right, and instructed Fethi Pacha to gradually retire with those of his troops which were not surrounded. When the bugles sounded the retreat the 7th Corps was exposed to a terrific fire from the Servian artillery. It fled panic-stricken, not knowing how to escape the murderous fire. The 7th Corps was annihilated: 150 cannon, ammunition and provisions were abandoned in the flight. The few remaining soldiers have arrived, terror-stricken, at Uskub. The strategy of Djavid Pacha has therefore failed. On his right the battle continues, but he is not strong enough to drive the enemy back, and I fear his resistance will be brief. I lack news of his division. The 5th Corps of Kara Said Pacha and a division of Nizams are fighting near Kotchana. They have inflicted severe losses on the Bulgars (?), but are broken and will retire to Istib. It is with the greatest sadness that I announce officially that our great battle is lost. We are plunged into dire affliction."

To the reader, this will seem but a mere notification of defeat; to us, who knew the man, and who bid him adieu as, light-hearted and gay, he set out to take command of his great army, it was a tragic message from a broken heart.

Next morning set me a difficult task. News of the defeat had, of course, been carefully hidden from public knowledge, and it was necessary for me to appear a blissful innocent when I made my customary visit to headquarters. The door had been rigorously barred against the inquisitive, but my intimate relations with the staff served me in good stead on this as on a subsequent occasion. And so, as the sentinel stood aside to let me pass, I squared my shoulders, put on a jovial exterior and burst unannounced into the chamber. There was little need for the play-actor. There before me lay a drama of real life. The laughing, chattering comrades of yesterday were to-day saddened, tear-stricken, broken-spirited men. Drawn up in pathetic, woeful groups, they gazed in silence as I shed my mask and, reflecting as I must have done the anguish of my environment, I asked what meant this sudden change from joy to sorrow.

"You'll excuse us," faltered one, "but we have nothing to tell you."

I was fortunate, however, in obtaining a fair amount of news from Turkish sources, which, coupled with the information I have since gleaned from the Servian authorities and residents in Uskub, enables me to trace, I believe authentically, the subsequent movements of the Turkish Vardar army.

On the morning of the second day of the battle of Koumanovo (24th October), the Serbs brought up two divisions which had been hitherto held in reserve, and an artillery duel took place over the entire front—from 18 to 20 kilometres in length. At this epoch there must have been some two hundred and fifty guns in action, and their deafening roar can scarce be imagined by those whose experience is limited to the perusal of such inadequate descriptions as the most brilliant pen can draw. It was the turn of the Serbs to assume the offensive, and the infantry steadily advanced under cover of the artillery, which had already succeeded in inflicting enormous losses upon the Turks. After a combat of some seven hours' duration the Ottoman lines were forced and, the retreat once sounded, the troops of the 7th Army Corps flew pell-mell in all directions, the while the now victorious Sneider cannon raked them with shell fire. Guns were abandoned, rifles flung aside, provisions and ammunition and accoutrements were discarded as the army scattered in the wild rush for safety. The large proportion of Turks who were wounded in the back told its own story. The remnants which arrived at Uskub were formed by Fethi Pacha into a few battalions to aid in the defence of the town.

The turning movement which Zeki Pacha had ordered the 6th Army Corps to operate failed in like manner. Led by a division of Albanian Redifs —who took to their heels upon the retreat being ordered—the entire corps rushed headlong from the battle-field, having no thought save that of escape from the Servian fire. Zeki Pacha subsequently reported that all that was left to him of these two great army corps amounted to less than 40,000 men.

The Turks abandoned on the field no less than one hundred and twenty cannon, together with thousands of rifles and enormous quantities of stores and ammunition. Kara Said Pacha's 5th Army Corps fared somewhat better, and, battered and beaten, succeeded in retiring to Istib.

Uskub was, however, not yet lost, and Zeki Pacha, sending out the Hodjas to scour the country-side for volunteers, succeeded in collecting 15,000 of these useless irregulars with whom, plus the 40,000 terror-stricken soldiers left to him, he intended to put up a forlorn defence. Fethi Pacha was placed in charge of this already beaten horde, and massing them with the garrison artillery of Uskub at the station, he prepared to entrain for Zelenico, there to offer battle. The men had little enough stomach for the fight, but were about to entrain when a Bosnian Moslem, crying aloud that the Albanians were cowards and traitors, fired a revolver and killed an officer and an Albanian. "The enemy!" cried the distracted warrior, and the defenders of Uskub took panic again and bolted, the majority of them down the railway line towards Kuprili (Veles), abandoning what remained of their cannon and discarding rifles and any other impedimenta which might hinder their flight. Fethi Pacha and Djavid Pacha arrived at Kuprili later, and Kara Said having conducted an ordered retirement to the same centre, all that remained of the 5th,

6th and 7th Army Corps of the Turkish army there congregated.[1]

THE OCCUPATION OF USKUB.—Throughout the Macedonian campaign, the Consulates of the Great Powers, always the refuge of the oppressed Ottoman subject, played a notable rôle, and few, perhaps, had a more exciting time than those established in the flourishing market centre of Uskub. Immediately following the precipitated flight of the remnants of the Ottoman army from Koumanovo, the Consulates were invaded by a conglomerate mass of humanity: Christians, Jews and Mussulmans; men, women and children; officers, soldiers and non-combatants— all vied with one another for the protection of foreign flags. The Consulates were speedily packed with this nondescript mass, and, be it said to their credit, the representatives of the Powers not only opened

---

[1] Zeki Pacha's official announcement of the flight from Uskub read as follows :

" Fethi and Djavid Pachas, having calmed the panic among the troops who had retreated to Uskub, re-formed them into companies and concentrated them at the station with the cannon, ammunition, provisions and effects which had been saved from Koumanovo, together with the armament in depot at Uskub. The trains were ready and the locomotives under steam when a Bosniac among the soldiers commenced to blaspheme the Albanians, calling them traitors and cowards. He fired a revolver, and having killed one officer and one Albanian, cried : ' The enemy is coming.' The troops, again seized with panic, cut the traces which attached the horses to the cannon, and discarding all the cases of ammunition and provisions, took to their heels, unarmed, in the last stage of demoralisation. Djavid and Fethi, despite religious exhortation and prayers, were unable to stop the flight of the soldiers. All the cannon, horses, effects and ammunition were abandoned at the station. The idea of defending Zelenico had to be given up."

wide their doors, but to the utmost of their ability
provided nourishment for their affrighted guests.
The Valli (Governor-General) of Uskub sought
sanctuary at the Russian Consulate.

In the town itself authority was absent, and
plunderers were given a free hand until the French
Consul organised a police force whose members,
replete with tricoloured cockades which cannot have
failed to have evoked memories of the French
Revolution, re-established a reasonable measure of
security.

Nothing was left to the remaining Turks but to
surrender the town to the conquerors who were yet
in ignorance of their conquest, and to request them
to make a speedy entry. Thus it happened that the
Consuls put on their medal-bedecked uniforms, and,
with the Russian doyen at their head and the
Turkish Mayor of Uskub in their train, set off for
the Servian camp. The skies wept; the roads were
in quagmire; and a bitter north wind swept across
the plain as the international " parlementaires " set
off in dilapidated carriages in quest of Prince
Alexander. After a two hours' jolting journey they
encountered a Servian patrol, whose commanding
non-com, having no special orders to treat Consuls
in any way different to ordinary mortals, dragged
them from the seclusion of their landaus, blind-
folded them, and drove them, their gold-braided
trousers knee-deep into the muddy morass and their
cocked hats and gaudy tunics exposed to the ruinous
effects of the pelting rain, right up to the fringe of
the camp. Here the Crown Prince, advised of their
arrival, sent his automobile to conduct them to head-

quarters, and, formalities ended, a detachment of the Servian army was ordered to Uskub, which it formerly occupied in time for five o'clock tea.    In most of the foreign Consulates there the visitor may see, hanging on the wall, a mud-stained handkerchief folded in bandage—the most prized of many relics of the great Balkan War of 1912.

The reconquest of Uskub marked a red-letter day in Servian history.

# CHAPTER VIII

## THE WORK OF THE GREEK NAVY

DESPITE the defeats inflicted upon them at Saran-daporon, Koumanovo, and simultaneously in Thrace, the fight would have by no means been lost had the Turks been able to draw upon their immense reserves lying inactive in Asia Minor. The 400,000 men they had engaged in the war in Turkey-in-Europe represented only a fraction of their fighting force. Under more favourable conditions than those which actually existed, the Ottoman General Staff would, from the outbreak of hostilities, have been pouring reinforcements, stores and food into Dedeagatch, Kavala and Salonika, and instead of being practically over by the end of October, the Turco-Balkan War would have been only at its beginning.

The unfavourable condition which prevented this operation was, of course, the presence of the Greek fleet, and it would be well not only for the allies of Greece, but for the Greek army itself, to remember that if they succeeded in inflicting so overwhelming a defeat upon the Osmanli, they owe the completeness and cheapness of their victory almost entirely to the Hellenic Navy. At a rough estimate it may be said that the Turks could have doubled the strength of their European army, and it is not unlikely that, under such circumstances, they would have turned the tables on their conquerors despite disorganisation and lack of preparation. Certain it is that the Greeks would have found it difficult to advance beyond Sarandaporon, that the Serbs would have been stopped at Kuprili (Veles), and that the advance of a newly landed Turkish column from Dedeagatch would have kept the Bulgars north of Adrianople.

The foundation of Hellenic sea power was laid by that eminent Greek statesman, Tricoupis, who got together a fleet composed of three cruisers of doubtful value and five torpedo-boats. Several destroyers were added in 1906 and, four years later, the *Georgios Averoff* was ordered by the Government. Contrary to general impression, the ship was paid for out of the funds of the Treasury of Defence and not by Mr Averoff; it bears his name as a tribute to the great and patriotic services he rendered to his country. Four British-built ocean-going destroyers, bought on the eve of the war, and two further ships of similar but lighter design presented by the Greek Americans, together with sundry other unimportant units, brought up the navy to its composition in 1912. Apart from training ships and other units of no fighting value, the Greek fleet was, upon the outbreak of the war, made up as follows:

TURKISH CRUISER "MESSUDIYEH" AT SALONIKA.

GREEK CRUISER "GEORGES AVEROFF" AT SALONIKA.

| Type | Name | Built | Tonnage |
|---|---|---|---|
| Armoured Cruiser | Averoff | 1910 | 10.118 |
| Cruiser | Psara | 1890 | 5000 |
| ,, | Hydra | 1889 | ,, |
| ,, | Spetsai | ,, | ,, |
| T.B. Destroyer | Thycela | 1906 | 400 |
| ,,     ,, | Sphendoni | ,, | ,, |
| ,,     ,, | Lonchi | ,, | ,, |
| ,,     ,, | Naukratoussa | ,, | ,, |
| ,,     ,, | Aspis | ,, | 350 |
| ,,     ,, | Niki | ,, | ,, |
| ,,     ,, | Doxa | ,, | ,, |
| ,,     ,, | Velos | ,, | ,, |
| ,,     ,, | Keravnos | 1912 | 560 |
| ,,     ,, | Nea Genea | ,, | ,, |
| ,,     ,, | Leon | ,, | 1050 |
| ,,     ,, | Panther | ,, | ,, |
| ,,     ,, | Altos | ,, | ,, |
| ,,     ,, | Jarax | ,, | ,, |
| Torpedo-boats | 5 | 1885 | 85 |
| Submarine | Delphin | 1912 | 310 |

In addition there were six merchant ships transformed into auxiliary cruisers.

In 1911 a British Naval Mission was sent out to Athens at the request of the Greek Government, but with the exception of Commander Cardale and Engineer-Commander Watson, the officers do not seem to have given very great satisfaction. In fact, one of the points which the late King George impressed upon me during the first interview which I was privileged to hold with him after the Greek conquest of Salonika, was his dissatisfaction with the then existing naval mission and his desire that the British Admiralty should send out a new staff composed of officers on the active list. This was, fortunately, subsequently arranged, and upon the

F

suggestion of the Greek Government, Admiral
Mark Kerr's new mission again includes Messrs
Cardale and Watson, but is otherwise composed of
active officers, with the result that extraordinary
progress is now being made by the Hellenic Navy
towards perfection.

The Turkish fleet, which had an overpowering
superiority on paper, at the same time consisted of
the following vessels:

| Type | Name | Built | Refitted | Tonnage |
|---|---|---|---|---|
| Battleship | Hairredin-Barbarosse | 1891 | 1904 | 10,600 |
| ,, | Torgud Reis | 1891 | 1904 | 10,600 |
| ,, | Messudiyeh | 1874 | 1906 | 9140 |
| ,, | Assar-i-Tefik | 1869 | 1905 | 5000 |
| ,, | Muin-i-Zaffer | 1869 | 1906 | 2400 |
| Cruiser | Hamidieh | 1905 | | 3830 |
| ,, | Medjidieh | 1903 | | 3442 |
| T.B. Destroyers | 12 | Modern | | |
| Torpedo-boats | 5 | Old | | |
| Torpedo-boats | 11 | Modern | | |
| Gunboats | 10 | Antiquated | | |

It is not my intention to give a complete history
of the naval campaign, nor do I intend to refer to the
occupation of the Ægean Islands accomplished by
the Greek fleet.   I rather wish to deal only with the
aspect of naval supremacy in the Ægean in so far as
it affected the course of military history in Macedonia.
The obvious duty of the Turkish fleet was to come
out, defeat the Greeks, and clear the way for the
transport of Asiatic troops to Thrace and Macedonia.
Conversely, that of the Greek fleet was to blockade
its enemy in the Dardanelles or defeat it in open sea.

As a base of operations, the Greeks seized the Island of Lemnos on 21st October, and forthwith inaugurated a strict watch over the mouth of the Dardanelles. Contrary to all expectations, the Turkish fleet showed no inclination to leave its hiding-place, and when, after the first great defeats in Macedonia, the need of reinforcements became increasingly manifest, the astonishment of the Turks themselves turned to disgust. " Our fleet must leave the Dardanelles," said a Turkish colonel to me, " and either send the Greeks to the bottom or go there itself. Either solution would be more compatible with national honour than its present inactivity."

The Turkish fleet, however, remained in its sanctuary until, on 14th and 15th December, when there was little hope of retrieving the fortunes of the Ottoman armies, the *Medjidieh* appeared at the mouth of the Dardanelles, surveyed the situation, and forthwith retired. The following evening—15th-16th December—the *Messudiyeh*, accompanied by the *Barbarosse* (flagship), *Torgud Reis*, and *Assar-i-Tefik*, sailed out in battle formation. The Greek fleet set off to meet its enemy, and after some firing at long range, the Admiral decided to take advantage of the superior speed of the *Averoff*, and proceed to the attack single-handed. He therefore signalled to his fleet to follow, and getting within close range (3500 yards) of the *Barbarosse*, got home with a salvo of 9.2 projectiles. The Turk then set her course for the Dardanelles, which, followed by the rest of the fleet, she succeeded in reaching safely. During the retreat a desultory fire was kept up by both fleets. On the Turkish side the *Barbarosse* was placed *hors de combat*, and the *Messudiyeh* was also considerably battered. The damages sustained by the Greeks were negligible. The *Averoff* was struck by one large shell, probably fired from the land forts, and fifteen times by shell from guns of a smaller calibre. Her casualties were one officer and four men wounded. The *Spetsai* was struck four times, and the *Hydra* once, with insignificant results.

There were afterwards one or two ineffectual demonstrations by the Turkish fleet, as a result of one of which the *Hamidieh*, either by mistake or design, escaped into open sea, and in addition to bombarding the town of Syra, and sinking the Greek auxiliary cruiser *Macedonia*, considerably worried the Greek authorities, particularly when, at a later date, they began the transport of Servian troops from Salonika to the Adriatic coast. For the rest, however, the exploits of the *Hamidieh* concern neither us nor the historian, and provide but a semi-comic interlude to a tragic story.

Thus, thanks to her command of the sea, Greece was able to render an inestimable service both to herself and to her allies. The beaten Turkish armies were left to their own resources, and obliged to give up all hope of retrieving their fortunes.

The Greek fleet limited the initial strength of the Ottoman forces; it effectually prevented their reinforcement; it permitted the transport of nearly 30,000 Bulgarian soldiers to Dedeagatch, and a like number of Servians to Albania; it would, aided by the proffered assistance of the Greek army, have enabled the allies to force the Dardanelles and dictate terms of peace in Constantinople; it, in short, rendered possible the Balkan War of 1912. And yet we find Bulgaria ungrateful for this assistance, desirous not only of assuming all the credit for the defeat of Turkey, but, at a later stage, treacherously attempting to rob her ally of her share of the conquest.

# CHAPTER IX

## THE BATTLE OF YENIDJE-VARDAR

FROM SERVIA TO VERRIA.—After its arrival at Servia,
the first necessity for the Greek army, which had been
marching and fighting for eight consecutive days
under the worst of climatic conditions, was rest; and
it is but natural that one of the first orders issued by
headquarters was to mount a strong guard over the
bridge which crosses the Vistritsa River, some miles
north-west of the town. The neglect to destroy this
important bridge demonstrates either that the Turks
were ignorant of the most primitive military tactics,
or that their defeat had been so complete that they
thought of little save to put a safe distance between
themselves and their enemy. Its destruction would
have delayed the Greek army for at least two days,
since the river at this point is very wide, and bordered
on either shore by extensive marshland. The troops
were camped out in and around the town, where they
remained for three days, while the Duke of Sparta
and his staff occupied themselves with preparations
for the continuance of the hunt—for hunt it had now
become.

On the Turkish side we received but the scantiest
information as to the march of events. Not only
had the terrorised remnants of Hassan Tahsin

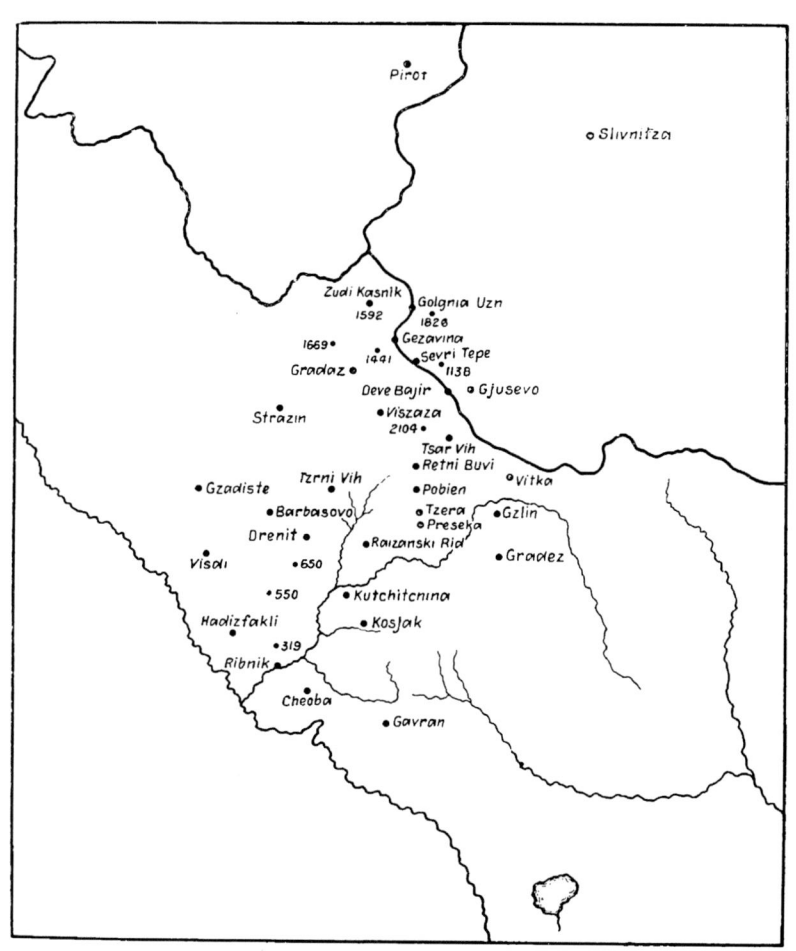

JENIDJE VARDAR.

Pacha's army eventually re-formed into two columns, but the enterprising Greek peasantry developed a playful habit of interfering with the telegraphic communications, with the result that only a small proportion of the General's dispatches ever reached Salonika. He did, however, succeed in acquainting the staff that his army had been reduced to fragments and that his Redifs were so overcome with cowardice that they were absolutely useless as fighting material. " If, however," he added, " you can send me adequate reinforcements and more cannon, I may yet be able to retard the Greek advance."

Hassan Tahsin Pacha, however, was still able to maintain communications with Djavid Pacha at Monastir, and his subsequent movements were doubtless decided upon after consultation with that most capable of Ottoman Generals.

The Turks now determined that Hassan Tahsin's army should retire on Verria (Karaferia), in the vicinity of which it was again reinforced by eight battalions and two batteries from Sorovitch, and four battalions and one battery from Katerina. In addition, the Struma army, whose occupation had hitherto been to oppose a Bulgarian advance down the Kresna Pass, was ordered to come south from Demir Hissar and assist in the defence of Salonika. In Salonika itself the garrison consisted of a scratch lot of 10,000 troops of various categories, whom it was decided to retain in the town in view of a report that two transports had already disembarked a mixed force of Greek regulars and volunteers in the Chalcidic Peninsula.

It must be remembered that at this time the

Turkish army, cut off as it was from communication with the outside world, was ignorant of the misfortunes which had befallen the Osmanli in Thrace, and they, in their blissful ignorance, still cherished a more optimistic view of the situation than was warranted by the facts. They therefore considered that the moral effect of the capitulation of Salonika would be more destructive than even another defeat in the interior.

On the other hand, the Turks determined to send a strong force south from Sorovitch. In this fashion it was hoped to catch the Greek army between two fires, and proceed to its undoing.

It is not difficult to understand, therefore, that the Greek staff, deprived even of the scanty information at our disposal, was for some time undecided as to its future movements. To them also there was a doubt as to whether their enemy would retreat upon Monastir or make for Salonika via Verria, but the same arguments appealed to them as to the Turks, and it was considered more probable that Hassan Tahsin Pacha would elect to hasten to the defence of the Macedonian seaport. They therefore decided to advance on Verria with the main army of five divisions, and to dispatch the V Division to Kozani, with the object both of covering any flank attack from the direction of Sorovitch, and protecting their unique line of communication with Larissa via Elassona. Another vital consideration which carried much weight with the Greek staff was, that once masters of Verria and district, they would be able to open up an alternative, quicker, and safer source of supplies from the sea via Katerina or Lefterohori.

On 27th October preparations were made for a resumption of the advance, and the V Division set off in its important—and as subsequent events proved—perilous errand. The Hellenic army was now, thanks to the mountainous nature of the territory, and the paucity of roads, able to thoroughly scour the country over a front of more than forty miles. In the west centre they advanced the I, II, III, IV, and VI Divisions, while the left was covered by the V *en route* to Kozani. On the right, the VII Division, which had originally been left in reserve at Larissa, had moved up to Elassona, and from thence, following the road leading through the Olympos and Flambouro ranges, had successfully occupied the famous Petra Pass. This one fact reflects sadly upon the intelligence of the Turkish staff, for a very small force could have held the Petra Pass against an army, and the march of the VII Division, which outflanked the Ottomans at Yenidje-Vardar, and which was the first to actually occupy Salonika, would have thereby been considerably delayed. The only opposition encountered by the VII Division until it arrived at the Kara Azmak River, was that offered by a few Bosnian immigrants from Katerina, who were installed at the exit of the pass.

Early on the morning of 28th October the Greek centre commenced its march to Verria. The II and III Divisions, with the artillery, took the high road; the I Division followed the right bank of the Vistritsa River, while the IV and VI Divisions crossed the mountains to the left. Before the Hellenes lay the long, tortuous, and difficult Pass of Tripotamos, and in the hands of any but the contemporary Turkish army they would have found it an expensive expedition. Hassan Tahsin Pacha had reached Kastagna, a position of great military value which dominates the road, on the 26th, and confided the principal defence to the new reinforcements received from Sorovitch (eight battalions and two batteries). The following day he reported to headquarters that the morale and discipline of his army had been restored, and that his actual position was good. The next morning, 28th October, the Greeks attacked, and the Turks, although they occupied heights from which, given average energy and pluck, they could have inflicted heavy losses upon their enemy, bolted after firing a few rounds, and left behind them eight ammunition carts fully charged.

The Greek army passed a bitterly cold night in the mountain pass, at an altitude of over 3000 feet, and the following day reached Verria without further incident.

The Battle of Yenidje-Vardar (Yenitza).—If the reader will glance at the map prepared to illustrate the progress of this battle, which sealed the fate of Salonika, he will gain an instructive idea of the problem which confronted the Greek staff upon the arrival of the Hellenic army at Verria. The road and railway, it will be observed, run almost parallel along the plain and cross the Kara Azmak River over a narrow neck of land which bridges the marshes lying north-west and south-east. The advance of an army in this direction could be effectively blocked by the destruction of the two bridges, which are but a little over one mile apart, for the marshland which flanks the stream and the

THE GREEK ARMY   ARTILLERY IN ACTION.

THE GREEK ARMY   ON THE SHORES OF LAKE YENIDJE.

nature of the surrounding terrain would prohibit the building of a pontoon bridge were the operation opposed by a comparatively small force.

It will not, therefore, surprise even the tyro in military tactics to learn that the Duke of Sparta, now in possession of the railway, decided to profit by same and move his divisions north towards Vertekop. Thence he could take advantage of the carriage road leading from Vertekop to Salonika via Yenidje-Vardar, and of the wagon tracks across the fields which several days of frost had rendered suitable for the transport of artillery. The VII Division had reached the Bridge of Nisel on the Vistrica River on 30th October, and was accordingly told off to protect the main army from a flank attack by the Turks advancing over the Kara Azmak bridges.

Yenidje-Vardar, however, is in itself a naturally strong position, for the town lies on the foothills of a range of precipitous mountains which it is impossible to outflank, and which are easily fortified to command the approaches until the lake and swamp which split the plain in twain are reached. It is a position, therefore, which, in the hands of a defending army, would naturally be used to bar any attempted advance on Salonika.

These deductions, so elementary in their nature should have been obvious to Hassan Tahsin Pacha, and it might have been expected that, on evacuating Verria, he would have proceeded across the plain to Yenidje-Vardar and have there placed his guns in position and thrown up formidable earthworks. Instead of so doing, he apparently decided that the

Greeks would endeavour to advance their entire force via Plati, for he fixed his headquarters at Culhalar, near the Kara Azmak River, and there concentrated what remained of his own army, together with the reinforcements from Sorovitch and Katerina, and the 10,000 men, which was all that remained of Ali Nadir Pacha's army on the Struma. The Turkish forces totalled about 30,000 men.

The news of the Greek advance towards Vertecop was, as far as I was able to ascertain, brought by the Salonika Redif Division, which had also been entrained south from Sorovitch to Vertekop to the assistance of Hassan Tahsin, and it was apparently the precarious plight in which this force found itself as it hurried along the road to Yenidje-Vardar that forced the Turkish Commander to move his army westward to the same destination. My theory, if it is, as I believe, correct, would explain the hurried and inadequate entrenchments which were thrown up on the Turkish positions.

When, on the morning of 1st November, I took a military train to Kirdjalar—the Turkish *point de résistance* to an advance along the railway line from Verria—the thunder of the guns could be heard at Salonika, and we knew that the great battle had commenced. Packed in a horse-box with fifty other atoms of suffering humanity, I reached the scene of action a little before midday, and, leaving the railway station, struck north-west across the plain to a point parallel to a line drawn between the opposing armies. The Turks were, as I have already indicated, in command of the heights behind Yenidje-Vardar, while the Greeks had marched in five divisions across the plain in a north-east direction. The Greek II Division, keeping to the main road, was brought to a halt at Bourgas, at which point a river some seventy-five feet wide blocks the way. The Turkish batteries rained a murderous fire upon the bridge, with the result that the Hellenes could do no more than bring their own batteries into action. Simultaneously the III Division on the Greek right joined in the mêlée, and for some hours a fiercely contested artillery duel continued. The mist from the marshes unfortunately prevented me from observing the actual results of the fire, but whether owing to indifferent gunnery or inferior material, it was obvious that while the Greeks were making exceedingly effective practice, a great proportion of the Turkish shells failed to explode.

During this time the Greek IV Division was threatening the Turkish right, and in the early afternoon the Osmanli endeavoured to relieve the pressure by a counter attack. The Hellenes were greatly inferior in number on this flank, and would possibly have been obliged to retreat had not the Turks overlooked the presence of the VI Division, which, holding the extreme left of the Greek front, swung round on their flank in turn and inflicted a severe defeat upon them.

The unsuccessful sortie had the effect of diminishing the strength of the Turkish fire on Bourgas, and taking advantage of the lull, the Greeks forced the bridge and got within effective range of the Ottoman positions.

At dusk I made my way back to Kirdjalar, and, clambering on to the top of a railway wagon, sat counting the flashes from the rival guns until as night fell and the firing ceased, a torrential rainfall drove all and sundry to shelter.

Despite a report, received with tremendous joy in the camp, to the effect that the Greeks had been driven back with a loss of four guns, it was evident that the game was up; but the General commanding the three battalions and two batteries posted at Kirdjalar would not hear of my departure. "To-night," he told me with enthusiasm, "I am going to make a night attack in order to dislodge two battalions of Greeks who are lying at Plati." My suggestion that there might be a division behind these two battalions, and that his own force was inadequate for the defence of such a vital strategic point as the Kara Azmak River, he found amusing. "Look," he cried, with perhaps reasonable confidence, "the bridge is already mined with dynamite. I have but to press a button and the whole structure will be blown to atoms. How then can the enemy pass?"

And thus, under cover of night, the battalions, which had all day bivouacked in the shadow of the straggling trees, were moved down to the bridge, and at daybreak, to the accompaniment of pelting rain and a biting north wind, the rifles began to spit out their messages of death and destruction. The issue was not long in doubt. It was a soldiers' battle, and the unhappy Turks were mown down by the score as they retreated before the Greek fire. Then from somewhere in the invisible distance there came the roar of cannon, and the Greeks, making excellent practice, rained shrapnel around the station. The Turkish gunners brought their guns into action with commendable bravery, but they were an already beaten rabble, and with a *sauve qui peut*, officers and men rushed pell-mell for the shelter of a departing train. And, in that panic-stricken flight, the Commandant forgot to press the famous button and that same afternoon the Greeks passed the river.

Simultaneously the "victorious" Turkish troops of the yesterday were flying in disorder from Yenidje-Vardar. I had left Kirdjalar to seek our horses and heard but a cannonade of short duration before the Ottoman army was seen to be retreating towards the Vardar Bridge. It was the same old story of retreat. A battalion of Redifs, throwing aside their rifles, took to flight; the infection spread, and the entire force was soon with its back to the enemy. In vain did Hassan Tahsin Pacha send a detachment of cavalry to the bridge to drive back the fugitives, and the Commander was obliged to transfer his headquarters from Culhala to Topsin and prepare his last line of defence before Salonika. On the field of Yenidje-Vardar the Turks left 3000 prisoners and fourteen cannon, with the full complement of ammunition wagons. The Greek losses totalled about 2000 killed and wounded.

# CHAPTER X

## THE TURKISH DEBÂCLE

THE cause of the Turkish flight from Yenidje cannot be better explained than by repeating a conversation which I held with some fugitives whom I met *en route*:

"Where have you come from?"

"From Yenidje-Vardar."

"Why did you run away after your victory of yesterday?"

"What else could we do, Effendi? We had fought for four days without food, the Greek fire was slaying our comrades on every hand, our ammunition was spent, and when our officers began to run, we ran too. We have had no chance to fight."

And so, with the Turks retiring across the Vardar to Topsin, and the Greeks advancing unopposed from Yenidje, I onsaddled and returned to Salonika.

.        .        .        .        .        .

I have seen many memorable sights in Macedonia, but none so heartrending and distressing as that ride back to Topsin the following morning (3rd November). The crowd was as thick as upon the road to Epsom on a Derby Day, but misery had taken the place of happiness, and sorrow was substituted for joy. I can but pick out typical instances from the mournful throng that I met wending its way from the theatre of war. First there was a mud-bespattered party of horse artillery minus their guns and horses.

"Where are your guns?" I cried in passing.

"At Yenidje; the Dushman (enemy) took them," they replied.

Then came a troop of barefooted Moslem peasants leading donkeys upon which were piled mattress and quilt and coffee-pot, all they had saved in the rush from Yenidje, when the Greek guns set fire to the rude huts they called home. Then a richer home. Two weedy oxen were dragging a creaky wooden wagon, which threatened to break asunder at every dip in the road. The worldly goods and chattels of these fugitives—beds, mats, the inevitable prayer rug, the shallow copper utensil which serves alike as cooking pan and salver even now as it did in Biblical times, a dozen unhappy ducks strung by their webbed feet to the frame—were piled high on the conveyance, and on top of this conglomeration of household effects sat wives and mothers, their sorrowful faces hidden from the sight of man, weeping and wailing as they ineffectually tried to comfort aged parents or to hold suckling babes to their breasts. They, even they who owned fields of maize in their native village, stopped me and begged for bread for the starving children who walked with torn, bleeding feet by the side of the primitive caravan, and who here and there ran to the roadside and lapped up the stagnant water left by the autumn rains.

There were sons leading their widowed mothers

G

to the great city, where tramcars run without horses and where lamps burn without oil; weary fathers carrying in their tired arms the infants they had lifted from beds of sickness; Mohammedan Hodjas urging along the stubborn mules which bore their veiled hanums; boys assisting crippled fathers; husbands carrying pick-a-back their exhausted wives. There were thousands of such scenes in this panorama of desolation.

Intermingled with this motley throng of homeless fugitives, wounded soldiers trudged painfully along—weary, sad, wan, khaki-clad figures who had dragged their ruined bodies through the long and bitter night. One barefooted, yellow-faced soldier with a bullet in his shoulder led an ass upon which was huddled his brother with a shattered thigh. The pitiable spectacle arrested me and I offered them a few piastres; they asked but for food, and devoured the sparse repast of bread and cheese I had put into my saddlebags, like hungry wolves.

"You are an English Effendi," said one in his Anatolian patois.

I nodded an affirmative, and he added:

"My father fought beside you in the Crimea; he always told me that the English were our friends. Allah reward you for what you have done to-day."

I could write without end of such sights, and repeat a hundred stories of woe and suffering; I could tell of the cold, stiff bodies of wounded soldiers who had succumbed to their injuries *en route*, and lay with the brown earth for a bier. Farther along the highway were the corpses of two women who, driven from their sick-beds, had

breathed their last during the cold of the bitter
November night; and anon I passed at a canter,
for I dared not stay to look, the small frail body
of a little child, its lifeless eyes gazing wistfully
up to the heavens. These poor martyred creatures
received but a shrug of the shoulders from the
fugitive throng which passed them by.

Moving in my own direction was a stream of
weary, dejected soldiers. They were men who,
having fled from the battle-field, had succeeded in
reaching Salonika, and were then being driven back
to the fighting line. Unwilling warriors, without a
fight left in them, they went to seek their battalions
only because fresh desertion meant starvation and
death. Muddied and often bootless, ready to
renew their flight at the first crack of a Greek
machine-gun, they were themselves utterly worthless as soldiers, and constituted, in addition, a
menace to the *esprit de corps* of their companions.

My first meeting with the troops was at the River
Gallico. Here a division of 8000 to 10,000 men
(nobody knew exactly how many) was massed as a
second line of defence. I can perhaps best describe
them as "very Redif." Their quality was poor,
and infantry, cavalry and artillery, all jumbled up
together, bore witness to the lack of organisation,
which, possibly more than anything else, was the
cause of the utter rout of the Turkish arms. The
men, who had touched no food for twenty-four hours,
were cold and hungry. They had neither bread,
nor water, nor tents, and they were destined to sleep
again in the biting north wind on the fields from
which they had already gathered every blade of sun-

baked herbage to feed their horses. What stomach had they, these poor hungry souls, to fight the last fight for the defence of Salonika? There was here no enthusiasm for war, none of that determination to die in the first trench for the honour of Islam that one reads about in Turkish journals, and which one had thought a short fortnight previously was one of the attributes of the Moslem soldier. On the contrary, the double line of sentinels which surrounded the encampment was ever busy repelling, often *corps-à-corps*, the deserters who sought to break the lines and fly from hunger and death.

From Gallico to Topsin the conditions on the road were much the same as those I have already described. At length I came again in sight of the Turkish headquarters, and found the defending army entrenched on exposed ground on the eastern bank of the Vardar. The great bridge which spanned the river had been destroyed, but at certain points, in spite of the heavy rains, the waterway was apparently still fordable. The troops, some 15,000 all told, were obviously unfit to fight. Their *moral* was gone, the men were deserting in droves, and not even officers brandishing revolvers and wielding whips were able to keep them within the lines. The General Staff was busily engaged re-forming into battalions the remnants who had escaped from Yenidje.

Across the river, some three miles distant, I saw the Greeks advancing along the road to Menteche, where they finally encamped. Against the 60,000 Greeks, the Turks had in their two camps but 25,000 demoralised, tired, and hungry men, whose numbers were being daily diminished by wholesale desertions from the ranks.

Returning once more to Salonika, I saw troops digging trenches upon the slopes which rise to the hills covering Langaza, thus indicating Hassan Tahsin Pacha's line of retreat. He obviously intended to skirt the mountains to the north-west and make for Serres.

The Greeks had advanced their VI Division on the left flank and had seized Gumendze, town and station, thus commanding the bridge which crosses the Vardar River at that point. It was doubtless this strategy which caused Hassan Tahsin Pacha to reject his first plan of offering resistance at Topsin, and to fall back on Salonika. His sun had, however, already set, for with the Servians at Demir-Kapou and the Bulgarians at Drama, he was but staving off the evil day at the cost of intense suffering on the part of his army.

.      .      .      .      .      .      .      .

The Turk had shot his last bolt in Macedonia. Except for his personal charm, there were few qualities left to him except that of a born warrior; but now he had been shorn even of his martial glory. It is still almost unbelievable that this warlike nation, the stories of whose valour fill some of the most thrilling pages in the military history of the world, could have degenerated into a beaten rabble flying before the onslaught of despised Servians and Greeks, people who till yesterday scarce dared to lift their voices when questions affecting their most vital interests were discussed and settled. The Greeks had most effectively wiped out the stain of 1897. They had shown themselves the superior of the Turk in organisation, strategy and even in personal courage.

Undoubtedly one of the chief causes of the Turkish debâcle was an entire absence of preparation and forethought. Men cannot be expected to fight on an empty stomach, and it was the rule rather than the exception for the troops to be left three or four days without food. No attempt was apparently made to grapple with the difficulties of feeding the armies. I have already described the starvation existing at Gallico and Topsin; yet these encampments were but a few kilometres from Salonika, where there was bread and water in profusion, and where the Government had ample cash in hand to make the necessary purchases. There surely existed no logical reason why carts should not have taken out bread and water and brought back the wounded soldiers who had been left unaided to drag their maimed bodies along the highway. The medical service was distinguished by its inadequacy or total absence, and it was unfortunate for the wounded that the Red Cross and Red Crescent detachments sent from England and other countries were unable to arrive by some more expeditious route.

Nor do I wish to dwell too strongly upon the lack of courage exhibited by the Ottoman soldier. It was lamentable, deplorable and unimaginable. Words fail me to describe the utter demoralisation I found in the ranks of the Turkish troops after the defeats at Kirdjalar and Yenidje-Vardar. Let me give one instance from another field, for the

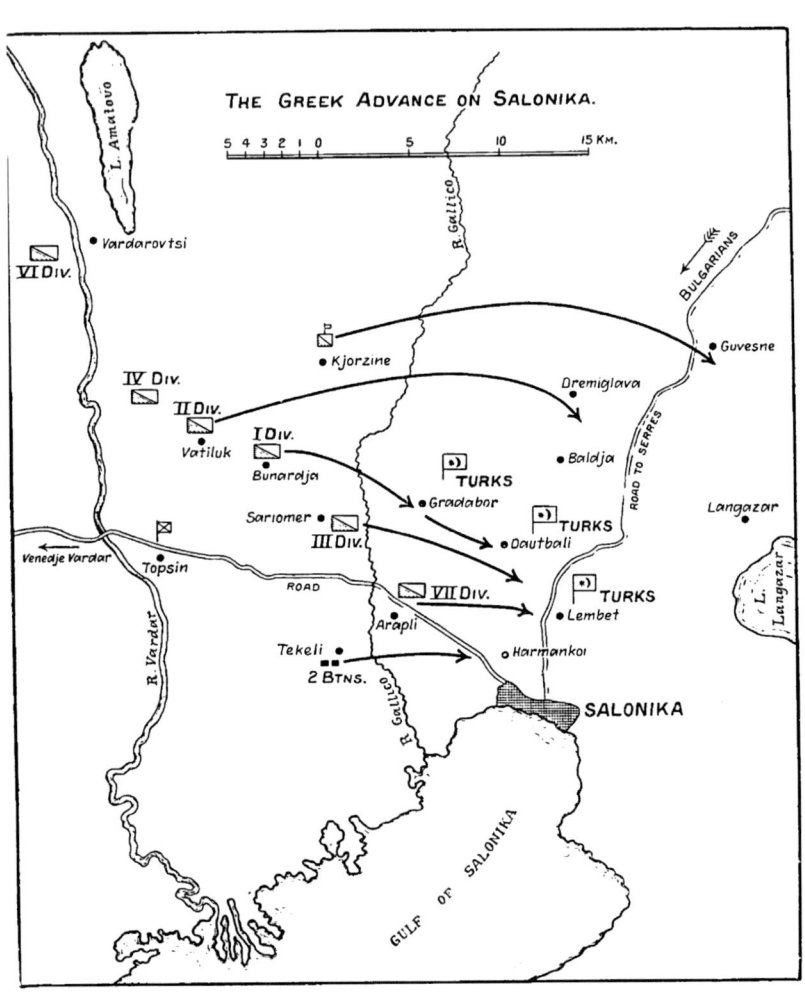

THE GREEK ADVANCE ON SALONIKA.

5 4 3 2 1 0          5          10          15 Km.

truth of which I can vouch. An exceedingly bright Turkish officer, who spoke perfectly seven languages, and who had passed through the artillery school directed by one of the German instructors with a first-class certificate, was given the command of a regiment of artillery at Kozhani. His batteries were mounted on a well-nigh impregnable position on a hill-top, and yet, immediately the Greek forces came in sight, he hoisted the white flag and surrendered with his men without firing a single shot. In many instances entire divisions of Redifs bolted from the battle-field and apparently never stopped running until they reached their homes.

*Sic transit gloria.*

# CHAPTER XI

I QUESTION whether, throughout its kaleidoscope history, Salonika has ever passed through a period of greater interest or import than those last few days which preceded the Greek occupation. We were cut off from all communication with the outside world, and surrounded by hostile armies. At Yenidje there were Greeks, at Kuprili (Veles) Servians, at Strumnitza and Demir Hissar Bulgarians, while outside the range of the guns at Karaburun lay the Greek fleet, eager to rush in and seize its impotent prey. Provisions were at famine prices; wise housewives had laid in stores of flour; Consulates had made necessary arrangements for sheltering threatened subjects. Greeks were exultant but terrified; Jews downcast and fearful for their worldly possessions; Turks broken-spirited but stoical; Europeans indifferent but anxious.

In the cold, muddied streets men wandered aimlessly hither and thither, discussing the eternal "situation" in entire ignorance of facts or details. On the outskirts of the town outgoing reinforcements jostled unconcernedly with incoming refugees. At the British Consulate, the representatives of the Great Powers sat and discussed the measures to be taken

104

for the protection of their subjects in the event of panic, pillage or massacre, for the position of the Christian inhabitants was critical, and there was still no news of a pending arrival of the prayed-for European warships. Yet until the Turkish gendarmery was disbanded some days after the capitulation, and the Greek and Bulgarian troops entered in force, the town was perfectly quiet—nobody was molested, no houses were looted, there were no epidemics; and this, let it be noted in justice to the Turks, despite the fact that there were at times within its walls thousands of starving soldiers who begged but never demanded bread.

So occupied, however, were the Saloniciens with their own immediate security, that few eyes were turned towards the palatial prison at the south end of the town, where an Imperial captive lived in ignorance of the calamity that had befallen the Empire over which he had once held undisputed sway. And it was not until the evening of 29th October, when the German stationnaire *Loreley* dropped anchor in the port, that the people deigned to concern themselves with the fate of Abdul Hamid. Yet it was obviously unthinkable that the ex-Sultan should be allowed to fall into Greek hands, and the Germans added another to their long list of diplomatic successes at Constantinople when they proffered their stationnaire for the conveyance of the fallen despot to safer climes. There was little in the way of ceremony. The following morning Hamid, his thirteen wives and his suite, were driven down to a landing-stage in closed landaus, and from thence rowed out to the German ship. It was the first glimpse of the outside world that his imprisoned Majesty had had for three years, and if one could judge from his continued and animated conversation, he appeared to mightily enjoy the experience. He had aged considerably since I had last seen him, but, nevertheless, was as active and alert as of old. No sooner was the illustrious traveller aboard, than the *Loreley* weighed anchor, and Abdul Hamid's sojourn in Macedonia was brought to its interesting close.

At 11.30 o'clock the next evening the already highly strung nervous systems of the Saloniciens were subjected to a further strain. At that hour, when citizens were confined to their houses and streets were deserted save for military patrols and a few scavenging pariah dogs, the silence of the night was broken by the report of a terrific explosion. A frail little Greek torpedo-boat,[1] braving the big guns at Karaburun, had run into the bay and torpedoed the dismantled Turkish gunboat, the *Fethi Boulen*,[2] amidships. Then, an hour later, when the forts had been advised of the catastrophe by telephone, she cheekily ran the gauntlet again. What Karaburun was doing is another question, but the sleepiness of the Salonika defences does not in any

[1] Torpedo-boat No. 11, built in 1884 and commanded by Lieut. Votsis. It fired an old 1870 Whitehead torpedo, so obsolete in pattern that it was impossible to purchase a fuze for it. The fuze was, as a matter of fact, ingeniously manufactured at Piraeus by Lieut. Waring of the British Navy.

[2] The *Fethi Boulen* was built in 1871. She was refitted in 1907, and during the Turco-Italian was re-armed with up-to-date Krupp artillery; but just prior to the Turco-Balkan war she was partially dismantled.

way detract from the courage of the handful of men
who risked their lives for their country's glory, or limit
our appreciation of the successful manner in which
they accomplished their mission. That the hull of
the *Fethi Boulen* was scarcely worth the torpedo
which sank it, was of little account, for the effect
upon the *moral* of the Turks was most noticeable.
It was the eve of the crucial battle of Yenidje-
Vardar. Salonika was in danger, but the Ottomans
at least felt that the elaborate fortifications and
powerful searchlights of Karaburun rendered them
safe from attack by sea. But now Greeks had
stepped in where Italians had feared to tread, and the
Turks would henceforth have manifested little surprise had the heavens themselves opened and rained
down shrapnel. It was a disconcerting little episode
which rendered resistance increasingly hopeless.

Next morning H.M.S. *Hampshire* steamed slowly
and majestically into port. Seldom, I think, has
the appearance of even a British warship produced
such a marked effect upon a cosmopolitan population. The Saloniciens breathed again, and many
who for a week past had not crossed the threshold
of their doors, put on their gala dress and sauntered
along the quay as if " fear " was the one word absent
from their vocabulary. Consular precautions, however, were by no means relaxed, and British residents
received private notice of an official rendezvous
where they were to forgather at the first sign of
trouble.

British and foreign battleships continued to arrive
until the port of Salonika harboured an imposing
international fleet. And here I must anticipate

events somewhat in order to relate an amusing anecdote. The Turks had effectively mined the entrance to the port, and had provided two pilot tugs, which served to guide incoming and out-going vessels through the mine field. Fearing the capture of these exceedingly useful auxiliaries, the Commanders of the foreign warships, assembled in solemn council, decided to place them under the protection of the French flag. When, then, follow-ing the capitulation of the town, the *Sphacteria* led in the Greek fleet of flour-laden transports, her Com-mander hailed the pilot tug. But it was too much for Captain Effendi. French flag or no French flag, his Moslem soul would not permit him to conduct a Greek warship into Salonika, and he declined the summons. A blank shot fired across his bows failed to influence the Turk, but when the Greek followed up with a live shell, he surrendered and got to business. All might then have ended without further ado, but the Commander of the French cruiser *Bruix* is a man of action, and, scenting an insult to the French flag, he cleared his decks for action and threatened to ram the *Sphacteria* unless satisfaction was immediately given to his outraged national honour. Thus the *Sphacteria* surrendered in her turn, and guards of honour from the English, Russian, and Austrian battleships having been solemnly paraded upon the deck of the *Bruix*, apologies were tendered, and the tricolour cere-moniously saluted.

Eloquent testimony of the overwhelming nature of the Turkish defeat were the thousands of refugees who descended upon Salonika as a plague of locusts.

Frenzied and terror-stricken and flying for their lives before the Serbo-Bulgarian advance to the north and east, they had held up southward-bound trains, and, clambering upon the engines, footboards, buffers, and wagon roofs, had faced the cold of the winter nights, and suffocation in the sulphur-laden tunnels, in their haste to reach sanctuary. Not more than fifty per cent of those who set out upon the perilous journey ever reached their destination. The rest were trampled underfoot or left sticking helpless in the muddy morass as the mass pressed forward towards safety. The race was to the strong; the weak were abandoned to their fate. Not a few, benumbed with cold, slipped from their insecure foothold on the trains and disappeared, unheeded and unregretted by their terrorised companions.

The first arrivals were quickly housed in the local mosques and schools, but, as the numbers rapidly augmented, the available accommodation was speedily exhausted, and the immigrants were thrown upon their own resources. The hardship thus entailed would have been approximately slight under favourable climatic conditions, but the weather was unusually inclement and the poor wretches were forced to seek an exposed haven against sheltering walls, and to rig up nondescript rags as a protection against the incessant downpour and the bitter north winds which swept down from the snow-clad mountains.

For Salonika it was a new danger, more potent than the advance of hostile armies, and the possibility of an outbreak of contagious disease caused the gravest anxiety. Wallowing in the mud and filth engendered by an entire absence of sanitary arrangements, one saw expectant mothers without so much as a mat upon which to lie, and women and children starved for want of bread. The camps presented a truly heartrending spectacle: numbers lay dying of hunger and exposure, while small-pox and other still more insidious diseases had already made their dreaded appearance. Charitable ladies and gentlemen, armed with European funds, sacrificed themselves in an effort to alleviate the general suffering, and worked among conditions of appalling squalor. They even succeeded in establishing a small hospital for the treatment of female patients, but their efforts were necessarily insignificant when spread over the 40,000 odd fugitives who had incessantly flowed into the town.

Simultaneously with the arrival of the first inrush of refugees had appeared train after train packed with the Turkish wounded from Koumanovo. Many were already dead from their wounds and subsequent exposure; the rest were evacuated to the military hospitals, where they at length broke a fast in many instances of four days' duration.

The paper organisation of the Turkish Army Medical Corps was fairly satisfactory. With each division there were two mobile field hospitals, each with a capacity of two hundred beds and staffed with four doctors, two officers and one hundred and eight men. One operating table was provided with each field hospital. The transport of serious cases was to have been effected, according to the existence or non-existence of roads, by the primitive and uncomfortable ambulances with which the Turkish army was equipped, or in stretchers slung over the backs of pack-mules. By the latter method two men could be carried by each mule. The base hospitals were provisionally situated at Ipek, Pristina, Uskub and Monastir. None but serious cases were intended to be brought to the central hospitals at Salonika, where a total of seven thousand beds had been provided. For railway transport, the authorities were dependent upon thirty well-fitted German ambulance wagons, each containing eight beds, but in view of the obvious insufficiency of the provision, the Turks decided to improvise further accommodation by slinging stretchers from the roofs of ordinary closed goods trucks. In addition to the Army Medical Organisation, the Red Crescent Society, under the direction of Dr Nazim Bey, the well-known Young Turk leader, provided a further two hundred beds in a large school recently erected in Salonika by the Committee of Union and Progress.

It is almost superfluous to remark that the Medical Service, like all other Turkish army organisations, rapidly went to pieces. The wounded who reached the railway dragged themselves there, and were thereupon shipped down to Salonika in any goods trucks which happened to be available. The two hundred who were fortunate enough to secure accommodation in the Red Crescent hospital— which had funds to spare at its disposal—received adequate and even excellent attention. The rest were huddled on the floors of the dirty military hospitals. These latter institutions presented a

revolting spectacle.    In the first military hospital
I saw seven hundred suffering Ottoman warriors
lying groaning on the filthy floors in their field
uniforms, their wounds swathed in dirty blood-
stained bandages.    The sole nourishment consisted
of mouldy bread.    Bandages, medicines, articles of
comfort and suitable food were all lacking, and
the hospital was lamentably understaffed.    It was
perhaps characteristic of the absence of camaraderie, which distinguished the Turks at this time,
that though the Red Crescent Hospital, over-
stocked with medical necessities, was but a stone's
throw away, its principals refused to raise a hand
to aid their less fortunate brethren who had fought
for the common cause.

In the town the population awaited the now
inevitable ringing down of the curtain on the
Turkish reign in Macedonia.    Hope had been
abandoned in the Moslem breast, and the only
question was how long it would take the Greeks to
cross the Vardar River.

# CHAPTER XII

THE occupation of Gumenze by the Greeks, referred to in Chapter X, enabled them to threaten the flank of the remnants of the Turkish army encamped upon the left bank of the Vardar River. Hassan Tahsin Pacha, after his experiences at Sarandaporon and Yenidje-Vardar, had no doubt by this time cultivated a wholesome dislike for Greek flanking movements, and he at once signalled the hopelessness of defence and struck panic into the hearts of the Salonika Turks, who forthwith insistently demanded the capitulation of the town. He then gave up the idea of defending the river, and retired to Yenikoiy, where he took up a position stretching practically from the sea to the Derbend River, east of Daoutbali. Here he was reinforced by the ragtag and bobtail of the Turkish army—some 7000 men of all ages and sizes—who had been collected in and around Salonika and hurried off to the front. But few of them knew anything of the discipline or arts of war, their military education having been necessarily confined to eleventh-hour instruction in the methods of holding and loading a rifle. However, roused to action by the fervent appeals of the Moslem Hodjas, they went forth to war to join an already beaten, unwilling horde, to whom their presence but constituted an additional danger.

Before deserting the Vardar, however, Hassan Tahsin Pacha had successfully accomplished one obvious duty—he had fired one of the spans in the wooden bridge across the river and thereby blocked the Greek advance. The railway bridge across the Kara Asmak was, of course, intact and in the hands of the Hellenes, but its surface required planking to permit the passage of artillery, and the Greeks were thereby kept back until 7th November, upon which day their army of six divisions crossed the Vardar, when headquarters were installed at Topsin.

Meanwhile, the Chalkis Peninsula, lying to the south-east of Salonika, was overrun with bands commanded by Greek officers, augmented by several battalions of Greek soldiers who had been disembarked upon its, for them, hospitable shores. From farther north, around Nigrita and Orfano, and from the Panghaion district, came news of the presence of Hellenic troops, while the Bulgarians were reported to be descending, practically unopposed, in three columns. Small wonder then that the population of Salonika, Turks, official and unofficial, Jews and Europeans, brought their influence to bear upon Hassan Tahsin Pacha with the object of inducing him to give up a hopeless fight and surrender the town to the Greeks. Capitulation, with or without a combat, was considered inevitable and beyond doubt. When returning from a visit to the Turkish camp on 6th November, I met numerous detachments of gendarmes who had quitted their post and fled, carrying with them their arms and effects. They had, they told me, to think of their wives and families, and were not going to remain to be taken prisoners by the Greeks. The policing of Salonika was thenceforth entrusted to patrols of volunteers chosen by the overseers of the various districts. Government funds, together with the receipts of the post and telegraph offices, were deposited in the Ottoman bank, and all through the night into the early hours of the morning a cursing, swearing mob of Government employees besieged the Konak, clamouring for salaries due to them for the past month.

In the midst of all this panic and despair, there was one calm, tranquil personality. Proceeding to the Konak on the evening of 8th November, I found Nazim Pacha, the Governor-General, sitting on a divan with his legs curled up under him, calmly writing his last letter as Valli of Salonika. His nation had lost its reputation; Islam had been driven out from Macedonia, and he had lost his post; but he nevertheless sat there serene and apparently unaffected by the tremendous history in the making around him, as if wishing to show to all the world that if his people were no longer invincible soldiers, they yet retained that quality of passive indifference to misfortune which has ever been one of their most striking characteristics.

In obedience to the wishes of the population of Salonika, Nazim Pacha had upon several occasions requested Mr Harry H. Lamb, H.B.M. Consul-General and *doyen* of the Consular Corps, to bring his influence to bear upon Hassan Tahsin Pacha in order to obtain his consent to an early capitulation of the town.  Mr Lamb, however, considering that his position did not entitle him to interfere in military questions, abstained from all action save that appertaining to the preservation of public order, until, on 7th November, the Turkish Commander-in-Chief himself requested him to open *pourparlers* with the Duke of Sparta.  Then, accompanied by the representatives of the Powers signatory to the Treaty of Berlin, he set out for the Greek headquarters.

# CHAPTER XIII

## THE CAPITULATION OF SALONIKA

[INTRODUCTORY TO CHAPTER.—The capitulation of Salonika has been the subject of much controversy, and the facts have been so maliciously distorted, that I have thought it well to amplify my own notes by a careful investigation, during which I have been able to collect not a little documentary evidence. I therefore feel justified in asserting that the following history of the events connected with the surrender of Hassan Tahsin Pacha's army and the capitulation of the great Macedonian seaport is in every respect authentic—AUTHOR.]

THE Greek army of six divisions crossed the River Vardar on 7th November, when headquarters were installed at Topsin. At 4.30 p.m. the Crown Prince was advised that a special train had reached Tekeli (where two battalions under Lieut.-Colonel Konstantinopoulos were by then quartered) carrying delegates with a letter from Hassan Tahsin Pacha, Commander-in-Chief of the Turkish forces defending Salonika. This document advised the Crown Prince that the Consuls of the Great Powers, in company with some Turkish officers, desired to meet the General commanding the Greek army, and begged him, at the same time, to postpone the attack on Salonika until such meeting had taken place. The Crown Prince having notified his willingness to receive the deputation, the Consuls-General of Great Britain, France, Germany, and

117

Austria, accompanied by General Shefik Pacha, proceeded to Topsin. The Consuls declared that they had urged upon Hassan Tahsin Pacha the desirability of avoiding a military engagement, in order to avert the danger threatening Salonika, and that the Turkish Commander was prepared to do so on the condition that he was allowed to retire with his army to Karaburun, there to remain until the conclusion of peace. The acceptance of these terms would, of course, have given the Greek army possession of Salonika on 8th November. The Crown Prince replied to the effect that he fully realised the danger, was desirous of sparing the town and obviating any loss of life or damage to property, but that his first and foremost object being to overpower the enemy, he must insist upon the surrender of the Turkish army, its disarmament, and the capitulation of Salonika and Karaburun; he added that he would be willing to allow the Turkish officers to retain their swords and to accept their *parole d'honcur* to refrain from further action against the allied armies. Shefik Pacha expressed his inability to accept these conditions on his own authority, and stated that it would be necessary for him to return to Salonika and there consult his commanding officer. He was informed that, failing a satisfactory reply by 6 a.m. on the following morning, military operations would be resumed.

Shefik Pacha returned at 5 a.m. next day (8th November), and conferring with Colonel Dousmanis and Captain Metaxes, the plenipotentiaries of the Crown Prince, advised them that Hassan Tahsin Pacha was disposed to accept the proffered conditions with the exception of the clause relating to the surrender of Karaburun, and that he further desired to retain 5000 men under arms to protect the unarmed prisoners. Upon the Duke of Sparta refusing to entertain any modification of his original terms, the Turkish delegates requested a renewed delay of six hours to permit a further consultation with Hassan Tahsin Pacha. This, however, was refused, and Shefik Pacha was notified that an order for the immediate advance of the Greek army would be forthwith issued.

We now come to the dispositions of the Greek army on 8th November, for the better understanding of which reference should be made to the sketch map. The positions on the morning of this day were as follows:

> Extreme right—Two battalions of Evzones (light infantry) at Tekeli.
> Right.—VII Division at Arapli.
> Centre.—III Division at Sariomer.
> Centre.—I Division at Bounardja.
> Left.—II Division at Vatiluk.
> Extreme left.—Cavalry brigade at Kjorzine.
> IV and VI Divisions in reserve at Vatiluk and Vardarovci.

In the early morning the cavalry brigade had left Kjorzine with orders to advance to Guvesna on the Serres road, with the object of intercepting the Turkish retreat. The II Division, under General Kalaris, was ordered to march from Vatiluk to Dremiglava and Baltza. The remaining divisions, I, III, VII, crossed the line Arapli-Sariomer-

Bounardja, and advanced to attack the Turkish positions on the line Lembet-Daoutbali-Gradobor. The extreme right proceeded towards Harman-keuy-Salonika, and at about 2 p.m. the entire army was developed in battle order against the enemy's position.

At 12.30 p.m. the Crown Prince with his staff set out to witness the advance of the Greek troops in the direction of Siamli. At this time, no members of the staff anticipated that the Turks would offer battle, all their information pointing to the fact that the enemy was unfit to make any serious resistance. It was felt, therefore, that sooner or later the terms offered by their Commander-in-Chief would be accepted. No sooner had the staff ridden off from Topsin than Shefik Pacha returned and was received by two officers, who subsequently reported to H.R.H. that the Turks held out for their original conditions. The Crown Prince and staff then took up position upon a hill situated near to Siamli, from whence a broad outlook on the territory lying north-west of Salonika is to be obtained. They were there able to observe the advance of the I and VII Divisions.

At 3 p.m. a Lieutenant of Cavalry rode up, bearing a message to the effect that at 11 a.m. that morning the Greek Cavalry Brigade had encountered a mixed cavalry regiment of Bulgarians and Servians at Apostolar (32 kilometres north-west of Salonika). This advance guard was followed at a distance of three hours (12 to 15 kilometres) by a mixed brigade, with a division three hours again in the rear. The mixed regiment had reported that it would spend the night of 8th-9th at Golobasi. It is important to note that this was the first intimation received by Greek headquarters of the proximity of a Bulgarian force.

The Crown Prince then wrote the following letter to the Bulgarian General (I received the copy from Bulgarian sources):

" HEADQUARTERS OF THE GREEK ARMY,
" BEFORE SALONIKA,
" *8th November* (n.s.),
" 3 *p.m.*

" MON GÉNÉRAL,—I have just learned that your cavalry has arrived at the village of Apostolar, and that it is followed by you at a distance of 10 kilo-metres—your destination being Salonika. While expressing my joy at this juncture of our armies, I have the honour to inform you that I am already at the head of my army before that town, which, as I do not anticipate any serious resistance, I shall probably enter this evening. I hasten to communicate this information to you in order that you may spare your troops the march on Salonika, and, if you think such a course advantageous, direct your forces where the military need is more pressing.

" (*Signed*) CONSTANTINE, DUKE OF SPARTA,
" *Commander-in-Chief of the Greek Army.*

"Addressed to GENERAL THÉODOROFF, Kilkish."

The Greek Commander-in-Chief then rode north to the point at which his centre was crossing the River Gallico. From there the Turkish positions

at Daoutbali and Gradabor could be plainly dis
cerned, and it was observed that the enemy was
making no preparations to offer battle.

On the morning of this day I had left Salonika,
and ridden out to the proximity of the Greek outposts. Damp, foggy weather prohibited any detailed
inspection of the lines, and the French aviators
who were whirring above assured us that the inclement conditions had prevented them from gleaning
any information concerning the movements of the
Hellenes. It was, however, clear that the principal
column was advancing along the road from Topsin
with a flanking party already well east of Tekeli.
The Greeks were at midday exactly 8 kilometres
from Salonika. Early in the afternoon I perceived
a Turkish officer, bearing a flag of truce, riding over
the hills towards the Greek lines. At 3.15 p.m. he
reached the Greek outposts and handed a letter
addressed to the Crown Prince from Hassan Tahsin Pacha. This communication was received by
H.R.H. when he reached the vanguard of the III
Division, and was worded as follows:

" SON ALTESSE LE PRINCE CONSTANTIN,
    "*Chef de l'Armée Hellénique.*

" J'ai l'honneur d'informer votre Altesse que
j'accepte la proposition de votre Altesse faite hier.

    "(*Signé*) HASSAN TAHSIN,
    "*Le Général de Division et Commandant du
    "huitième Corps de l'Armée Ottomane.*"

("I have the honour to inform Your Highness
that I accept your proposition of yesterday.")

Upon this the further advance of the army was suspended, the VII Division on the Greek extreme right and the detachment of two battalions under Lieut.-Colonel Konstantinopoulous being, however, instructed to continue their march to Salonika in order to occupy the outskirts of the town.

Meanwhile, the Duke of Sparta had dispatched two officers of his staff—Lieut.-Colonel Dousmanis and Captain Metaxes—to Salonika, there to discuss and draw up the protocol of capitulation. The Crown Prince rode to Tekeli, where he intended passing the night, and there arrived, wrote a second letter to the Bulgarian General commanding, to the effect that the Greek advance guard would shortly enter Salonika, the army taking entire possession on the following day. One of the conditions of the surrender being that Hassan Tahsin Pacha would effect the disarmament of his troops himself in forty-eight hours; the Crown Prince was desirous of avoiding the entry into the town with a very large force, his wish being to avert any danger of disturbance.

Colonel Dousmanis and Captain Metaxes having been directed by a Turkish officer to meet the Ottoman Commander-in-Chief at Daoutbali, proceeded to that village, where they were informed that Hassan Tahsin Pacha had meanwhile returned to Salonika. They followed immediately, and reached the Government Konak between 9 and 10 p.m. *Pourparlers* were immediately begun, and the protocol of the capitulation was drawn up on the base of the terms proposed by the Crown Prince in his capacity of Commander-in-Chief of the Greek army. The complete understanding was facilitated by the discussion being carried on in Greek, a language of which Hassan Tahsin Pacha possesses a perfect knowledge. The dragoman of the vilayet—Djelal Bey—was invited to draw up the document in French, and towards 11 p.m. same was signed by Hassan Tahsin Pacha and the Greek plenipotentiaries. No copy was made either in Greek or Turkish.

Upon the Turkish Commander expressing some apprehension lest the Greek II Division, in the course of its turning movement, should come into contact with some part of the Turkish army which was ignorant of the capitulation, Colonel Dousmanis immediately dispatched an officer with a written message acquainting General Kalaris (commanding the II Division) with the fact of the surrender. Throughout the discussion no mention was made of the proximity of a Serbo-Bulgarian force.

At this point it is interesting to note that up to this time no news whatever concerning the advance of Bulgarian troops along the Serres road had reached headquarters, and that if Hassan Tahsin Pacha was aware of the fact, he kept the information strictly to himself.

During the night, information reached Greek headquarters to the effect that the two battalions of Evzones had reached the town and were quartered in the suburbs (to be exact, adjacent to the brewery). At 10 p.m. on 8th October, a detachment of two officers and ten men were partaking of refreshments in the Olympos Café, Salonika's principal rendezvous. The entire VII Division reached the western entrance to Salonika towards 2 a.m. on the morning of the 9th, and later entered and took possession. Simultaneously, the new military and civil officials were appointed, and the quarter of the town in and around the railway station occupied.

A great deal has been written regarding the presence around Salonika of the Bulgarian army on the 8th and 9th November.

The officially ascertained information which reached the Greek headquarters was as follows:

Up to 3 p.m. on 8th November the Crown Prince and his staff had not the faintest idea of the proximity of the allied army. On 8th November, as already stated, the first meeting with a presumed mixed Serbo-Bulgarian force of cavalry was reported from Apostolar. On the same date, towards 5 p.m., the Greek cavalry brigade advancing from Yenikeuy on Guvesna encountered a Bulgarian column of all arms on the Serres road. Lieutenant Staikos, of the Greek cavalry, who had been present at Topsin during the first discussion regarding the capitulation of Salonika, was ordered forward to meet the Bulgarians. Nearing Guvesna he found their column coming to a halt, General Petroff and Mr Stancieff (Bulgarian Minister at Paris) having just dismounted. Lieutenant Staikos hastened to impart to General Petroff the information that the Turkish army was encircled by the Greek advance, and that *pourparlers* for their surrender and the capitulation of Salonika had been commenced the previous day. To this General Petroff responded that he knew nothing of that, and added that he was resolved to attack and bombard Salonika early the following morning. It should here be noted that though the

Bulgarians were aware that the Greek army, after the battle of Yenidje-Vardar, was operating on the right side of the Vardar River, they apparently made no attempt to communicate with the Greek headquarters; on the other hand, the Greek General Staff was under the impression that their allies were still at Demir Hissar or Serres, as no rumour even of a victorious battle or important resistance on the part of the Turks had heralded their advance.

The interview between Lieutenant Staikos and General Petroff was reported to headquarters on 9th November.

In the early hours of 9th November, the Greek II Division was at Demiglava and Baldja, and preparations were being made for an advance towards Aivatli, when Captain Georghiou, of the Greek Infantry, accompanied by a Turkish officer, hastened up to the Commanding Officer (General Kalaris), and handed him the order, written in the name of the Commander-in-Chief and forwarded by Colonel Dousmanis after the signature in the Konak of the protocol of capitulation. The tenor of this communication was to apprise General Kalaris of the Turkish surrender on the previous evening, and to order him to suspend all further operations. Almost simultaneously, General Kalaris observed to his left, in a north-westerly direction, a column of infantry approaching from Guvesna, and marching south in the direction of Aivatli. This he first imagined to be Turkish troops falling back on Salonika, but at that moment a Bulgarian officer rode up and revealed the nationality of the approaching column. To this Bulgarian officer General

Kalaris immediately handed a translation, written in pencil, of the communication which he had just received, and urged upon him the necessity of its immediate delivery to the General commanding the Bulgarian forces.   Meanwhile, the Bulgarians marched past the front of the Greek division, and developing a small detachment in battle order, opened fire against the retiring Ottoman troops. A few rounds of artillery were fired and, notwithstanding General Kalaris's communication, the Bulgarian column continued to advance upon Aivatli.

Much capital has been made out of this so-called battle between Turks and Bulgarians outside Salonika.   The Bulgarian story, as given officially to the writer shortly after their entry, was to the effect that at 5 p.m. on 8th November their forces, descending on Salonika in three columns, encountered resistance on the part of the Turkish army. Their 49th and 50th Infantry regiments, together with the 7th Artillery regiment and 2nd Mountain Battery, engaged the enemy in an action which continued until 9 p.m.   At 2 a.m., on 9th November, two columns advanced and occupied the foothills of Aivatli and Laina.   At 9 a.m. the Turkish artillery opened fire, the battle ceasing at 2 p.m.   The engagement was described as a great battle, in the course of which the Bulgarians suffered heavy losses. They did not, however, bear any evidence of this, and a subsequent visit to the alleged battle-field disclosed the fact that only three Turks had been killed on the top of one of the hills as a result of the explosion of a Bulgarian shell.   The Turks themselves persistently alleged that they had been fired upon during their retirement, and while it is true that a certain amount of cannonading was heard both on the evening of the 8th and the morning of the 9th, it is equally beyond doubt that nothing in the nature of a " battle " ever took place.

The same day (9th November) another officer, Captain Papadiamandopoulos, was dispatched by motor-car, bearer of a further letter from the Greek Crown Prince to the Bulgarian General.

While the Greek General Staff was yet without knowledge of the afore-mentioned incident, the Turkish Commander-in-Chief, now a Greek prisoner, protested against an unwarrantable attack on his troops after they had surrendered, and it was further ascertained that the Bulgarian commanding officer had demanded of Hassan Tahsin Pacha the same protocol of surrender as had been drawn up between him and the Crown Prince of Greece.   To this request Hassan Tahsin Pacha replied that having already surrendered to the Greek army, he could not do so again to a second adversary.

In order to protect the now defenceless Turkish army from a second attack, the Greek VII Division was ordered, before dawn on Sunday, 10th November, to occupy the northern entrance to the town.   It further received instructions to supervise the disarmament of the retiring Ottoman troops, and to prevent anyone entering or leaving Salonika.

Upon the events which had transpired at Aivatli being reported to the Greek Commander-in-Chief, he dispatched Captain Mazarakis to the Bulgarian General, with instructions to express his (the Greek

Commander-in-Chief's) surprise and regret that not-withstanding his repeated intimations of the surrender of the Turkish army and the capitulation of Salonika on 8th November, the Bulgarians had opened fire on the Ottoman troops, and had also demanded from Hassan Tahsin Pacha a similar protocol of surrender to that contracted with the Greek army. Captain Mazarakis encountered General Petroff at Aivatli and delivered his message. The Bulgarian General replied that he knew nothing of what had transpired, and had taken the communication of the II Division as a ruse on the part of the Turks to permit of their making an easy retreat. He added that it was only at 4 p.m. (9th November) that he observed that the Ottoman army was actually falling back, and then realised that the communication from the General commanding the II Division was genuine. General Petroff further admitted that he had requested Hassan Tahsin Pacha to surrender to him also. Upon Captain Mazarakis expressing his astonish-ment at General Petroff's ignorance of the facts with regard to the capitulation, the General insisted that he had received no advice of same from the Greek Commander-in-Chief. (There exists, however, at the Greek headquarters, a receipt, signed by a Bulgarian officer at 2 p.m. on 9th November, acknowledging a letter from the Greek Crown Prince concerning the capitulation of Salonika.) Captain Mazarakis replied that he considered this inexplicable, as the Greek Commander-in-Chief had repeatedly sent him special notifications, but added that Greek head-quarters could not possibly have sought to enter into communication with the Bulgarian army before

I

7th November, as they were totally ignorant of its presence in the vicinity.

It is well known, of course, that the Bulgarians carried out not one, but a series of forced marches in their endeavour to arrive first at Salonika. They, moreover, encountered but the most feeble resistance on the part of the Turks *en route*. The Ottoman " Struma " army had, owing to the rapidity of the Greek advance, been withdrawn from its positions against the Bulgarian columns and had been sent to reinforce Hassan Tahsin Pacha's command. The Greeks had, on the other hand, to overpower Hassan Tahsin Pacha, against whom they had been pitted since the outbreak of hostilities, and who had been continually reinforced throughout the duration of the campaign.

Towards 11 a.m. on 10th November an officer arrived at the Greek headquarters (then at the Government Konak at Salonika) with the object of requesting the Crown Prince to allow two Bulgarian battalions to enter the town. The staff officer present replied that he felt it would be more seemly were the General commanding the Bulgarian division to come and make known his wishes to H.R.H. personally.

About 1 p.m. a deputation of Bulgarian officers, comprising General Théodoroff, Mr Stancieff and a subaltern officer, was announced and was immediately received by the Crown Prince. Speaking through Mr Stancieff, General Théodoroff complained that his troops had been stopped at the northern entrance to the town by Greek outposts, who stated that, at the order of the Greek Commander-in-Chief, nobody was permitted either to enter or leave the town. He added that the army under his command had fought a heavy battle of four to five hours the day before (9th November), and that he had sustained heavy losses in killed and wounded.[1] General Théodoroff now requested permission to enter Salonika with two battalions, stating that his soldiers were tired and wet, having been exposed to the rain all the previous day and night. The Crown Prince expressed his surprise at the mention of a serious battle on the 9th, as the Turkish army had surrendered at 3 p.m. on the 8th, and he asked whether the General had not received his several letters advising him of the Greek advance, the *pourparlers*, and the surrender and capitulation of Salonika. General Théodoroff replied that the fact of the Turkish surrender was made known to them by a note brought to them by an " orderly "— (we have previously stated that General Kalaris had personally handed it to a Bulgarian officer)—that it was scribbled in pencil and signed by a " certain Kalaris." He further explained that little importance was attached to this note, as it might well have been a ruse on the part of the Turks. The Crown Prince admitted his astonishment at this statement, and forthwith enlightened the Bulgarian General as to the advance of the Greek army on 8th November, and the subsequent surrender of the Turkish army, concerning both of which events he had hastened to notify Bulgarian headquarters. He added that the

[1] I still possess a report, written for me by a Bulgarian staff officer, which distinctly states that there were " *no* Bulgarian casualties."

Turkish army had begun to fall back on Salonika as soon as Hassan Tahsin Pacha had notified his various units of his decision to surrender, and that the force encountered by the Bulgarians must certainly have been the retiring Ottoman troops. General Théodoroff, however, insisted on the fact of a hardly won victory which had cost him many casualties. Mr Stancieff then stated that he had himself entered the town the day previously (9th November), and that he had found Hassan Tahsin Pacha at the Konak, surrounded by his staff, busily issuing orders. The Crown Prince suggested that the Turkish Commander-in-Chief might possibly have been engaged in giving instructions regarding the disarmament and other similar matters. Mr Stancieff further admitted that he had encountered Greek officers and soldiers in Salonika on 9th November.

Upon the Bulgarian General repeating his request that permission be granted for two battalions to enter the town, the Crown Prince replied that to his great regret he could not accord this upon his own responsibility, it being a question that he must needs report to his Government, and concerning which he must demand special instructions. He added that, in accordance with a promise previously given, he wished to avoid molesting the inhabitants by bringing too many troops into the town, as such a course would inevitably necessitate the forcible requisitioning of suitable lodgings for the soldiers, and might conceivably lead to looting and other disorders. For this reason he himself proposed to quarter only two battalions in Salonika, the rest having received orders to find quarters in the surrounding district. General Théodoroff thereupon replied that he could answer for the good behaviour of his men, that he had sufficient lodgings provided for them by the Bulgarian community, and that, recognising the authorities appointed by the Greek Commander-in-Chief, he would submit in every way to the rules and regulations prescribed by the Commander of the garrison. The Crown Prince again submitted that on a matter of such importance, which might eventually lead to a " condominium," it would be necessary to demand instructions from the Hellenic Government. The Bulgarian General continued to argue that he did not consider that the Greek Government could have any objection to his request being granted, and pressed his point by stating that he asked but for the hospitality of an allied army for only two battalions. The Crown Prince promised to refer the matter to Athens immediately, and stated that he trusted to receive an answer by nightfall. The Bulgarians assented and withdrew. At this interview Princes Nicholas, Andrew, Christopher and Prince George (son of the Duke of Sparta) were present.

At this time the Greek staff were under a distinct impression that the Bulgarians were using every possible argument to enforce their entry into Salonika. The necessity of bringing two battalions of tired and rain-sodden troops into the town, while 30,000 equally tired and rain-sodden men would, according to their own arrangements, have to stay outside, certainly could not have been very apparent. The staff even go so far as to state that had the

Crown Prince been definite in his refusal, the Bulgarians would have entered, if necessary, by force. In this connection it is interesting to remember that the Bulgarians claimed to have sent an ultimatum to the Greeks, wherein they threatened to enter the town by force. Though the importance of the document in question was no doubt exaggerated, I believe that the Bulgars did actually train their cannon upon the town, and that, so great was their chagrin at finding themselves a day late, they would have been prepared to shell their allies had permission to enter Salonika been refused them. In such an event, the Crown Prince and the Greek army alike would have found themselves in a distinctly critical position, and Europe would have viewed the matter in a very unpleasant light. And, on the other hand, had the Bulgarians accepted the refusal as final, they would have kept a trump card up their sleeve, for the Duke of Sparta, the Greek army and the entire Greek nation would have been mercilessly chided for having refused hospitality to two battalions of an allied and friendly nation.

As matters developed, however, they were spared the risk, for on the evening of the same day Mr Stancieff called at Greek headquarters and stated that after the interview which he and General Théodoroff had held with the Crown Prince, a military council had been called together at the Bulgarian headquarters, at which it had been decided that in case of a refusal on the part of the Hellenic Government to grant the desired permission, General Théodoroff should be given ten hours' notice, when he would withdraw his two battalions.

In the meantime the necessary permission had been granted by the Government for the two battalions to enter the town, and on Monday, 11th November, towards midday, they marched in, *followed by eight others, with cavalry and artillery in addition.*

The lodgings prepared by the Bulgarian community being insufficient, many other buildings, including the Hamidieh School (prepared by Greek headquarters for a military hospital), the mosque of St Sophia, etc. etc., were violently seized and converted into barracks. During a week or ten days the orders of the *Commandant de la Place* were respected, but were eventually overlooked, and the Bulgarians then inaugurated their own military patrols, who continually interfered with the Greek police arrangements.

The text of the protocol of capitulation is as follows:

PROTOCOL OF 26*th October*, 1912 (v.s.)

Between H.R.H. the Commandant-General of the Greek Army and H.E. the Commandant-General of the Turkish Army the following has been agreed to:

*Article* 1. The arms of the Ottoman soldiers will be taken and deposited and kept under the responsibility of the Greek Army; a minute will be made to this effect.

*Article* 2. The Turkish soldiers will be quartered part of them at Karaburun, the other part at the so-called Topdji barracks; they will be fed by the Salonika authorities.

*Article* 3. The town of Salonika is surrendered to the Greek Army until the conclusion of peace.

*Article* 4. All the high military officials and officers are authorised to keep their swords and will be free in Salonika. They will give their word not to take up arms again against the Greek Army and its allies as long as the present war will last.

*Article* 5. All the high civil officials and employees of the vilayet will be free.

*Article* 6. The gendarmes and the policemen will carry their arms.

*Article* 7. Karaburun will be used for quartering the disarmed Turkish soldiers; the guns and instruments of war of Karaburun will be put out of working order by the Turkish Army and handed over to the Greek forces.

*Article* 8. The contents of Article 1 will be executed within 2 days (two days) from Saturday, 27th October, 1912; this delay may be still further extended with the consent of the Commandant-General of the Greek Army.

*Article* 10. The gendarmes and the Turkish police will continue their service until further notice.

HASSAN TAHSIN,
*The Commandant-in-Chief
of the Ottoman Army.*

DOUSMANI,
JEAN P. METAXES,
*The Delegates of
H.R.H the Prince Royal of Greece.*

RIDER TO PROTOCOL, *27th October*, 1912

*Article* 1. Two battalions of the Greek Army will enter the town this afternoon and will be quartered in the infantry barracks.

*Article* 2. The food of the Turkish soldiers and that of the horses and beasts of burden will be supplied with the co-operation of the Corporation by the local Greek authorities. The costs involved thereby will be borne by the Greek Government. The supply of the food will be begun as soon as a formal demand to the effect will have been made.

*Article* 3. Three thousand Turkish soldiers will be left with their arms to effect the disarming of the others. Once these have been disarmed they will themselves lay down their own arms; the clearing of the arms laid down will be undertaken by the Greek troops; the disarming will take place in the presence of two delegates of the Greek Army.

*Article* 4. The Commandant of the Greek Army will give strict orders so that all the villagers, the disarmed soldiers, their proprietors, their property are not attacked by any bands, and are respected by the allied troops.

*Article* 5. Strict orders shall be given to take great care to respect the traditions, the customs and the religions of the inhabitants; the religious tribunals of all religions will continue to perform their duties.

*Article* 6. The service of the Customs may

continue to act until further notice, under the control of the Greek authorities.    Likewise for the Régie and the Public Debt.

HASSAN TAHSIN,
*The Commandant-in-Chief*
*of the Turkish Army.*

DOUSMANI,
JEAN P. METAXES,
*The Delegates of*
*H.R.H. the Prince Royal of Greece,*
SALONIKA, 27*th October*, 1912.

# CHAPTER XIV

## SALONIKA AFTER THE CAPITULATION

WITH the entry of King George of Greece on 11th November, another chapter was opened in the history of the Macedonian capital. It was an event of vast political, historical and sentimental importance. But few of the onlookers remembered they were celebrating a victory over the Turks. The thoughts uppermost in their minds were that once again the Greeks were masters of Salonika, that a long exile was ended and that a dream had been realised. The imagination of the King, too, must have been fired as he entered, conqueror, into this town where ancient walls and churches tell of Byzantines, triumphal arches stir up memories of the Roman conquest, and the round, white, circular tower on the sea front speaks of the Venetians. The Turks have left us few landmarks save a wanton destruction of the old city walls and an attempt to smother up, by continual applications of whitewash, the beautiful mosaics of the Byzantine churches which they had converted into mosques.

The previous day had seen memorable sights. I found the road out to the marshes, which lie to the west of the town, alive with Greek enthusiasts *en route* to greet the victors. Here, as I gazed upon the camp of the 7th Division under General Cléoménis (the men who have been opposed to us at Kirdjalar), and saw the Creusot artillery lined up along a road flanked on either side with V-shaped khaki tents almost indistinguishable among the rushes, the Greek army made a good first impression. The men were in excellent condition, happy and bright, as befits conquerors, well clothed, booted and equipped, and ate ravenously of the raw cabbages they had plucked from the vegetable gardens which dot this district of the town. Amidst the everlasting brown of the khaki clothes and the Sneider guns of the army, the sun-baked grass of the fields and the muddy tracks which serve for roads, the landscape was gladdened only by the thousands of red fezes which denoted the Ottoman nationality of the majority of the visitors.

A comparison of this picture with that of the weary, demoralised and undisciplined Turkish troops, tentless and starving, within sight of Salonika, went far to explain why the Greeks had been able to reach their goal in a hop, skip and a jump. The order was excellent. I followed a regiment along the road and watched them bivouac in Beshtchinar Gardens. They entered the gates, split to left and right in companies, piled arms, sat down, unpacked their dinner and commenced to eat, all in perfect order, without even a word of command.

It was well into the afternoon ere a detachment of cavalry led the Evzones through Salonika's streets and gave the Greek population of the Macedonian capital their opportunity to "demonstrate." The occasion was well seized. The "Star and Crescent" had disappeared as if by magic, and in its place flew the blue-and-white flag of Greece; fair damsels showered roses upon the warriors until they marched over a flower-carpeted street, and crying "Zeto!" "Zeto!" the crowd pressed upon the khaki army until the men had to fight their way in single file. Thus commenced, the enthusiasm grew.

Like most continental towns, Salonika lives in its cafés, and it was to the cafés that the exultant mob repaired. It needed but the introduction of a Greek uniform into one of these spacious refreshment halls for the assembly to rise to its feet and shout itself hoarse. I was fortunate in being present in one of these establishments when Matzoukas, the Athenian street poet, who had cheered the soldiery with Hellenic rhyme throughout the campaign, was caught, set upon a marble-topped table and put to work. What Matzoukas failed to do in verse, subsequent speakers effected by more prosaic but none the less fervent oratory, and then the "maffe-king" began. Ottoman Greeks, till now condemned to wear the hated fez, *pour des raisons politiques*, tore them from their heads and shred them to ribbons. Other Ottomans, mostly Jews, who still retained this mark of Moslem rule, saw their head-gear summarily disappear, to be returned to them in rags; and horse-play, often of a regrettable nature, was freely indulged in.

It was as though a victorious Hellenic army was returning to its native Athens from a successful campaign abroad. It seemed incomprehensible that a Turkish defeat could thus be celebrated in a

Turkish town. In effect, it *was* more than a celebration of martial victory; it was the deliverance of the Greek population from the bondage of Turkish rule. It was only now that Georgio had been able to burn his fez; only now that this Greek café-keeper had been permitted to snatch down the red-and-white flags that had hitherto adorned his tavern, and hoist in their place his own white-and-blue emblem; only now that the Greek Ottoman had dared to proclaim from the house-top his hatred of the Turk and all his works. It was a strange, wonderful sight that one can see only in Macedonia, because there is but one Macedonia.

In comparison with all that had passed, the King's entry, in company with the royal princes and the Princess Alice (who worked heroically with the Greek Red Cross throughout the campaign) was tame. Several reasons combined to rob the royal progress of its splendour. The drenching rain was sufficient to damp the most ardent patriotism, and the enthusiasm of the preceding thirty-six hours had burned itself out. Apart from this, the show was very badly stage-managed. There was an entire absence of martial display, bands and banners were conspicuous by their absence, and it seemed to me that a great opportunity to fittingly impress the Oriental mind was thrown away. Albeit the King and his sons were affectionately welcomed. Even the Bulgarians, who after days of forced marches and a night previously spent with mud for a bed and rain for a cover, managed things better. At least they had a band—dirty and weather-worn though it was—and a torn banner to add a touch of military

colour to the proceedings, and as the young princes,
Boris and Cyril, followed a detachment of business-
like cavalry, and led in three regiments of muddied
soldiers, one felt that victorious troops had really
arrived. On the day's showing, the Bulgars had the
best of it.

In the days that followed there was much to
interest the passer-by. The martial music on the
water-side, very creditably rendered by a Greek
regimental band, the soldierly bearing and funereal
uniforms of the Cretan gendarmery, the usually filthy
condition of the streets, the tolerably clean Government Konak, the rush of military motor-cars, the
International fleet, the tramcars crowded with
soldiers until no room was left for civilian passen-
gers, the coming and going of masses of khaki-clad
troops, the blazing off of the guns of the battleships
until one knew not whether one was in the centre
of a pyrotechnic display or a pitched battle—all added
new zest even to the varied excitement to which the
Ægean town had grown accustomed. Of the many
strange sights, I saw none more curious than a band
of Greek "komitadjis," headed by a priest holding
aloft a cross, leading in a body of Turkish gendarmes
whom they had captured in the Chalkis Peninsula.
So had the tables been turned.

The streets were full, the cafés crowded ; everybody was apparently happy, and it was only when
one strolled around the shuttered market-place,
visited the camps of starving refugees, or climbed
the hill to the military hospitals, that one realised
that all was not well in Macedonia, and that the
reverse of this medal of gaudy uniforms and ani-

mated street scenes was poverty and wretchedness and suffering.

The occupation of a city of over 150,000 inhabitants, even under the most favourable conditions, is admittedly a task calculated to test the organising capacity of the most experienced of General Staffs. At Salonika the normal difficulties were increased tenfold. The Greeks found themselves preoccupied with the serious complications presented by the disconcerting behaviour of the Bulgarians. They had become the unwilling hosts of ten instead of two battalions of the allied troops ; several public buildings and one of the largest mosques had been commandeered by the Bulgars ; General Théodoroff had hastened to inform his King and the whole world that the Bulgarians had conquered the town ; and the normal population of Salonika had been subjected to a sudden increase by the addition of some 80,000 soldiers, 40,000 refugees and 25,000 prisoners of war. Moreover, Sandansky's " komitadjis " had entered the citadel, and while the Greek staff must have recognised that they were entertaining visitors who were not famous for their respect of the rights of man or beast, they found their allies disinclined to accept the measures they had framed for the preservation of public security.

There was consequently more disorder than was agreeable, and it was regrettable that the conduct of some of the more indisciplined elements of the Greek army, ably assisted by lower-class native Greeks, was highly reprehensible. The Bulgarians, defying the Greek military patrols, gave themselves up to loot and pillage, and even worse offences, diplomatically choosing the higher and less public quarters of the town for their operations; but fortunately they refrained from a repetition of the bloody savagery of which they had been guilty during their march to Salonika. The excitement, however, speedily quietened down, and there was soon little to complain of save the inevitable inconveniences resulting from the abnormal situation brought about by the dual occupation and the doubling of the population of the city.

For some time considerable bad feeling was manifested between the Greeks and the Jews. The Israelites, who form the bulk of the population of Salonika, were naturally, for sentimental and commercial reasons, displeased with the Greek occupation, and the Hellenic Press, unable in its ecstasy to appreciate any sentiments other than its own, inaugurated a campaign of anti-Semitism. This little inter-racial quarrel had its origin in the somewhat lukewarm reception accorded to King George by the Jews. The Chief Rabbi put the Jewish case to me clearly and frankly when he explained that his people were Ottoman citizens, felt the keenness of the Turkish defeats as such, and it was but natural that they should appear more mournful than jubilant. The Hellenes, on their part, insisted that the Jews should at least have hung out a few Greek flags as a sign of recognition of the conquest, if not of actual welcome. Like so many things, it all depends upon one's point of view. However, with the appointment of a Greco-Jewish Committee for the promotion of harmony between the two elements, the cloud of bitterness was soon dispersed and happier relations

K

were quickly established. The *rapprochement* was, moreover, materially assisted by the arrival of details of the misdeeds committed by the Bulgarian forces *en route* to Salonika. The Jews began a comparison of their lot with that of the populations conquered by the Bulgars, and their well-known sense of proportion did not fail to make them very contented with the fate which had befallen them.

Among the European residents at Salonika the belief was almost universally held that the task of administering the cosmopolitan Ægean seaport would prove too difficult for the Greeks, and it must be accounted them a triumph as noteworthy as their martial victories, that they quickly belied this hastily drawn conclusion.

It is my desire, in writing this story, to as far as possible avoid either favourable or unfavourable criticism of individuals, but I cannot refrain from special mention of the small band of officials who did so much to evolve order out of chaos, and who, in the doing, earned the gratitude of all and sundry.

Salonika will, I venture to assert, ever cherish the happy initiative which led the Duke of Sparta to appoint his brother, H.R.H. Prince Nicholas, to the post of Military Governor. It will be my duty, in a subsequent chapter, to treat of the masterly ability with which the Prince dealt with the difficult situations created for him by the Bulgarians, and it will suffice here to record that the kindness and consideration which H.R.H. meted out to those who were thrown into contact with him, and the impartiality with which he decided the many vexed interracial questions with which he was continually confronted, endeared him to all and sundry.

As Governor-General, Mr Ractivan, the Greek Minister of Justice, allowed neither friendship nor prejudice to influence his rulings. Perhaps, in view of the peculiar circumstances of the hour, he was lacking in elasticity, and there were times when I think he might well have tempered law with diplomacy, but none were able to complain of unjust treatment. The efforts of the Civil Governor were ably seconded by his Secretary-General, Mr Tsorbatzoglou. Here was surely the right man in the right place. An experienced Consul-General with years of experience in Turkish territory behind him, he spoke the language and sympathised with the mentality and customs of the conquered people, and was well versed in the privileged treatment to which the Consuls of the Great Powers are accustomed in Ottoman territory. Suave, *coulant* and considerate, he earned golden opinions.

It was, however, on the shoulders of the newly appointed Prefect, Mr Argyropoulos, that the burden of administering the town itself fell, and, working in close sympathy with Prince Nicholas, he handled the many thorny problems with which his office was beset with consummate skill. He showed himself able to appreciate "the point of view of the other fellow," and Turks and Jews were assured of a sympathetic hearing to their complaints, and a speedy righting of any wrongs. True, he never lost sight of the fact that he had been called upon to preside over an alien population, or forgot that hostile plots were likely to be hatched under his very nose. Thus

when Hassan Tahsin Pacha's officers, in defiance of
the terms of the protocol of capitulation, associated
themselves with the Young Turkish intrigues of the
ubiquitous Dr Nazim Bey (then in charge of the Red
Crescent Hospital) the Prefect played his part in
the evolution of a scheme, as a result of which some
five hundred of these troublesome spirits, including
the Doctor himself, were suddenly captured in street,
house or tramcar, and hustled aboard a waiting
transport.

To the unravelling of the Macedonian financial
tangle, with its maze of responsibilities towards
European interests, Mr Venezelos sent Mr Cofinas,
and it was doubtless largely upon the intelligent
advice of that able functionary that the privileges
enjoyed by the *Dette Publique* and the Tobacco
*Régie* were observed, the customs tariff of Turkish
days maintained and the existing currency recognised.   Mr Cofinas likewise inaugurated the system
of a Free Customs " Zone," which is likely to remain
a feature of commercial activity in Salonika.

It would, I think, have been impossible for the
Greek Government to have selected personalities
more fitted to carry the tremendous task imposed
upon them to a successful conclusion, and to the
sagacity of this choice must be attributed the exceedingly favourable opinion of Greek administration,
which was impressed upon all but the most bigoted
of individuals during those difficult months which
followed the entry of the Hellenic army.

# CHAPTER XV

THE reader will remember that after the Turkish rout at Koumanovo and Uskub, the remnants of the Ottoman forces retreated to Kuprili (Veles). The Serbs halted a while at Uskub for the twofold purpose of giving the troops a little necessary repose and repairing the breaches in their own armour. The Ottoman General Staff remained installed at Salonika, and it was generally understood that the next resistance would be offered at Kuprili, an exceedingly strong and easily fortified position, and one which not only commands the descent by the railway and Vardar Valley to Salonika, but would be exceedingly difficult to outflank.

What idea the Turks had in mind when they decided to evacuate this excellent strategic position, retire to a comparative cul-de-sac such as is Monastir, and leave Salonika to the mercy of their enemy, I have not yet been able to understand, the more particularly as they were at this time under the impression that the forces they had dispatched south from Sorovitch would succeed in catching the Greek army in the rear. Had Zeki Pacha's troops been maintained at Kuprili they could have been retired at any time for the defence of Salonika, and had the entire

149

Ottoman army concentrated at Monastir been sent south against the Greeks, they would have stood a greater chance of success than was rendered probable by the tactics actually adopted. The capture of Monastir would have availed the Servians little had the Turks been able to re-establish their military position, while Salonika could undoubtedly have been defended for a considerable time by the combined efforts of the armies of Zeki Pacha and Hassan Tahsin Pacha.

My surprise may, therefore, well be imagined when, on 28th October, I arrived at the Turkish headquarters, only to be informed by the sentry that the building was empty. He had strict orders to give no information, but, "as an old friend," he whispered the astounding news that the staff had left at 4.30 o'clock that same morning for Monastir. It was, then, farther north that the last scene of the Macedonia drama was to be played, and Salonika was left to the mercy of the first comer. I subsequently learned that Kuprili, the base of the great Vardar army, had been evacuated. Twenty-five thousand of the mixed crowd of Nizams (regular troops) and Bashibazooks, concentrated there after Uskub, had been sent to Kalkandelen under Fethi Pacha, and the rest, commanded by Kara Said Pacha, had left for Monastir, via Prilip.

When the Servian army marched south to Kuprili, they found the town already evacuated. News was received that the Turks were flying, via Prilip, to Monastir, having left a strong rearguard in position on the heights of the Babouna Mountains, in order to retard the progress of their enemy. On 1st Novem-

### PASHITCH.

As a young student, M. Pashitch inclined towards Socialism and saw in the "Zadruga," or Servian peasant community, a ready-made "terrain" for the application of his doctrines. Servia has partly grown out of the "Zadruga" and Pashitch entirely out of Socialism. Today he is one of the cleverest diplomats in Europe and an enormous asset to his country. He has been aptly called "The Grand Old Man of Servia."

ber, therefore, the Serbs set out for Prilip, one of the most famous towns in old Servian history. They had at their disposition the excellent military road which, running at first over open, monotonous country, at length, ever rising, enters the narrow gorge between the well-wooded mountain ranges amidst a wealth of magnificent and savage grandeur.

Half-way to Prilip is situated a dirty, dilapidated han which, once the hunting-box of a wealthy Turkish lord, now serves as a resting-place for weary travellers and tired horses. From Abdi Pacha's chiflik, as the han is still called, the road winds upward through the pass until it at length reaches the top of the range; after which the country falls away down to Prilip and the Plain of Monastir.

It was upon this range, which commands the road over the whole of its winding ascent from Abdi Pacha's chiflik, that the Turks had prepared their defence. It impresses the traveller as one of those naturally impregnable positions designed by nature with the object of permitting a beaten army to pull itself together, and I am still unable to quite realise how the Serbs were able to storm the precipitous and entrenched heights from which the Osmanli sought to stay their advance, the more especially as the assault was carried out in broad daylight, and not, as one would have imagined more practical, by a night attack. One's first idea is that a battalion or two of boy scouts with a few maxims could have kept an army at bay.

To the left, the Turks held a mountain summit 1458 metres high; their centre and right covered a string of positions stretching from summit 1458 to summit 1534, the latter being turned slightly to the south-west to oppose any turning movement by the Servian flank.    Additional opposition to such strategy was provided farther to the south, on the summit of Kojan, from whence the road from Gradsko could be commanded.    Upon all these heights they had placed field and mountain batteries. In advance of their main line of defence the Ottomans had fortified a commanding hill 1200 metres high.    Their entire position was exceedingly strong, trenches and stone walls having been constructed in order to complete the work of nature.

The attack on the Pass of Prilip, or, as it is sometimes called, Prissat, was entrusted to the Servian Morava division—which was split up into three columns for the purpose.    Two regiments left the main road and advanced along the crests of the hills to the west, with the intention of attacking the left flank of the Turks entrenched upon summit 1200; one regiment, short a battalion, was ordered to proceed over the crests to the east of the main road and march, via Nikodin, against the right of the enemy's main line; the central column, consisting of one regiment, with one battery of horse artillery in its rear, kept to the main road, and had for its primary object a frontal attack on the summit 1200; the cavalry division, with one battalion of infantry, and the unique mountain battery belonging to the Morava division, formed the extreme left of the Servian advance, and was destined to outflank the entire Turkish position.

Owing to the mountainous nature of the country, and the winding roads, the Servian field artillery was useless; their mountain battery had, as we have already noted, been attached to the cavalry division. The infantry were, therefore, called upon to make an unaided attack on the fortified Turkish positions.

As the Servian centre swung round the bend in the road, they came within short range of practically the whole of the Ottoman artillery and infantry. Seeking whatever cover they found available, the Slavs kept up a sustained rifle fire on the Turkish position on height 1200 throughout the day (3rd November), but at night had made no progress, despite heavy losses. The same day the left column suffered enormous casualties before Nikodin.

The following day (4th November) a second Servian division (Drina) joined in the fight. Coming from Kuprili, one column of two regiments crossed the hills between the main road and the left wing of the Morava division. A further column of two regiments made a detour to the extreme right of the Servian lines. Thus reinforced, the Serbs attacked the Turks on 1200 with great violence, the infantry being now aided by the battery of horse artillery, which had taken up a position on the main road. At last the order went forth to storm the mountain, and the Servians rushed up the steep slopes (which took me nearly an hour to climb), taking the successive lines of opposing trenches at the point of the bayonet, under a veritable hail of bullets from the Turkish rifles and maxims. Cover was scarce—almost non-existent—and the men had to climb like goats. They succeeded in driving out the enemy, however, and once in possession of this commanding position, were able to turn their own fire against the rest of the Turkish lines. These were subsequently captured after a tremendous effort, and Kara Said Pacha retired his troops to the heights of Kosjak, from whence he commanded the descent into the Plain of Prilip. Night had now fallen, and the armies guarded their positions until the next morning, when the Turks, after a final effort to recapture the lost vantage points, and finding their retreat now threatened from the east, retired south of Prilip.

The battle of Prilip cannot, of course, be compared in importance to those of Koumanovo and Monastir, but it was a fight of a most desperate nature, and effectively demonstrated the superb excellence of the Servian infantry. One after the other, the strongly defended and almost impregnable positions had been taken at the point of the bayonet, and it is little wonder that the casualties of the victors totalled nearly 2000 killed and wounded.

The Servian peasant is a simple idealist, steeped in tradition and superstition. I well remember discussing the battle of Koumanovo with a schoolmaster who served his country as a private soldier.

" What gave you," I asked him, " such tremendous *élan* after the severe gruelling you received during the first day's fight? "

" Well," he replied quietly, " during the combat we all saw St Sava, robed in white, and seated in a white chariot drawn by white horses, leading us on to victory."

A strange story to hear from the mouth of a warrior—and an educated man to boot—in the twentieth century, and yet he was firmly convinced of its

actuality. At Prilip there was another spirit working in the Servian imagination, and it was perhaps the
legend of Marko Kraliévitch which, more than anything else, rendered possible the heroic deeds which
marked the combat. Any Serb will tell you the
story of his national hero, Marko Kraliévitch. He
was born at Prilip, and died in 1394. According to
the legend, the hero and his horse, Charatz, are
still living in a near-by cave. There, Marko, having buried his sword in the vault, lay down and
sleeps. Charatz nibbles at the moss before him,
while little by little the sword is edging out of the
stone. And when Charatz shall have finished eating the moss, and the sword shall have fallen to
earth, Marko will awaken and reappear in the
world. He has declared, so goes the story: " In
a marvellous grotto in the mountains I await the
hour when I shall again take up my sword and
mount my Charatz, in order to reassemble all the
Serbs 'neath my banner, and, at their head, I shall
rush upon the Turks, crying, " Forward, my
brothers! in the name of our motherland and the
cross, exterminate the enemy."

There, hard by the Pass of Prilip, in the shadow
of the black, forbidding mountains, is the legendary
tomb of Marko Kraliévitch, and, talk to who you
will of the wonderful sacrifice of the Servian soldiers,
they will assure you that in those self-same shadows
they saw Marko, astride his Charatz, leading them
on to victory. These stories of Servian mysti-
cism, like the tales of fanatical patriotism which
illuminated the Hellenic campaign during the second
war, sound strange to Western ears, but they are

workers of victory perhaps more potent than modern shrapnel.

The Servians entered (re-entered perhaps one should say) Prilip with bands playing and colours flying. There is little enough to see now. Low white-washed shacks, narrow cobbled streets, trellised windows and high-walled gardens—the usual features of Turkish occupation. But the men made merry, as do victors; when suddenly, from the hills of Bakarno-Gouvno to the south, came the thunder of Turkish cannon. The Serbs had been caught napping. There was a momentary panic, and transport trains began to retire northward; but the General rallied his men, and deploying one regiment on each side of the main road, set out to the attack. There, on the shelterless plain, they offered an ideal target to their enemy. But soon the Servians batteries unmasked to cover the advance of their infantry, and then, full of the confidence born of victory, the peasant soldiers rushed at the Ottoman trenches, and drove the Osmanli *en route* for Monastir. There was again a heavy toll of killed and wounded, but the capture of Prilip had been definitely accomplished, and the Turks were thrown back upon their last stand at Monastir. Kara Said Pacha had indeed stayed the Servian advance, but at a cost of innumerable lives and nearly sixty cannon.

THE BATTLE OF MONASTIR.—The subsequent insignificant rearguard actions fought by Kara Said Pacha, in order to cover his retreat, concern us but little. He had himself no other object than to arrive at Monastir as quickly as possible, there to unite with the forces of Djavid Pacha. The Serbs waited again at Prilip, and thus facilitated his programme. Whether they could have advanced more quickly is questionable in view of the terrible condition of the roads, and the fact that incessant rain had caused the rivers which water the plain to overflow their banks, and set up a watery barrier to the Servian descent. While the Turks had been delaying the advance of their foe to the east, Fethi Pacha had descended, via Kalkandelen and Kruchevo, to Monastir, and the Turks had, therefore, a goodly force of troops and generals with which to defend their last remaining stronghold in Macedonia.

Had Monastir been a position of any strategic value to the Turks at this time, had there been any hope that a prolonged resistance at this central Macedonian fortress could have in any way affected the course of military history in the peninsula, its choice by the Turks for their last stand would have been highly logical and indeed praiseworthy. The situation as it unrolled itself after the battle of Prilip, however, but confirmed the criticism I outlined at the commencement of this chapter. With the Servians enveloping the town from the north, and the Greeks advancing from the south-east, the only way of escape was along the western road which led to Ochrida, and thence to the Albanian Mountains.

Monastir, in peace time, was the garrison of the VI Army Corps, and it played an important rôle in the military, commercial, and political history of Macedonia. Its 40,000 inhabitants, of whom Turks and Greeks were in great majority, plied a profitable trade with Albania. Situated at the foot of an amphitheatre of glorious, snow-clad mountains, it resembles, in aspect, a big, overgrown village. As a citadel it offers great advantages to a defending army. Its covering mountains effectually guarantee it from attack from the south-west, while on the north and west Nature has provided many vantage points of great strength. The approaches from the east lie over the great, well-cultivated, and well-watered plain, whereon man or beast can with difficulty find leafy protection from the summer sun; it is entirely bereft of cover for an advancing army.

When, on 13th November, ten days after the battle of Prilip, the Servians eventually moved off against Monastir, they found that Nature had set up yet another barrier to their progress. Snow and rain, which had fallen in abundance, had rendered the single road almost unfit for transport. It had, further, caused the Tserna River and its tributaries to overflow their banks, with the result that the plain had been turned into an immense lake. The tremendous obstacles which confronted the Servians on their march to Monastir will, therefore, be easily imagined.

Moving forward their divisions, now increased by the Morava (II) which had descended via Kruchevo, where it had a serious tussle with Fethi Pacha's retreating Turks, they drew an immense semi-circle around the Ottoman positions from east to west. The intention of the General Staff was to gradually draw in upon Monastir, special stress being laid upon the necessity of cutting off the Turkish retreat towards Florina to the south-east, and towards Ochrida to the west.

The Turks had confided the principal northern and western defences to the intrepid Djavid Pacha, who had placed cannon and entrenched his men on the commanding heights.   Fethi Pacha's nondescripts held the hills just to the north of the town, from whence he commanded the approaches from the plain, while Kara Said Pacha was detailed off to repulse any attack coming from the west along the short road leading from the township of Novak.

Particularly in view of the inundation of the plain and the Greek advance on Florina, the obvious strategy for the Servians would seem to have lain in a determined attempt to break the Turkish resistance on the west, and cut the line of retreat to Ochrida.   As a matter of fact, the Servian right was comparatively weak, and the staff planned the chief attack along the main road from Prilip. This decision appears to have been dictated by the mountainous nature of the country around Oblakovo. The Servian army was notoriously weak in mountain cannon, and the employment of field guns being out of the question, any concerted operation by infantry and artillery was accordingly impossible. Consequently, the principal offensive was directed against the Turkish positions due north of Monastir, where the heavy artillery, placed on the road, could render the desired assistance.

On 16th November the Serbs drove in the Turkish outposts, and the Morava (I) division, having seized the height 1200 between Lisolaj and Beranci, by a superhuman effort succeeded in placing a battery of horse artillery on the southern slopes of the mountain. To accomplish this it was necessary to dismount the guns from their carriages and drag them over bridle paths. Then occurred a development which frustrated the plans of the General Staff, for the Servian right, having crossed the Semnitza River, and having engaged the Turks at Oblakovo, found itself the object of a sustained counter attack, and obliged to demand reinforcements. Oblakovo then became the chief objective. Two regiments sent to the aid of the threatened right wing spent the whole day of 17th November traversing the overflown Semnitza, under the combined fire of the Turkish artillery and infantry. So swift was the current that the troops were obliged to form a human chain in order to avoid being swept away by the rushing waters. Towards midnight the regiments halted, and entrenched themselves in preparation for the attack of the morrow.

By day and night (17th and 18th November) Djavid Pacha, who realised the necessity of driving back the Servian right in order to preserve his way of retreat along the western road, delivered a series of counter attacks, which were heroically sustained by the Servians, numerically inferior, and practically without cannon. Thirteen times, I was informed, were the Turks repulsed, but so great was the exhaustion in the ranks of the Slavs that it is admitted in some quarters that had the Ottoman General been able to make but a fourteenth onslaught he would have accomplished his object. So persistent had been the coming and going of attack and defence that the opposing forces often occupied trenches but ten to fifteen yards distant the one from the other. On many occasions, moreover, the adversaries

actually fought *corps-à-corps*. Eventually, on
19th November, the Servians succeeded in obtaining possession of the heights of Oblakovo, where,
utterly fatigued, they rested. From their positions
they were, however, able to threaten the road to
Ochrida.

While this fierce combat had been going on, amid
execrable climatic conditions, on the western side,
the remaining Servian forces had been slowly closing
in on Monastir from the north-east. Before the
Danube division lay the dire task of fording the lake
formed by the flooded Tserna River. For a distance
of a mile and a half the men were obliged to wade,
often waist deep, through the water. Before them,
all the time, lay a precious bridge, but swept as it
was by the fire of the Turkish machine guns, the
choice lay between Scylla and Charibdis. So the
troops, under a hail of bullets and shrapnel, entered
the icy torrent and, holding hands to prevent their
being swept away, moved slowly forward. Every
man who loosed his hold, or who was struck by
shot or shell, was inevitably claimed by the rushing
torrent. Only one in three was able to fire; and
yet these brave peasants not only succeeded in
crossing, but having done so, fixed their bayonets
and carried out the assault against the Turkish
battery which had rained the leaden hail upon them.
" The finest infantry in Europe," said the attaché
of a great European Power to me, as he dwelt on
this deed of wonderful endurance and valour, which
surely deserves to be writ large in the military history of the Balkan wars.

It was on 18th November that the Danube

L

division got to close quarters with the eastern defences of Monastir, and the Turks, appreciating the hopelessness of further resistance, moved westward. Djavid Pacha, as we have already recorded, had succeeded in keeping the line of retreat more or less free until this date, and, aided by a thick fog, the bulk of the Ottoman army escaped into Albania. They left, however, 10,000 prisoners, scores of cannon, and an enormous quantity of stores to their victors.

With the capture of Monastir the Servian campaign in Macedonia was brought to its close. Djavid Pacha, together with Ali Riza Pacha, my good friends Zeki Pacha, Sulieman Faik Pacha, Kara Said Pacha, and the remains of the great Turkish army, passed the winter in Albania till, after the conclusion of peace, all were transported by sea from the Adriatic coast to Constantinople.

# CHAPTER XVI

### DEFEAT AND VICTORY

THE battle of Yenidje-Vardar, while it ensured for the Greeks the possession of Salonika, had not seen the completion of their military task in Macedonia. They had yet to do their part in the general sweeping up of the conquered territory, and, although the events which thereby transpired are technically interesting, their political importance was not always great, and a mere outline of the operations will suffice for the purposes of our story.

When, following the occupation of Servia, the Duke of Sparta dispatched his weak V Division along the road to Kozhani in order to protect the left flank of his advance on Verria, he did not anticipate that the divisional Commander would blunder into a superior force of Ottoman troops. It is difficult to imagine that a solitary division would have been sent into a country, ethnologically Turkish, with any other instructions than to keep in touch with the main army, and act strictly as a flank guard. The strategical necessity was that the troops marching on Verria and Yenidje-Vardar should be protected against the possibility of attack by a Turkish force advancing either along the railway or main road from Monastir. That object would apparently have been served had the V Division solidly occupied the Pass of Kili Derbend, north of Sorovitch, where rail and road meet, and from whence retreat to Kozhani would have been easy had scouts at any time announced the presence of a superior hostile force. The advance of the Hellenes still farther north was the result of an ill-starred initiative, which would seem to have had its origin in a desire on somebody's part to rush north to Monastir and bring off a *coup de guerre.*

Colonel Mathiopoulos reached Sorovitch with the V Division on 31st October, to find his troops worn out by their fatiguing march, and his ranks depleted by the necessity of maintaining a strong line of communication through a hostile country. He, nevertheless, pushed on beyond the Kili Derbend Pass to Banitza, which he occupied on 1st November.

There is little doubt that Djavid Pacha, who on 27th October had been ordered to Sorovitch to command the Turkish reserves there concentrated, had been carefully planning the downfall of his adversary, and he must have deliberately retired in order to entice the Greeks northward. During the night of the 2nd November Djavid, who had been awaiting his prey, suddenly flung his superior force upon the V Division, and caused it to retreat in some confusion with heavy casualties. Throughout 3rd November Mathiopoulos continued his retirement, fighting the while a rearguard action, and at night took up a position between Sorovitch and Sotir. Here the Greeks held their ground for two days; but, during the night of 5th November, they were again surprised—it is said that the outposts had

THE GREEK ARMY—SCOUTING.

THE GREEK ARMY AT REST.

fallen asleep from exhaustion—and retired in confusion with a loss of sixteen guns. The Turks did not follow up their victories, and what was left of the Greek V Division was, therefore, enabled to reconcentrate the following day, and to arrive safely at Kozhani on 7th November. This episode is said to have cost the Hellenes some 2000 casualties. All reports go to show that the troops, though overpowered, displayed great bravery, and the individual courage of the officers was worthy of the highest commendation.

Had the Turks, as I have suggested in a previous chapter, withdrawn Zeki Pacha from Kuprili to Salonika, and sent a strong force south from Monastir, the Hellenes would have been placed at a disadvantage. I do not consider that the ultimate result of the campaign would have been materially altered, for the Duke of Sparta was probably aware of the Ottoman concentration towards Monastir (28th October) before the battle of Yenidje-Vardar (1st and 2nd November), but the entry of either of the allies in Salonika would thereby have been considerably delayed, for the Greeks would have been obliged to move a large force westward against Djavid Pacha, and the Bulgarians would have been incapable of ousting Zeki Pacha from Salonika.

After his successful exploit against General Mathiopoulos, Djavid Pacha rushed back to Monastir to aid in the defence of that town against the Servians. He left, however, certain forces in this theatre, which moved eastward with the object of protecting the Turks against a renewed Greek advance on Monastir. Immediately the capitulation of Salonika had been assured, the Crown Prince ordered about two and a half divisions (III, IV, and part of the VI) to entrain for Sorovitch. They first encountered their enemy holding strong positions in the mountainous region west of Vodena, where fierce fighting occurred. The V Division, reinforced by a column of Evzones, was simultaneously ordered to advance towards Sorovitch, and though the retiring Ottomans fought rearguard actions at Kastranitza, on the south, and at Ostrovo and Gornitzevo, on the north of Lake Ostrovo, the Greek divisions were able to concentrate at Banitza on 20th November. The cavalry then advanced to Florina, where 3000 Turks and a number of guns, together with a large quantity of stores, were captured.

The remnants of the Turks found their way back to Janina—whence it was at this time anticipated that the Greeks would pursue them. It was found, however, that the movement of a thoroughly equipped army along this snow-covered route was impracticable, and the cavalry, having been dispatched to Biklista, the troops were ordered to hold the following positions:

> III Division at Kastoria.
> V    ,,    ,,  Kozhani.
> VI   ,,    ,,  Florina.

The I Division was thereupon dispatched to Epirus via Salonika.

Peace now reigned until 15th December, when the Turks delivered a smart attack upon the cavalry at Biklista, and obliged them to retire back to the shelter of their supports at Smrdes. A subsequent advance of the Hellenes to the much-discussed Korytsa proved to be the climax of the Greek Macedonian campaign, and before the end of the year the staff felt itself justified in withdrawing the VI Division to Salonika.

With the exception of the unfortunate catastrophe which befell the V Division at Sorovitch, the operations of the Greek army had been carried out with singular success. Like their allies, they were numerically superior to their enemy; but it must be admitted that they accomplished their given task uncommonly well.

# CHAPTER XVII

THE Bulgarian operations against the Turkish army in Macedonia furnish a testimony to the magnificent physique of King Ferdinand's soldiers. They provide little evidence of military prowess, because on no occasion, except during the engagement at Kotchana, where one column assisted the Servians, did they find themselves confronted with any organised resistance. In their race to Salonika, however, they carried out a series of forced marches under the most trying climatic conditions, and if, as I was informed by the medical officers, not one man fell out on account of any complaint more serious than sore feet, that fact alone is a sufficient tribute to the strength and endurance of this race of sturdy peasantry. So urgent were the orders to reach the Ægean seaport with no loss of time that the troops were, as far as possible, directed up hill and down dale "as the crow flies." Saturated by the incessant rainfall, they bivouacked in the mud and slush by the wayside, with the clouded heavens for their only cover, and, since even the convoy had been abandoned because it delayed the progress of the columns, the famished soldiers seized the cattle

168

which strayed across their path, and slaughtered
them with pocket-knives. Yet, despite these sufferings, the details of which were communicated to me
by Bulgarian officers, the troops arrived in Salonika
in prime condition.

The Bulgarian descent was operated by three
columns. One of them left the Servian second army, to
which it had been attached, at Kotchana; the other
two crossed the Rilo Mountains and worked south.
After the engagement at Kotchana with Kara Said
Pacha's division, the Bulgarian Colonel commanding
advised the Servian General that, having received
information to the effect that a very strong body of
Turks had concentrated at Radovishte, he proposed to
attack in force. He therefore requested the Servians
to delay at Kotchana pending the result of the battle.
Whether the alleged information had actually been
received or whether the statement was a mere excuse
to leave the Servians in order to undertake a march
on Salonika, it is impossible to say; but it is significant that after discovering that the reports were unfounded the Bulgarians did not return to the assistance of their allies, as was apparently their duty, but
continued their advance to the Ægean. According
to contemporary Turkish official reports, it appears
that after an attack by Bulgarian irregulars on
Radovishte—then defended only by the armed
Moslem peasantry—the garrison of Strumnitza, consisting of one Redif battalion, marched north and
recaptured the village. This battalion was subsequently surrounded by a Bulgarian regular force of
one regiment of infantry and eleven guns, and
forthwith destroyed. The Bulgars then advanced on

and occupied Strumnitza. Between Strumnitza and Salonika there were no Turkish troops.

It is somewhat more difficult to follow the movements of the Bulgarian columns descending from the north-east, for the country above Serres is largely inhabited by Bulgarians, and there was a continual interference with the telegraphic communications. The Turkish "Struma" army of about 25,000 men under Ali Nadir Pacha was originally concentrated at Demir Hissar. Almost immediately following the outbreak of hostilities the wires from Djumaia, Petritch, and Nevrecop were cut, and the Ottoman Commander found himself deprived of information from his outlying detachments at these points, which, it may here be added, consisted almost exclusively of territorial battalions.

On 20th October the Ottoman army was ordered to advance on Djumaia, and successfully reached the heights commanding the Kresna Pass. The following day a Bulgarian brigade attacked the pass, where the Turks offered a stout resistance, and, having destroyed the bridge over the river at Krupnik, they succeeded in delaying their enemy for five days. Ali Nadir Pacha had apparently anticipated that the Bulgars would confine themselves to an advance along the main road through the pass, and, by reason of the absence of communications, he was unaware of the advance of a further hostile column over the mountains to Pechevo. When he ultimately received this information he found himself obliged to move the bulk of his forces to the defence of that town. As was to have been foreseen, he arrived too late, and on 21st October Pechevo was in flames and its inhabitants in terror-stricken flight. Thereafter the Turks seem to have made a considerable advance in the direction of Djumaia without any serious fighting until, on 28th October (one week after their advance from headquarters), they were ordered to descend to Demir Hissar, there to entrain for Salonika and reinforce the army of Hassan Tahsin Pacha against the Greeks, which they joined on 31st October.

The *moral* of this section of the Turkish army is well illustrated by the fact that upon their arrival at Demir Hissar the Serres Redif division mutinied, and, refusing to accompany the army to Salonika, marched back to Serres, from whence the Mussulman population telegraphed to the authorities that they intended to retain the division for their own protection. They were leaning on a broken reed, however, for on 2nd November these patriots, hearing of the impending approach of the Bulgars, fled from the town in panic and returned to their individual homes.

On 6th November, Nadji Pacha, the Commandant of Serres, having received information to the effect that hostile columns were descending from Djumaia, Drama and Zelhova, massed his garrison force of 2000 bayonets, thirteen guns and one maxim company, and, leaving the town to the mercy of the invaders, hurriedly withdrew to Ligovan. The following day he continued to Salonika and joined Hassan Tahsin Pacha, without having put forward the slightest effort to stay the Bulgarian advance.

It will be observed, therefore, that throughout the duration of the Macedonian campaign these three

Bulgarian columns took part in nothing more serious than a few skirmishes, and that from 28th October onwards their march to Salonika was unopposed by Turkish troops. They arrived at Salonika twenty-four hours after the Greek entry—after, in fact, a detachment of Servian cavalry had also ridden in from Doiran.

The complications which then ensued have been dealt with at length in previous chapters, and it here remains only to be added that, as subsequent events have demonstrated, the Bulgarian entry into Salonika was a political blunder of the first magnitude. Their descent to the Ægean was not dictated by any military necessity, for the forces opposed to them had been withdrawn, Hassan Tahsin Pacha was already the unhappy Commander of a beaten army, and the Greeks were well able to take care of the interests of the allies on the littoral; for it is manifestly certain that had the Greeks so desired they could without the slightest difficulty have occupied Kavala and Dedeagatch by landing naval detachments. The march was, therefore, dictated solely by political considerations. Had Bulgaria stopped short of Salonika, she would have occupied an undisputed zone, the second war would have been avoided, and she might have obliged Servia to evacuate a part, if not the whole of the " arbitration " territory which King Peter's army had occupied. In grasping the shadow of Salonika, Bulgaria lost the substance of Macedonia.

It may reasonably be asked whence these 36,000 Bulgars should have gone if their action in penetrating to Salonika was so greatly at fault. They

should, of course, have been transferred immediately
to the Plains of Thrace, where their presence would
doubtless have enabled the Bulgarian army to drive
home its initial victories in that theatre. Thus might
peace have been forced upon the Turks, and the
wastage of money and human life entailed by the
subsequent weeks of negotiation and warfare would
have been avoided.

Yet, despite all these considerations, it cannot be
denied that by all save the Hellenic population of
Salonika, the Bulgarians were much more warmly
welcomed than the Greeks. Various reasons combined to produce this result. The Levantine Hellene
is, generally speaking, by no means a worthy representative of his nation. Whether this be due to
spasmodic intermarrying with other peoples, or to
the influence of environment—commercial, social and
racial—I know not; but it is an undoubted fact
apparent alike to foreigner and native. The Bulgarian physique and martial bearing without doubt
also counted for much. The Greek soldier is by
nature diminutive in comparison; he is less highly
disciplined, and until his uniform is re-designed and
he is taught how to wear it, the passer-by must be
pardoned if he fails to attribute to him that military
value which his deeds in these two wars have shown
him to possess in such high degree. This necessary
disciplining of the Hellene will not be easy of accomplishment. He is essentially democratic, and
the severity of Bulgarian or Prussian training would
destroy his " soul," while effecting no other useful
purpose. The Greek is possessed of an alert mind:
he is accustomed to think and to argue, and he will

never develop into a mere fighting machine. Rather must his individual intelligence be cultivated, and must he be taught to appreciate the logical necessity of precision in military movement. The Greek soldier of to-day is a magnificent instrument for attack; patriotism in its highest degree then replaces discipline, and officers are necessary to lead rather than to command. But these are characteristics which are thoroughly appreciated only after a close association with the people. What the Saloniciens saw were smartly attired Bulgarian guards standing rigidly at attention outside the residence of their General, and the Greek exemplar propping up a sentry-box before the palace of his Royal Commander-in-Chief—and they drew the obvious conclusions.

Yet the factor which counted for most in this preference was that the Bulgarian was accepted at his advertised value. King Ferdinand and his statesmen understand the value of the *réclame*. For years the Sofia Government has carried on a well-organised and expensive Press campaign in Europe, and has succeeded in enlisting the sympathies of well-known authors and journalists—in some instances quite gratuitously. The Greek Governments, on the other hand, have consistently failed to appreciate the power of the Press, and have not only omitted to ensure publicity to their virtues, but have permitted an unchecked exploitation of their failings. Any organised attempt to place the Greek cause before the European public is as conspicuous by its absence now, after the obvious lesson should have been learned, as it was before the Balkan wars.

Saloniciens believed the Bulgarians to be a nation of sturdy, hard-working, determined and unimaginative tillers of the soil, who had made wonderful strides of national progress since Russia made them the precious gift of independence. All this, with the exception of the alleged lack of imagination, is undoubtedly true. The race possesses many admirable and enviable qualities. Saloniciens had, moreover, so often read that the Bulgarian soldier ("who by his discipline and bravery has conquered the admiration of the whole of civilised Europe," once modestly wrote General Hassapdjieff to Prince Nicholas) was invincible, and that the Bulgars were at once the Prussians and the Japanese of the Orient, that they had become obsessed with the same idea. Lastly, the inspired reports of the victories over the Turks in Thrace had not at this time been trimmed down to truthful limits, and Lieutenant Wagner was still an undestroyed authority.

While for these and other reasons the Bulgarians became the darlings of the European colony, the sympathies of the Jews (who number about two-thirds of the population) turned in the same direction, chiefly because they feared the mercantile *savoir faire* of the Greek and regarded the Bulgar as their commercial inferior.

When, therefore, we listened to stories telling how the three columns had worked their way down to Salonika in clearing the country of hostile forces and protecting the peaceful Moslem populations against aggression, they so exactly coincided with preconceived impressions that they fell on willing ears. The Bulgarophile atmosphere thus created continued to exist until details began to arrive of the hideous atrocities committed principally by the Bulgarian irregulars who accompanied the regular army into Macedonia.    Then the native inhabitants with one accord sent up prayers of thankfulness that the town had capitulated to the Hellenes.    It is difficult to imagine why the Bulgarian Government found it necessary to play into the hands of these blood-stained auxiliaries and hand over the administration of the conquered territories to their tender mercies.    They must surely have appreciated the risk of allowing men who regard murder as a profession, and who, in many instances, had been outlawed from Bulgaria, to work their savage will upon the defenceless Moslem.    The result was a disgrace to Christianity, and immediately robbed the Bulgars of the sympathy that had hitherto been theirs.

The system followed by the three Bulgarian columns appears to have been invariable.    As the troops passed through the villages, Mussulmans were disarmed, Bulgars armed, and the lines of communication were left in the uncontrolled hands of the irregular bands.    The Bulgarian Government was, without doubt, much indebted to its *voivodes*, and these brigand chiefs were rewarded with appointments as governors of various towns and districts. This promotion of aforetime outlaws to posts of administrative authority was systematic, and a reign of terror for Moslem, and in a lesser degree for Greek, was thereby ushered in.    I well remember my astonishment at the proposal of a ci-devant Turkish Valli of Salonika to make the famous "komitadji" Tchernopieff a judge "to keep him out

of mischief," and it will therefore be understood that I
was no less surprised when I learned that the Bulgarian authorities had nominated this individual as
Governor of the flourishing tobacco centre of Kavala.

Kavala was occupied, without opposition, by a
mixed band of Bulgarian regulars and "komitadjis."
Tchernopieff, as I have already stated, was appointed
Governor of the town, and another of his felon breed,
Tchakoff, *caimakam* of town and district. A proclamation, promising to respect the lives and honour
of all citizens, was issued in the name of King
Ferdinand, following which over one hundred and
fifty innocent Moslems (including women) were
arrested on a trumped-up charge of having plotted
to massacre the Christians. At dawn on several
following days these poor wretches were led out in
batches, stabbed to death in cold blood, and left to
rot in the open air. Some of them received between
twenty and thirty bayonet wounds—others were
mutilated in a most disgusting fashion. Seven rich
Jews were arrested and imprisoned until a ransom
of £10,000 was forthcoming, and Ibrahim Pacha, a
wealthy Turk, paid a similar sum for his life. An
interesting comment on this barbarity is the fact that
most of the murdered Moslems were landed proprietors, whose ground was subsequently distributed
among the assassins.

After the flight of the Turkish garrison from
Serres, that town was surrendered to a Bulgarian
band captained by one Djankoff. Pretexting a
search for arms, the "komitadji" emptied the houses
of the Moslem inhabitants of their valuables and
outraged wives and daughters under the eyes of their

M

husbands and fathers. Several days later somebody
—whether Turk or Bulgar has not been established
—fired a rifle, whereupon a general massacre was
inaugurated, and one hundred and fifty victims fell,
often done to death in a most horrible manner.

Probably the most concentrated example of this
unspeakable savagery was perpetrated at Strumnitza. I give the story of Midhat Bey, the former
Imperial Procurator of the town, not only because
he is an educated Moslem and a personal friend,
but because I was able to confirm his report in its
essential details from no less than three independent sources, including the testimony of one of
those Protestant missionaries who labour among
the Bulgarians, and who obtained his information
from the Bulgarian inhabitants of the town themselves. Midhat Bey's report reads as follows:

"The Turkish troops evacuated the town on
22nd October, 1912 (v.s.). Four hours later a
Bulgarian band of thirty persons captained by
Tchakoff entered, followed the next day by a force
of 15,000 Bulgarian regulars and 2000 Serbs. I
was nominated Mayor. Although they had promised to respect the lives of the inhabitants, within
forty-eight hours eleven Moslems had been killed,
and one hundred shops and sixty houses belonging to Moslems and Jews had been looted by
the 'komitadjis.' Within four days thirty-four
Moslems were massacred, and I thereupon protested to the authorities. My protest being ineffectual, I resigned the mayoralty. During
twenty-two days following my resignation the

Mussulmans were summoned to the Konak by the Military Commandant and the Chief of Police, and there tried by mock court martial. Over five hundred and ninety of these people, including one doctor, two majors, four captains, four lieutenants and one hundred Turkish prisoners of war, were condemned to death. They were denuded of their valuables and clothes with the exception of shirt and drawers, and marched through the town in batches to the *abbatoir*, where, with eyes banded, they were killed, mostly by the bayonet, and buried in eight trenches dug near the barracks. Only four shops and houses belonging to Mussulmans escaped pillage, eighty cartloads of loot being dispatched out of the town. Greeks who had endeavoured to provide sanctuary for Mussulman friends saw their guests dragged out of their houses and slaughtered before their eyes."

Kilkich was the seat of a Bulgarian Roman Catholic bishopric.[1] The Uniate Church assured

[1] The Bulgarian State Church is schismatic and therefore accorded by Rome a tolerance which the Pope cannot extend to the Greek or Servian orthodox churches. Moreover, King Ferdinand himself is a Catholic and his Government welcomed the establishment of schools conducted by the sisters of Roman religious orders, just as, at a later date, it offered no opposition to the American Protestant missionaries who provided Bulgarian youths with technical instruction. This liberality of thought has stirred up considerable outside sympathy for Bulgaria, has brought to her people instruction which they lacked, but is unlikely to have any lasting effect upon the religious thought of the people. The Uniate Catholic Church is, in fact, a piece of political jobbery tolerated and protected by the Exarchate. On one occasion, when the inhabitants of a Uniate village requested the Exarch to accept their abjuration, he appealed to

a certain protection under the Turkish regime, and the Catholic missions were successful in obtaining a goodly number of professing converts. Consequently their sympathies are wholly Bulgarian, and we may, therefore, without hesitation, accept the statements of Père Gustave Michel, a priest of the French mission at Kilkich, when he tells of the abominations committed by the Bulgars in that district. He relates that he was an unwilling eye-witness to some of a long series of crimes committed in and around Kilkich. At Kurkut a band, captained by Dortchieff, drove all the men into a mosque, compelling all the women to stand around it. Then they set fire to the building and burned several hundred occupants alive. At Planitza this devilish perform-

them to remain Catholic, as they could thereby best serve the national cause. The same criticism may be applied in a lesser degree to the Protestant propaganda.

"Les Lazaristes de Salonique, en effet, ont converti bon nombre de ces Slaves au catholicisme : Kukus (Kilkich), avec son évêché catholique, est un des centres de l'église Bulgare uniate. Perdus, aujourd'hui, dans la masse des Bulgares exarchistes, ces Slaves catholiques tendent à disparaître. Mais l'Exarque Bulgare et ses prêtres ne font aucun effort pour achever la ruine de cette église. Ils semblent, au contraire, en protéger soigneusement les restes, ici, autour de Doiran, comme en Thrace autour d'Adrinople et de Kirk Kilissi. Les notables d'un village uniate étant venus trouver l'Exarque pour lui demander de recevoir leur abjuration, l'Exarque fit appel à leur patriotisme Bulgare et leur remontra qu'en restant catholiques, ils servaient bien mieux la cause nationale. C'était au moment des discussions avec la Russie pour le transfert de l'Exarque à Sofia ; l'Exarque ce servait du catholicisme pour effrayer le Russe orthodoxe, et lui montrer que les Bulgares connaissaient encore ou pourraient retrouver le chemin de Rome."—V. Bérard, "La Macedoine," p. 263.

ance was repeated by the same band, who afterwards burned the women who had witnessed the spectacle. At Rainovo hundreds of men and women were massacred, and a well was filled with corpses. In Kilkich itself the Mussulmans were massacred by the population and their mosques destroyed.

"I was called," says Père Michel, "to the death-bed of a Christian who had been beaten for having refused to deliver his little girl to a 'komitadji.' I applied to the French Consul at Salonika to have the massacres stopped, for they were a disgrace to humanity and to all Europe."

I, personally, asked a sister of the Order of St Vincent and St Paul at Salonika whether the conduct of the Catholic Bulgarians had been any better than that of the Exarchists, and she replied that "unfortunately it has been equally reprehensible."

The European steward of a large property in this district assured me that the Bulgarian peasants divided up the farms belonging to Turkish proprietors even before their owners were slaughtered.

I have cited these particular details as examples. I could increase them a hundredfold. All along the routes covered by these Bulgarian columns was left a trail of slaughter, outrage and pillage. There was a systematic attempt to exterminate the Moslems. One Bulgarian officer at least admitted and regretted these horrors.

"An engineer officer, a friend of mine," he further told me, "was in charge of a company of sappers who were repairing a bridge over the Struma River, when a convoy of six hundred Turkish prisoners was brought along in the charge of a band. The *voivode* approached him with a request that he would study the scenery behind him a few minutes. 'But why?' retorted the officer. 'Well,' continued the Chief, 'we have a few hundred Turks here, and if you will turn round we will throw them into the river.'"

An English volunteer with the Bulgarian army informed me that when Yaver Pacha surrendered near Gumuldgina, the only request he made was that his men should be placed under the charge of an escort of regular troops. "He had good reason," remarked my fellow-countryman, "for if they had been handed over to our division, not the half of them would ever have reached Bulgaria."

Simultaneously with the massacres, the Bulgarians carried out a series of "cold steel" conversions of Moslem peasants who had escaped slaughter. "Mohammed or the sword" gave place to "Christianity or the bayonet," and we were shown that acts considered as in the highest degree reprehensible when committed by victorious Moslems centuries ago can be condoned as justifiable when imitated by Christian conquerors in the present age of light and learning. I remember meeting in the streets of Salonika a wealthy Turkish tobacco planter from a village—which must be nameless because it has remained in Bulgarian territory. He had discarded the fez for the more prosaic bowler, and he answered to a Bulgarian name. Briefly, his story was that the inhabitants of the township had been called to the mosque, where it was ordered that those who desired to be baptised as Christians should lift up their hands. There being no response, several of the notables were led outside and dispatched. The invitation was then repeated and the congregation surrendered, were baptised and given Bulgarian names. In this manner were the ranks of Christianity swelled by thousands of forcibly converted adherents.

In view of the facts which I have here but briefly recorded, is it any wonder that I was constrained to telegraph to England that Macedonia was being drenched with the blood of innocents? The Bulgars first asked me to refrain from wiring over further reports, then warned me of the consequences which might follow my so doing—" Because our irregulars won't stand that sort of thing." To such requests and threats alike I had but one answer: " Stop the massacres and my telegrams will automatically cease." I find it poor excuse for this gross offence against humanity to assert that the Turks in past centuries committed similar deeds. If the Balkan War of 1912 had any justification, it was surely to replace the barbarism of the Crescent by the civilisation of the Cross. The events which transpired constituted an affront, an insult, and a disgrace to Christianity. Of protests there were many; but it was the Moslem who was being slain, and Europe would not lend us her ears and Foreign Offices carefully pigeon-holed the reports received from their Macedonia Consulates. When, at a later date, General Hassapdjieff informed the Salonika Relief Committee that the refugees might return to their homes, the Chairman (the British Consul General) felt it incumbent upon him to demand a guarantee that their lives would be respected. When, further, the correspondent of the *Temps* suggested that *La Lique des Droits de l'Homme* be petitioned to send out a commission of investigation, there was not a single representative of a European journal but felt himself compelled to join in the appeal!

Such, then, is the story of the Bulgarian march to Salonika. I have not overdrawn the picture. I have but supplied the outline and must leave it to others to fill in the details and deepen the shading. It is, even so, a sordid tale of cold-blooded savagery, and when, months afterwards, I heard a Bulgarian Protestant lecturer solicit the sympathy of an English Nonconformist audience on the ground that religious open-air meetings are permitted in the parks of Sofia, the hollow mockery of it all appalled and disgusted me. My mind inevitably wandered back to that charred mosque in which several hundred souls were burned alive, to that well choked with the corpses of slaughtered non-combatants, to those villages where terrorised Moslems renounced the religion of their fathers in order to save their unhappy skins, and to those dishonoured daughters of murdered fathers whose purity was sacrificed to gratify the lust of that army of conquerors who overran Macedonia carrying banners surmounted by a holy cross.

# CHAPTER XVIII

FOUR confederated Balkan States forming one military unit of imposing force, enjoying a free interchange of merchandise under a customs union, animated by the same ideals, owning allegiance to the same brand of Christianity, and differing only in race, language and custom. The Balkans in possession of the Balkan peoples. Such was the Utopia drawn for us by Balkan statesmen, and by many journalists and writers who had endeavoured for years past to convince the world that the one thing necessary to end five hundred years of misrule, disentangle a skein which had baffled European diplomacy for three decades and transform the danger zone of Europe into an Eden of peace and prosperity, was to drive the Turk, bag and baggage, into Asia. Yet it would be surprising to hear that there was a single soldier or diplomat in the whole of Europe who had the faintest idea that the Ottoman army would, within a few days of the outbreak of hostilities, degenerate into a hopeless, beaten rabble, or who believed that the allies would make more than a more or less successful fight, and, while gaining some extension of their frontiers, force the

Porte to grant a large measure of autonomy to Macedonia.

When the allied forces had driven their enemy from every important point in the battle area, and had beaten his armed hosts into starving guerilla bands, it was easy to talk of the inevitableness of it all, of the "course of history" and of the victory of Cross over Crescent. Even European statesmen, who had a few weeks previously solemnly warned the League that they would under no circumstances countenance any territorial changes, vied with one another in eating their words and in declaring that the *status quo*—that cherished old humbug of moth-eaten chancelleries—had vanished for ever. Thenceforth the world prepared itself for the surgical operation which should slice European Turkey into four pieces, and end, once and for all, the troublesome Near-Eastern question.

The laudable attempt of the Balkan delegates in London to preserve a united front before their common enemy was, however, so successful that for some time little was heard in Europe of the differences which had arisen between the allies, and which were to confront the plenipotentiaries when they set about the division of the spoils of war. Yet as early as November, 1912, the writer felt constrained to suggest that, far from approaching the end of the story, we had but turned the first page of a history whose unfolding will yet encompass many a tale of intrigue and bloodshed. The race to enter Salonika, the Greek success, the Bulgarian chagrin, the oft-repeated charges of bad faith on both sides, and the bitterness voiced by high and low, gave one

**VENEZELOS.**

A Cretan lawyer, who has taken his place in the first rank of European statesmen. To those who know him, he is distinguished by gentleness of manner combined with great will power and a faculty for seeing far ahead. Not the least of the outstanding characteristics of this truly remarkable man is the determination with which he has more than once defied Greek public opinion

a reminder of past Greco-Bulgarian hatred and a glimpse into the future race-struggle for supremacy.

To appreciate what the possession of Salonika meant to the allies it is necessary to remember that it is the key to Macedonia. It was one of the greatest, if not the greatest, prizes of the war. Its occupation would have permitted Bulgaria to economically swallow the whole of Macedonia, just as its annexation to Greece will enable the Hellenes to check any overpowering advance by their neighbour. Given Salonika, the Bulgars would have had, ready at hand, a great seaport with railway connections running through the vast territory they expected to annex; let it remain in the hands of Greece and they will find themselves obliged to construct a new port geographically inferior, and to lay down railway communications through a difficult country.[1]

Admittedly, after the great effort which they had put forward, it must have been exceedingly galling to the Bulgars to find themselves a day late in the race to the Ægean. There is nothing more exasperating than to be beaten by a short head. But it is really questionable whether the anger and disgust thereby engendered justified the attitude which they forthwith adopted towards their more fortunate allies. As we have noted in the history of the capitulation of Salonika, General Théodoroff had requested hospitality for two of his battalions;

[1] As long ago as 1885, Schopoff, the Secretary of the Exarchate, wrote : " Salonika ought to be the chief town of our country. Salonika ought to be the chief window of our edifice. Let us work then in Macedonia."

he actually marched in an entire brigade. He had assured the Crown Prince that the Bulgarians would only occupy the quarters provided for them by the Bulgarian community; he actually requisitioned a large number of houses and public edifices, including the mosque of St Sophia and the Turkish Law school.   He had promised that the troops should submit to the regulations of the Greek authorities; but the Bulgarians soon ignored the Greek gendarmery and inaugurated their own patrols, who, by their attitude, clearly demonstrated that they recognised no authority other than that of their own Commander-in-Chief.

Little wonder then that the relations between the two armies speedily became more unpleasant, and the visitor would have been inevitably impressed by the absence of any display of fraternity between Greek and Bulgarian troops.   It must have been strange, indeed, for any but a resident, to hear these two peoples, who till then had been engaged in the common task of slaying the Moslem, refer to the Turk as an impossible governor, but otherwise compare him favourably with Greek or Bulgar, as the case might be.   It was at best an inauspicious beginning.   Pan-Hellenism and Pan-Bulgarism were not dead, but sleeping, and signs were not lacking that the hatred between the two peoples was as living a force as when the rival bands of "komitadji" soaked the soil of Macedonia with Christian blood.

Within a week of the capitulation relations had become strained nigh to bursting point and the Bulgars were openly talking of the prospect of war with Greece. There had been trouble concerning the beautiful mosque of St Sophia—seized by the Bulgars to accommodate their surplus troops—and at one time there were Bulgarian troops in the mosque, Greeks outside in the mosque-yard and Bulgars again surrounding the whole. There had further been a serious dispute about the seizure of a Bulgarian locomotive from Serres.

Had the congestion of the rival troops continued, it is to be feared that a serious outbreak would have been unavoidable, but fortunately the exigencies of warfare in other fields necessitated the dispatch of most of the Bulgarians to Dedeagatch. The Greeks were able to provide the necessary transports and escort for the transfer of this army, but their action merits little recognition at our hands, for they would with equal or greater pleasure have transported the entire division. Simultaneously, there was a large exodus of Greek troops towards Sorovitch, and Salonika began to regain its customary calm.

Prior to his departure for Sorovitch to the relief of the V Division, the Duke of Sparta appointed his brother, Prince Nicholas, Military Governor of Salonika. This nomination gravely displeased the Bulgarians, but for Greece it proved to be one of the happiest events of the epoch. Indeed, it is not too much to say that Hellas owes a debt of gratitude to His Royal Highness for the diplomatic skill with which he handled the many critical developments during the joint occupation, and the foresight which led him, conscious of the breakers ahead, to conceive the idea of an alliance with Servia and open up *pourparlers* to that end with Prince Alexander.

One of Prince Nicholas's first initiatives was to invite King Ferdinand's sons, the Princes Boris and Cyril, to a reception at the Salonika Club, where, to the strains of military music, the healths of the Greek and Bulgarian Royal families were respectively toasted and washed down with champagne. The whole performance was, of course, a farce, but anything calculated to relieve the existing tension was, at the time, cordially welcome, and, as a matter of fact, relations were considerably improved.

Unfortunately, the new-born peace was but short-lived. In the outlying villages there had been considerable overlapping of occupation, due to the fact that the Bulgarians had marched through a country much of which had previously been occupied by Greek troops who had been landed on the gulf of Orfano prior to the capitulation of Salonika. Again at Langazar, after the Bulgars had marched through without signalling an occupation, and the Greeks had a day later hoisted their flag and inaugurated a civil administration, a band of Bulgarian irregulars under the notorious " komitadji " Dombalakoff arrived, and presenting his nomination as *délégué civile*, the chief demanded the withdrawal of the Hellenes. Dombalakoff had previously declared his sentiments towards the alliance by entering the church of the Greek village of Sohos during service, where, having warned the priest that no other sovereign than King Ferdinand was to be mentioned in prayer (the Greek custom was to name all four rulers) he cursed the Greek troops and ordered them to quit the village. Prince Nicholas subsequently retired his detachment from Langazar, and Dombalakoff, doubtless attracted by the revenues from the near-by fisheries, gave up brigandage and tried his prentice hand at civil governorship.

There were a thousand and one instances which clearly demonstrated the mutual hatred of the two races for one another, and it seemed that the Bulgars were determined to embrace every possible occasion of humiliating their allies. Thus at Likovan, on 11th November, a band of Bulgarian irregulars shot the entire Turkish male population under the eyes of a Greek detachment, who were obliged to protect the terror-stricken women and children who ran to them for sanctuary.

Though the Bulgarian forces at Salonika had been nominally commanded, first by General Théodoroff, and, after his departure with the division to Dedea-gatch, by General Andréeff, the man at the wheel was, in reality, General Petroff. Petroff's real position was always more or less veiled in mystery, but I was subsequently informed in the highest Bulgarian circles that he had actually no other office than that of guardian to the young Princes Boris and Cyril, and that subsequently, upon his own initiative, he had usurped the position of General Théodoroff and then endeavoured to control Bul-garian action. I cannot do other than agree with my informant that, although the General's spirit may be an admirable asset upon the battle-field, it was not calculated to lead to the happiest results when ques-tions sensible to amicable arrangement arose between the allies. It is not surprising, therefore (I continue to quote from highly placed Bulgarian sources) that reports emphasising the danger of General Petroff's diplomacy eventually reached Sofia, with the result that General Hassapdjieff—an experienced soldier-diplomat—was nominated as Bulgarian representative. This change of leadership arrived at a most opportune moment, when relations between the two armies were growing continually more delicate, and probably avoided a sanguinary struggle between the allies within a month of the occupation.

Early in December the dual possession of the Salonika-Serres railway led to serious friction. The Greeks held the line as far north as the 14th kilometre—where they had posted a small detachment. The Bulgars apparently coveted this position; but instead of entering into *pourparlers* with the Greek staff, they adopted the same tactics on this occasion as they months later made use of against their allies, and attempted to seize the post by force. At midday on 4th December a train coming from the direction of Serres drew up at the 14th kilometre and deposited a Bulgarian force consisting of three officers and sixty men, who ordered the Hellenes to quit. The Greeks naturally refused to obey, and telegraphed news of the incident to Salonika. There were no developments until 6.30 p.m., when another southward bound train stopped at the station. Then the Bulgarians fixed bayonets, surrounded the inferior Greek detachment, forced them to enter the carriages, bundled in their equipment after them, and sent the train forward to Salonika.

Prior to their departure, however, another act in the drama was being played in Salonika. The news of the arrival of the Bulgarians had roused the Greek staff to action, and orders were issued for the dispatch of two companies to the 14th kilometre. At 5.45 p.m. the reinforcements entrained and were on the point of leaving, when a Bulgarian officer, on the pretext that two trains were then on the single line, requested a delay. Scenting trouble, the Greek officer agreed to wait only fifteen minutes, at the expiration of which time preparations were again made for departure. Then the Bulgarian officer gave a signal and his men opposed the advance of the Greek train with loaded rifles. More Hellenic troops covered the Bulgars, however, and some " komitadjis " who were busy placing bombs higher up the line received appropriate attention.

Explanations demanded and excuses offered, the Bulgarian attempt to seize the 14th kilometre fell through. First the post was occupied by a mixed guard, but soon the Greeks were left in undisputed possession.

I have given the affair of the 14th kilometre perhaps more attention than it merits, not only because it was the first serious incident between Greek and Bulgar, but also because it marked the exit of General Petroff from executive authority. When the General heard of the failure of the Bulgarian strategy he was—so one of his brother officers of equal rank informed me—enraged, and ordered that a large force should be dispatched with orders to fire on the Hellenes. Then it was that the peacemaker, General Hassapdjieff, rose up and, flourishing the newly arrived telegram announcing his appointment to the command, declared that these were matters to be settled by diplomatic negotiation, that he had determined to follow his own plan, and that, if

N

he failed, he would perhaps then seek the aid of Petroff's battalions. It was thus that General Hassapdjieff came into our lives, and he remained a central figure in Salonicien history until, six months later, he was allowed, alone and unattended, to slip past the 14th kilometre into the Bulgarian lines.

Whether owing to his personal tact or as a result of orders from Sofia, the new Bulgarian chief immediately placed relations on a better footing. He called upon Prince Nicholas, expressed his regret at the tactics adopted by his predecessors, discoursed upon the necessity of harmony between the allies, and so impressed Greek higher circles with his sincerity and appreciation of what the ideal relations should be, that it was felt that the desired fraternity between the two races could not be far distant.

Slowly but surely, however, the breach widened again, and there developed not only antagonism between the two races, but, what was vastly more interesting to the political student, a battle of wits between the two leaders. It was my privilege to watch the sparring from very close quarters, and never was diplomatic warfare more fascinating. On the one hand there was the Greek Prince, young, polished, somewhat emotional, sincere to a fault, but a naturally brilliant exponent of honest statesmanship. If a certain inexperience was manifested in the manner in which he took unjust accusations to heart, his correspondence proved his perfect mastery of the art of diplomatic expression. Against him was matched Hassapdjieff, a soldier also, sharp, cynical, and perhaps at times a little unscrupulous, not without a certain charm of character and with

years of political service behind him; he, too, was
an accomplished French scholar, and if he erred, it
was that he sadly underestimated the value of his
opponent. General Hassapdjieff became infected
with the swelled head from which most of his comrades in Salonika suffered, and towards the end he
developed, in its most insidious form, that arrogance
which was perhaps the greatest of all causes of the
Bulgarian debâcle.

Had he been confronted with a less capable
adversary, Hassapdjieff would have added yet
another to his laurels, but Prince Nicholas, partly
because he was the cleverer diplomat and partly
because he generally had righteous argument on his
side, kept his antagonist against the ropes, and it
was only the fact that the General was present in a
civil rather than a military capacity which spared him
the knock-out blow upon the outbreak of the Greco-
Bulgarian War.

. . . . . .

It will be impossible for me, within the scope of
this story, to deal with all the many incidents which
arose to disturb the relations between the two allies.
Scarce a day passed but some cause of friction, som
more or less serious dispute, was the source of mutu
recrimination. At first the Greeks, unsure of themselves, showed a tendency to give way: but th
Bulgars took the pitcher too often to the well, with
the result that finally force was opposed by force
and the inevitable bloodshed ensued. There wer
sometimes faults on both sides, and while it is not
my object to beat any particular drum, it would
be inconsistent with my desire to lead my readers

to an understanding of the cause and effect of the Balkan wars were I not to state my conviction that, with very few exceptions, the Bulgarians were to blame for the untoward events which transpired. Their attitude towards their allies was openly hostile, and so obvious were the facts, that their attempt to cast the responsibility for their own misdeeds upon other shoulders went for naught.

Before I treat, in a succeeding chapter, with the most important of the incidents which marred the harmony of Greco-Bulgarian relations, it will be fitting for me to refer to the conclusion of the armistice with Turkey in December, 1912.

On 2nd November Kailmil Pacha, acting on behalf of the Sublime Porte, visited the Russian Minister in Constantinople, and made his first suggestion for the conclusion of an armistice. Russia, however, did not feel capable of acting alone, and Kailmil thereupon addressed himself to the Concert of European Powers. A few days later the Turkish statesman addressed a telegram to King Ferdinand of Bulgaria in which he renewed his request for a cessation of hostilities. But Bulgaria was drunk with victory and there were cherished dreams that peace would be signed within the walls of Constantinople itself. Thus far the Turkish opposition had been singularly ineffective and—well, it looked so easy to force the Tchataldja lines and encamp victorious on the shores of the Golden Horn.

The attack on Tchataldja was therefore ordered, and after three days of fierce combat (17th, 18th and 19th November), the invaders were at last repulsed with severe loss. Thereupon Bulgaria changed her tune and Mr Guéshoff declared that in view of the complications which it might entrain, his country had decided to sacrifice the idea of entering Constantinople, and he offered to sign an armistice upon the condition that Turkey should cede the Tchataldja lines and Adrianople (neither of which had been taken), together with the fortresses of Scutari and Janina, which likewise continued to resist attack. The Turks refused.

While the Bulgarian (acting also for Servia and Montenegro) and Greek delegates arranged to meet the Turkish representative at Tchataldja, Kailmil Pacha entered into negotiations with Bulgaria and Greece. The Hellenes were given to understand that their aspirations would receive satisfaction provided they would sign an armistice and withdraw their fleet from the Ægean. Had Athens agreed to this proposition (which, by the way, would have saved her thousands of pounds and months of uncertainty and anxiety) there is little doubt that the Turks would have profited by the occasion to throw reinforcements into Thrace, and matters might have gone ill with Bulgaria. Mr Venezelos, however, with that loyalty which is so characteristic of him, refused these enticing overtures and declined to abandon his allies. The result was to persuade King Fredinand's Government to insist upon the Greek conditions to an armistice which were:

1. The capitulation of Janina.

2. Maintenance of the Greek blockade of the Asiatic coast.

3. Release of Greek steamers seized prior to the war.

The Porte remained obdurate, and Bulgaria commenced to give way.  Her army was thoroughly fatigued and contaminated by cholera.  Moreover, the three days' unsuccessful attack on Tchataldja had given birth to a wholesome respect for the Turkish fortifications.  Greece, noting the weakness of her ally, appealed to her not to accept the Turkish counter proposals, and, going still further, offered to land three divisions on the Gulf of Enos, and, as a result of a combined attack on the Dardanelles by land and sea, to force the Straits and dictate peace at Constantinople in the name of the League. Bulgaria did not deign even to reply to this offer, but on 3rd December concluded an armistice with the Porte on behalf of herself, Servia and Montenegro.

Thus, while her allies rested, Greece continued the struggle.  Most happy was this for Bulgaria, for had the Hellenes left the Ægean open, Turkey would have poured reinforcements into Dedeagatch, to the immense discomfiture and perhaps certain defeat of King Ferdinand's army.  The story stands in little need of comment.  I do not know whether Mr Guéshoff deliberately planned the manœuvre which I have outlined, but it cannot but be admitted that, whereas loyalty and sacrifice characterised the attitude of Athens, that of Sofia was entirely governed by the particular interests of Bulgaria.

# CHAPTER XIX

AMID the innumerable incidents which testified to the embittered nature of Greco-Bulgarian relations during the eight months which elapsed between the two wars, the *affaires* of Subozko, Nigrita, and the Panghaion stand out in bold relief. Indeed, so clearly do they indicate the difficulties which ensued between the two nations, and the manner in which the respective authorities were wont to handle questions of so delicate a character, that their detailed consideration will relieve us from the necessity of examining the mass of minor quarrels which insistently checkmated any attempts to restore much-desired harmony.

SUBOZKO.—It speedily became notorious that the Bulgarian troops and irregulars in outlying districts were being left upon their own resources. Without pay and unrationed, they were expected to loot for a living—a proceeding which, in the case of the irregulars, composed largely of Macedonian " komitadji," was not entirely foreign to their habitual mode of existence. On 20th February a detachment of fifteen Bulgarians was installed at the little village of Pozar, which lies high upon the mountain-side, about seven hours north-west of Vodena. This village—in which the writer has more than once passed some very unpleasant days—is exclusively inhabited by the worst species of Macedo-Bulgars, who exist, rather than live, in a state of indescribable squalor and filth. The invaders belonged to a troupe of irregulars captained by one Djako, against whom the entire Moslem and Bulgarian population of the district had risen in complaint because, as the Turks adroitly put it, " he infests the villages of our district, employing sometimes threats, sometimes brute force, in order to usurp our fortunes."

The Bulgarians of Pozar ultimately found themselves compelled to appeal to the Greek authorities for protection against their own countrymen, with the result that a detachment of Hellenic troops was dispatched to clear the village of the armed intruders. Nigh into their destination the Hellenes encountered four of the " komitadjis " who, loading rifles and fixing bayonets, sought to impede their advance. With a loss of one Greek soldier wounded, the Bulgars were disarmed, the goods which they had stolen returned to the peasants, and the prisoners conducted to the near-by village of Tresino, where they passed the night. Djako, however, got together a band of fifty men, and set them off with the object of delivering their four comrades. But a Greek detachment of similar strength went in pursuit, and, encountering their foe near Pozar, they succeeded in avoiding a fight, and both bands returned to Subozko. The same day the four prisoners, with their escort, arrived at Subozko, but no sooner were they introduced into the Konak than the Bulgarian troops and irregulars garrisoned in the town attacked the building. The Greeks first shot into the air, but this demonstration proving ineffective, they directed their fire against the incoming enemy, and a general engagement took place, as a result of which one Greek and five Bulgars were killed, one Bulgar mortally wounded, and three slightly wounded. The following day the local Bulgarian authorities expressed their regret, explaining that while the *voivode* Djako was largely culpable, the origin of the unfortunate incident lay in the fact that their troops were left without food or money, and obliged to live by pillage and loot. Such then are the facts.

Whether as a result of ignorance or by design, this incident brought forward a remarkable epistle from General Hassapdjieff. With assumed pathos, he writes that he is " afflicted by the unqualifiable acts committed by the Greek troops," and asserts that " the Greek troops conduct themselves in a manifestly hostile and provocative manner." That which the inhabitants and Greek authorities call " loot and pillage," the General refers to as " a legitimate right to obtain supplies," and he asks that His Royal Highness will advise him of the measures which he will decide to take in order to " impose punishment upon the guilty persons, and avoid a future renewal of such very regrettable incidents." Incidentally, he laments that some subordinates are apparently " incapable of appreciating the great importance of the alliance between the two countries," and he begs the Prince, " in the name of the precious bonds of friendship and alliance which unite the two states," to give orders for the " immediate cessation of the arbitrary acts which prejudice our common cause."

The reader, who has the advantage of a prior knowledge of the facts, will appreciate the irony of this letter, and will, perhaps, understand the amazement which its reception caused. Prince Nicholas. The reply of His Royal Highness is so instructive that it deserves to be quoted in full. I must, however, content myself with the extraction of its most important passages. Writing to General Hassapdjieff, under date of 25th February, His Royal Highness says:

"In reply to your letter of 23rd inst., I beg to inform you that I entirely share your views. I can further assure you that the astonishment and affliction which your letter indicates are entirely justified if Your Excellency is convinced that, despite the correct attitude of your troops, obedient to the orders which they receive from their superiors, the Greek detachments act towards them in a hostile and provocative manner. If you are certain that the military authorities under my orders are incapable of appreciating the importance which I attach to the sacred obligations of our alliance, and act in contradiction to my convictions and formal instructions, believe me that I cannot find words with which to sufficiently brand such insubordination to my orders. If, as you assure me, my soldiers interfere with your troops in the accomplishment of their duty, and, without reason, prevent them from procuring their means of livelihood, that fact alone constitutes a most deplorable lack of camaraderie.

"If," again continues His Royal Highness, "my subordinates have acted in the manner you have indicated, you are entirely justified in charging them with the entire responsibility."

With this tactful admission as to the enormity of the offence which had been committed, Prince Nicholas's agreement with General Hassapdjieff ends, and he forthwith cleverly saddles the Bulgarian with his own condemnation.

"But unfortunately," he adds, "the facts are not as you would wish me to understand them. If your soldiers had been satisfied to use the authorisation to requisition in the villages surrounding Subozko, do you think that my subordinates would have opposed them? Are you not disposed to think that the manner in which your troops have sought to secure provisions has not always been in accordance with customary usage?"

Prince Nicholas then proceeds to point out that the Bulgarian victims do not belong to the regular army, and that even his own people were unanimous in the opinion that the author of the regrettable incidents was none other than the ex-"komitadji," Djako; he further reminds the General of his own declaration to Mr Venezelos that the presence of such individuals in the service of the army constituted an element of menace and danger. In accordance with this understanding, the Greek authorities subsequently desired to arrest Djako, but desisted at the request of Colonel Tsilingiroff, who assured them that this "komitadji," denounced as a brigand by all the inhabitants of the district, was, in fact, an officer of gendarmery, and, consequently, a functionary of the Bulgarian state. Had Djako proved to be a priest on holiday, no surprise would have been felt by those versed in Macedonian history, but to find a gendarmery officer masquerading as a brigand chief was truly Gilbertian. The story, however, served its turn, and the chameleon outlaw went unpunished.

NIGRITA.—I think 5th March, 1913, was the most memorable of the many memorable days which I have spent in Salonika. It was a day of double fête. In view of the close ties which bind Queen Olga to Russia, we had all prepared to rejoice at the Tercentenary of the Romanoff dynasty, and on that very morning there arrived the great news of the fall of Janina. Queen Olga was overcome with emotion.

"What a godsend we did not receive the news last night," observed Her Majesty to me. "The suspense would have been too cruel."

And so the Cretan gendarmery played the Russian anthem, and Greek royalty went to the Russian church; and as we left the church guns boomed out a salute for the victors of Janina; and then Russian officials went to the Greek church; and at night there was a ball at the Russian Consulate for the Romanoffs, and a torchlight procession in the streets for Janina; and everybody in Hellas was rejoicing everywhere—except in Nigrita.

Whether Nigrita can be held to have been theoretically occupied by the Bulgarians before the

**H.R.H. PRINCE NICHOLAS OF GREECE.**

A younger brother of King Constantine. He is a General of Division, an excellent artillery officer, and endowed with rare diplomatic talent. His negotiation of the Greco-Servian Treaty and his handling of the intensely difficult situation in Salonika, following the capitulation of the town, assure to him a prominent place in Greek history. He is beloved by all who enjoy the privilege of his friendship.

Greek army took the town after a two hours' skirmish with the local Turkish garrison, is not for me to decide. So far as we are concerned, it will suffice to know that it was captured from the enemy by the Greeks, and that its population is exclusively Hellene and Turkish. As its possession might under certain circumstances have been of considerable importance when the new frontier came to be drawn, the Bulgarian desire to remove the Greek outpost is not difficult to understand.

There had been frequent incidents and much discussion on both sides concerning the question of re-provisioning, as a result of which Prince Nicholas was constrained to write to General Hassapdjieff, under date of 4th March, that "our incontestable right to priority of occupation in the district of Nigrita prevents our allowing the Governor of Serres to interfere in the administration of these localities," and requests him to "give orders to cease the dispatch of Bulgarian troops into territory occupied and administered by us," which "may give rise to incidents which I should be the first to deplore, but for which I absolutely decline all responsibility." He adds that the Greek authorities have already assured the Bulgarian representatives that "no difficulty will be opposed to the transport of their post, or the re-victualling of their troops, provided that same is undertaken in a rational manner, and not as was done at Subozko."

The Bulgarians had, however, determined to seize Nigrita, and, by an unhappy chance, they chose the very day upon which the heart of the Hellas was palpitating with joy at the victory over the Crescent at Janina on which to turn their cannon against their friends and allies. " My indignation and my sadness," writes Prince Nicholas to Hassap-djieff, " are so great that it is impossible for me to describe my feelings, but I must utter a loud cry of protest against the attitude and conduct of those who are responsible for this act, which is without parallel in the history of nations."

It was, in effect, during the morning of 5th March that the Greek Commander at Nigrita learned of the approach of Bulgarian troops, who, upon their arrival, took up a position outside the town and opened fire. The hostile forces numbered 868 rifles, 66 sabres, 2 cannons, and 2 maxims. The Greeks had 807 rifles (only 507 of which took part in the combat), and were unsupported by cavalry or artillery. The company of Bulgarian soldiers in the town simultaneously attacked the Hellenes, but were speedily overpowered. The onslaught was so unexpected that the Greeks had no time in which to make adequate preparations, but they resisted their enemy during the whole of the day, with a loss of fourteen killed and twenty-six wounded.

The next day the Bulgarians, reinforced by two additional cannon, renewed the attack, but the defenders again held their positions. A third day the battle continued with a successful counter attack by the Greeks on the positions towards the village of Phytoki, and, with the arrival of reinforcements, the fighting ceased. The Bulgarian attempt to seize Nigrita had, however, failed, and two days later they began their retreat.

Needless to say, an incident of a nature so grave

as that of Nigrita gave rise to a considerable interchange of notes between the respective military
chiefs. While there does not appear to have been
any attempt on the part of the Bulgarians to justify
their action, the local Greek Commandant was informed that General Hassapdjieff had been requested
to arrange with Prince Nicholas for the dispatch
upon the scene of a mixed commission, with a view
to bringing about a cessation of hostilities, and after
some delay peace was once again established. The
situation had, however, been so obviously serious
that it led to an exchange of views between Athens
and Sofia, and Mr Venezelos ultimately proposed
the nomination of a mixed commission for the settlement of all questions in suspense between the two
allies. There was, it is advisable to add, not the
slightest hope that an accord would be thereby
reached, but it was recognised that the mere fact
of the existence of a commission would tend to delay
the prevailing and dangerous excitement.

Almost simultaneously it was decided that the
claims of priority of occupation should be submitted
to a mixed commission, which was also to be charged
with the delimitation of a temporary zone frontier.
Here again there was little chance of agreement,
for whatever might have been the idea in Europe
on the subject of the partition of Macedonia, both
the parties actually concerned were actuated by
Macmahon's famous precept: *J'y suis! J'y reste.*

These abortive discussions continued intermit-
tently until 10th May, when the respective delegates,
realising that a continuation of the sittings would
be unlikely to serve any useful purpose, agreed to

disagree.  Whereas, in order to ensure a satisfactory termination to their labours, it would have been necessary for both parties to have entered upon the discussion without any *parti pris*, the mutual and evident line of action had been to fix upon the desired ultimate frontier, and to make use of every argument, good, bad, or indifferent, to support the claims advanced.  Thus the Bulgarians attempted to substantiate an unchallenged descent to the Langazar and Besik Lakes, and the Greeks strove to theoretically push their rivals back to the Struma River.  The Bulgarian plan found expression in a disinclination to discuss any question of priority of occupation north and north-east of Salonika, regardless of the fact that the Greek skirmishes with the Turks at Nigrita coincided with the Bulgarian combat with the common enemy at Demir Hissar. The Hellenes, on the other hand, based their claims on actual prior penetration into individual villages. The theories which suited one line of argument were therefore challenged by diametrically opposed considerations from the other.  There had been, moreover, a tendency to put forward pretensions of a highly fantastic nature, and the Bulgarians' claim to have theoretically occupied Subozko by an advance guard of eighty irregulars, who had wandered a hundred miles from their main column through a hostile country, admittedly bordered on the ludicrous.

This and other similar arguments were probably advanced in preparation for the anticipated bargaining, which is apparently as inseparable from Oriental diplomacy as from Eastern commerce.  This became increasingly evident when the Bulgarians attempted to exchange their pretensions to Subozko for the Greek claims on Nigrita—a proposal which was not unnaturally met by a polite refusal, coupled with an advice that suggestions of such a nature merely entailed a repetition of oft-repeated Greek arguments. Thus the only practical agreement reached by the commission was that further negotiations were obviously hopeless. The crux of the question lay in the fact that both sides realised that there was too great a risk that a permanent character would subsequently be attributed to any temporary concessions intended to alleviate the then existing tension, and contemporary events combined to demonstrate that the parties concerned reposed more faith in the efficiency of army divisions than in the persuasive eloquence of their soldier-diplomats.

In the meantime, a tragic sequel to the combat at Nigrita served to further embitter Greco-Bulgarian relations. As the beaten Bulgars retired from Nigrita they passed through the village of Dimitritsi, from whence they carried off eight of the principal citizens. Circumstantial reports soon arrived to the effect that these unfortunates had been rudely done to death, and Prince Nicholas thereupon requested their liberation (15th March). To this request, General Hassapdjieff replied on 21st March that an order had been given to release ".the priest Dimitri, the schoolmaster Kapetanos, and the six other inhabitants of Dimitritsi arrested by our military authorities." Distressed at the non-execution of this promise, Prince Nicholas reiterated his request on 31st March. General Hassapdjieff was spared the necessity for further temporising with ugly facts, for

on 7th, 13th, and 15th April respectively, the Struma
River solved the riddle of the fate of the missing
peasants by washing up their dead bodies, all bearing
indisputable signs that the unhappy victims had been
bayoneted to death. Had these men been killed
in the fighting, it is obvious that they would have
borne gun-shot wounds, and have been either left on
the battle-field or buried there. To calculate what
actually happened to them requires but little imagination; they were undoubtedly arrested, marched one
and a half hours distant to the bridge, there bayoneted
(the body of Kapetanos bore five wounds) and thrown
into the river. But for the providential washing up
of their dead bodies by the waters of the Struma, the
truth of this dastardly deed would ever have been
hidden from the world.

Despite the continued sitting of the mixed commission, there now followed a period of mutual
recrimination. Scarce a day passed without its
complaint of aggression from one side or the other,
and while it is as impossible as it is unnecessary to
investigate every individual case, there exists one
exchange of correspondence which at once indicates
generally and fairly the rival claims, and the ability
of the respective chiefs of the two armies to conduct
their case.

Writing under date of 4th April, General Hassapdjieff repeats his assertion that the Bulgarian army,
" having driven out the enemy " (i.e. Turks), had
occupied all the territory lying north and north-east
of Salonika, as from the month of October. He
then proceeds to assert that while the Bulgarian
army, " which had been called upon to bear the

heaviest burden of the war," was engaged in what he modestly describes as its " admirable and glorious effort to overwhelm our common enemy before Adrianople, Tchataldja, and Bulair," Greek troops had " systematically ' filtered' into the regions watered by the blood of our valiant brothers." He claims further that " they (the Hellenes) have driven our weak detachments from the region of Nigrita and the majority of the villages around Pravista, and at the present moment are carrying out their penetration in the district of Langazar, and are endeavouring to advance towards Drama and Kilkich."

This system appeared to the General to be " full of danger and increasingly useless, since it cannot, in any case, serve as the basis of a claim to priority of occupation in the regions which have been for a considerable time occupied by our troops." He therefore again beseeches the Prince " to retire all the Greek troops recently sent into our territory, and to reinstate the Bulgarian detachment at Nigrita."

The imputations contained in this letter would have been, in any case, unpleasant enough, but, under the existing circumstances, they were calculated to arouse considerable annoyance. Moreover, the Bulgarian claim to priority of occupation in all the country lying to the north and north-east of Salonika was categorically laid down, and its immediate refutation was therefore essential.

In his reply, Prince Nicholas protests against the offensive insinuations, denies the pretended Bulgarian rights over Nigrita and the Panghaion, and draws the attention of General Hassapdjieff to some instances where his own army has been guilty of the actions which he deplores in the Greeks. Finally, he agrees to the suggested cessation of military movement in a paragraph which, nevertheless, leaves matters exactly where they were before. This, I may add, is diplomacy. I give a translation of the most salient portions of His Royal Highness's letter *in extenso*:

" Before examining the accusations made in your letter, permit me to observe that the question of the contested rights of priority of occupation and administration has already given rise to lengthy discussions between us, the result of which is the agreement arrived at between our two Governments that a mixed commission shall be nominated with the object of settling the differences which exist between us on certain points. In view of this, it seems to me unnecessary to recommence a discussion concerning what we consider our indisputable right of priority of occupation of certain regions.

" I regret to find myself obliged to refer to the phrase in which you make absolutely unmerited accusations against the Hellenic troops, and which I can only consider a grave offence—not to say insult—to the whole of our army. You accuse us of having systematically ' filtered ' into the territories lying behind your army at a moment when the latter was making admirable and glorious efforts to overwhelm our formidable and common enemy before Adrianople, Tchataldja, and Boulair. In other words you infer that, while the Bulgarian army was shedding its blood for our common cause, Greek troops, profiting by its absence, and having no more fighting to do themselves, penetrated behind the allied army, gave themselves over to brigandage and robbery, and stole from it that which it had already acquired. You must admit that the most elemental courtesy between brothers-in-arms should have led you to make insinuations less offensive than these.

"I am compelled to protest in the most energetic manner against this accusation, which, moreover, cannot be supported by a single fact. There exists no region or village into which the Greek army has penetrated as a result of the weakness or absence of Bulgarian forces; and I can further assure you that not a single drop of blood has been shed by the Bulgarian army in the taking of any of the territory which is to-day occupied by Hellenic troops. Thus, although you state in your letter that your troops occupied all the country lying to the east and north-east of Salonika (Nigrita and Panghaion) after driving out the enemy's forces, I can prove to you not only that it was actually our soldiers who there fought against the common enemy, and drove them out from the above-mentioned territory, but that your troops found it completely free from hostile forces on the occasion of their advance towards the south.

"You accuse me, in addition, of having driven your feeble detachments from Nigrita and Tsaigesi. I challenge this as a fallacious and unjust assertion, for the established fact is that Bulgarian troops were the first to attempt to seize Nigrita by force, and to hinder our customs authorities at Tsaigesi in the execution of their duty. You seem to have very speedily forgotten the incident at kilometre 14, as also that at Anatolin, where the Bulgarian army, profiting by the weakness of our detachment, arrested and disarmed it, and transported our soldiers to Poroy, where, I may add, they were left for forty-eight hours without food or water.

" Since that date the Greek troops have not proceeded to occupy any villages situated outside of the zone of which they have been in possession since the month of October. So far as concerns the disembarkations of which you speak, and which, as you correctly state, continue to-day, these have no new conquest for their object, but are simply intended to relieve certain detachments or to reinforce others, a necessity which has naturally been brought about by the provocative and hostile manifestations made by the Bulgarian detachments at Nigrita, Tsaigesi, and Panghaion.[1] Here there has been a consistent attempt to penetrate into territory conquered by us from the Turks. If you assert that the occupation of a district after an engagement with the enemy is ' filtering,' what may you be disposed to call the clandestine entry of Bulgarian soldiers into the villages situated to the north of Yenidje-Vardar as far as Gumendze, and also at Subozko? These are districts occu-

---

[1] The letter written by General Savoff to the Bulgarian Prime Minister on 6th May, and which is reported as a footnote to page 270, clearly demonstrates that the Bulgarian army was determined to pick a quarrel with the Greeks, of which we may presume that the incidents in the Panghaion were an outcome.

pied by us immediately after our sanguinary victory at Yenidje-Vardar.

" I repeat that no movement has been operated beyond the zone which we have occupied either in the direction of Kilkich or Drama, for our detachments have never ceased to receive strict orders not to cross the line in question. So far as Langazar is concerned, I am at a loss to understand how you can characterise a permanent occupation of this district, dating from the month of October, as ' filtering.'

" I am willing to order a cessation of the dispatch of reinforcements, but on the condition that this action is reciprocated by you. It must be understood, however, that I cannot assume such obligations with respect to all the districts which you consider are yours, and which we, on our part, claim to have been occupied by us. In the same manner I shall consider that you have the right of free movement of your troops in regions in which your occupation cannot be contested."

PANGHAION.—A comparative calm followed the storm at Nigrita until the month of May, 1913, when a series of very disconcerting incidents transpired in the Panghaion region lying between Orfano and Kavala. The *raison d'être* was the everlasting question of " filtration." The district had been first occupied by the Greeks, and when the Bulgarians subsequently descended they placed their outposts in close contact with those of their allies, thus sowing the seed of future friction. The Greek occupation of this territory was additionally distasteful to the

Bulgars, because even had the Hellenes been ultimately prepared to evacuate it, they would obviously have demanded compensation elsewhere—perhaps at Langazar—and they accordingly manifested a determination to seize the country by force and negotiate about it afterwards. They were actuated, in short, by the same idea as had governed their tactics at Nigrita, and which, at a later date, led them to inaugurate the "War of the Allies." A Bulgarian threat to seize Paliohora led to the strengthening of the Greek outposts and to the issue of an order to the effect that any advance on that town by way of Portos was to be resisted. When, therefore, during the night of 4th-5th May, a company of Bulgars pushed their way towards Paliohora, they were forthwith attacked and captured. On 8th and 9th May a Bulgarian desire to seize a bridge at Vulcista also led to skirmishes in that locality. The following day an engagement of a much more serious nature took place over the whole front from Tovlyani to Leftera, when the Greek casualties amounted to thirty killed and forty-three wounded.

This dispute, however, was not without its saving grace, for a military commission was at once appointed, and a frontier line between the two armies verbally agreed upon. The temporary cessation of aggression which followed does not, unfortunately, appear to have in any way altered the determination of the Bulgarians to make themselves masters of the region, for further and more sanguinary incidents followed upon the arrival of reinforcements. Then, entirely disregarding the boundaries of the agreed-upon frontier, they commenced an advance along the road to Vulcista during the night of 19th-20th May. The Greeks, though in greatly inferior force, opposed this movement, and for two days fighting of a most determined nature continued between Vulcista and Kolcak. Cannon were employed by both sides, and the casualties were so heavy that a hospital ship was necessarily dispatched to Tsaigesi to evacuate the Greek wounded. The Hellenes then moved up a regiment of infantry and a battery of artillery to strengthen the two regiments which had thus far borne the brunt of the defence, but the army was, nevertheless, driven back towards Semaltos. On 23rd May the units retreated on Provista, and the troops were ordered to as far as possible avoid a further effusion of blood until the results of the diplomatic representations which had been made at Sofia transpired. During the three subsequent days there were skirmishes of an insignificant nature: a Bulgarian column advanced down the Ilidze Valley to Mustenia (thus threatening the communications of the Greek detachment at Leftera with their base at Tsaigesi) and various points of strategical importance were arbitrarily seized.

Doubtless as a result of the protests of the Greek Government and of the representations made at Sofia by more than one European monarch, the Bulgarian armed " filtration " ceased on 30th May, and the following day the Greek Governor of Leftera was informed that " the movements of the Bulgarian army were due only to the necessity of altering their front," and that they "had no intention of making any further advance." Little enough reason, one is tempted to add, for the maiming of hundreds of humans. The Hellenes who had been taken prisoners during the combats were marched to Serres and there delivered to the hardships of the " corvée," in striking contrast to the treatment accorded to the Bulgars captured at Nigrita, who were liberated immediately upon the cessation of hostilities.

The seriousness of the events in the Panghaion was undeniable, and they brought both King Constantine and Mr Venezelos hot haste to Salonika. Both sides now realised the urgent necessity of fixing a neutral zone between the two armies, and Mr Sarafoff having arrived as a delegate from the Bulgarian Government, conversations took place between the two statesmen. The Greek Premier desired then and there to settle the whole question of the partition of the conquered territories. He considered, he told me, that it would be an untold disgrace if, after successful co-operation against a common enemy, the allies were now to engage in fratricidal warfare, and he felt it desirable that, as peace with Turkey had then been signed, the statesmen should sit around a table and regulate their differences uninfluenced by the ultra-chauvinists of their respective countries. " If," he added, " agreement be found impossible, the solution of the difficulty must be referred to arbitration."

These views Mr Venezelos expressed very clearly to Mr Sarafoff, who replied in a similar vein. To General Ivanoff and Colonel (now General) Dousmanis was set the task of drawing up anew a frontier between the two armies. Like its predecessor, it was foredoomed to speedy violation, but it appeared probable at the time that the four premiers would proceed to St Petersburg without delay, and the chief object of the contracting parties was to peacefully bridge over the intervening period.

# CHAPTER XX

WHEN the biography of the late King of the Hellenes comes to be divided into chapters, the most glorious and happy will be that opening with his triumphal progress through the streets of Salonika one drenching November morn, and ending with that tragic moment on Tuesday, 18th March, 1913, when an assassin's bullet brought to a close a notable reign.

His was a noble life, full of incident, pathos and joy; his a kingship which founded a dynasty and saw a nation fashioned neath its dais; his a monarchy now the victim of immature statesmanship, then the butt of political intrigue; his a martyr's death suffered for the cause he held more dear than life itself. Of all this much will be written, but I rather wish to tell of the King as I knew him, as we knew him, during this happiest period of his sovereignty.

When on 1st November, 1912, King George's charger pranced over the badly laid granite pavings of Salonika's streets, the monarch's imagination must have been fired as he entered, conqueror, into that town where on every hand rise memories of the old Greek domination which nearly five centuries ago gave place to Turkish rule. What sad, solemn memories those five hundred years! The Cross trampled 'neath the heel of the Crescent; the nation

THE SPOT WHERE KING GEORGE FELL.

On the right is the stone on which the assassin sat until his victim had passed.

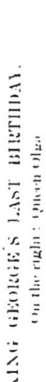

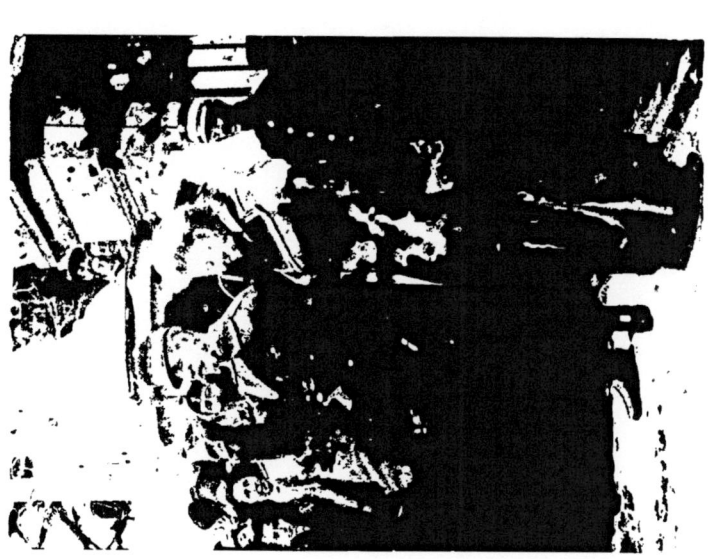

KING GEORGE'S LAST BIRTHDAY.

On the right: Queen Olga

shattered and then re-moulded; the people enslaved and then re-liberated. This was no victorious army marching into a foreign citadel; this no mercenary rabble overrunning an alien land. It was but a chastened exile returning to his home; the actual realisation of a vision that every infant Hellene had learned to dream at his mother's knee.

And I thought, as I looked down upon that kingly figure that made his royal progress through the rain-soaked throng, what a day of days for him! At such times as that, when emotion plays havoc with the heart, the panorama of history rushes inevitably before the eye. What must it have meant for that King, who for fifty years had striven midst ignorance, midst party passion and midst wild, uncontrolled chauvinism, to break down the barriers of prejudice and lift his people to a higher ideal of citizenship, to lead them back victorious into their own land.

From the hour of his arrival, King George took a very special interest in Salonika, losing no time in studying its antiquities, its commerce and its industry. He led, as in his own capital, a simple, unostentatious life, and demonstrated so kindly a solicitude for the welfare of the population as quickly enthroned him in the hearts of the people.

He was a great patriot. To him, alien though he was, the prosperity and progress of Greece was his chief concern. He had no love for the etiquette of Court life. A simple democrat, he wished always to mingle with his people, be over them, and yet of them. His outward simplicity was but the demonstration of his inward sentiment.

Every morning found him, from an early hour,

occupied with his voluminous correspondence and affairs of State. While he never presumed upon the limitations of a constitutional monarch, King George took a great interest in the political position of his country. His tremendous experience, his intimate knowledge of European diplomacy, his personal acquaintance with rulers and statesmen alike, rendered him most competent to advise his ministers, and it might be said that Greek diplomacy was successful in such degree as it heeded the councils of the chief of the State. During his residence in Salonika he was in constant communication with his Government, and closely followed each move in the complicated political game in the Balkans. He was an assiduous student of the European Press, and kept intimately in touch with contemporary thought.

Correspondence and State business once finished, His Majesty devoted the rest of the forenoon to the reception, in audience, of various officials and foreign visitors. He had a remarkable facility for putting those whom he honoured immediately at their ease, his personal magnetism being greatly aided by his ability to converse in most European languages, and an intimate knowledge of almost every possible subject of discussion.

My first interview with the late King of the Hellenes was on 9th December, 1912. A plain, sincere English welcome awaited me.

" This is not to be a formal interview; sit down, and let us talk."

The King opened with a few leading questions, the while I noted my own impressions. I found myself face to face with a stately gentleman in General's field uniform, who bore his sixty-seven years but lightly. A kindly, genial face radiated enthusiasm when he talked of his beloved Greece. His Majesty knew at once the topics which would interest me. England, Queen Alexandra (his sister), British statesmen, Balkan politics—all had their turn. King George gave me his impressions of the British Foreign Ministers he had met during his fifty years' reign, alternately admiring the strength of some and criticising the weakness of others. He knew well that the peace of Europe would be seriously endangered as a result of the Balkan War, and he anxiously awaited the appearance of a statesman sufficiently strong to grapple with the situation and bring the concert to a harmonious conclusion. What he feared most of all was an indefinite patchwork settlement which would usher in an era of strife and anxiety of long duration.

King George had no doubt as to the unanswerable nature of the Hellenic claim to Salonika. Historically, geographically, ethnologically, he considered it Greek, and he held up the right of conquest as not the least important of his many arguments. He was at this time very anxious to return to Athens, but despite the many inconveniences which life in the Macedonian capital imposed upon him, he refused to quit his post.

" I feel it my duty," he told me, " to stay here, lest my departure be interpreted as a weakening of our determination to remain. I do not intend to leave Salonika until its annexation by Greece is assured."

Poor King George! He indeed departed thence

before he willed, but who shall say that the manner of his going had not accomplished that which he wished far more surely than his staying? Did he not seal the fate of Salonika with his life's blood?

The King was very strongly opposed to the conclusion of the first armistice with Turkey. Even at that early date he foresaw, in some measure, the inevitable and fatal result.

"Mark well what I tell you," he said. "This cessation of hostilities will enable the Turks to pull themselves together; they will hurry fresh troops from Asia Minor, and the conclusion of peace will be set back indefinitely. If the Bulgarians feel that they cannot carry on without assistance, we are prepared to send 60,000 men to their aid, effect a landing on the northern shores of the Gallipoli Peninsula, attack the forts from the rear, force the Dardanelles and send the fleet up to Constantinople."

Bulgaria, however, declined this help, with what unfortunate result all the world now knows.

Luncheon was the occasion of the family reunion. Day by day all the members of His Majesty's family assembled at the kingly table for the midday meal, to which ofttimes guests were likewise invited. It was my privilege to be so honoured exactly seven days before the monarch fell victim to the assassin's bullet. At the head of his table, King George was the personification of kindness and good humour. His conversation was a continuous flow of merriment and wit. An incident which happened on this occasion has now a melancholy significance. The first *plat* was oysters, a dish which locally has a deservedly unhealthy reputation. The memory of

friends dead from oyster-eating pardoned the liberty
I took in begging His Majesty to refrain my partaking of the unhealthy dish.

"Well," said the King, "if you think they are
risky, I will not eat them, for I have no desire to die
just as I have reached the happiest period of my
reign."

Then but a passing pleasantry, it became invested
with a tragic significance one short week later when
the life he had wished to live had been so cruelly
cut down.

Luncheon over, His Majesty proceeded to the
smoking-room, and then again demonstrated his
never-failing consideration for those he honoured.
Handing me a cigar, he said:

"You'll like this, it is one of the cigars of your
late Sovereign, Edward VII."

As we smoked, I was privileged to hold a further
long conversation with the King. Again the deep
concern for the welfare of Greece; again the whole-
souled enthusiasm for his adopted country. Nothing
annoyed him so much as the studied attempt made in
some quarters to belittle the assistance the Hellenes
had rendered to the alliance during the war.

No record of King George's last days would be
complete without a reference to the fall of Janina.
To the thoughtfulness of Prince Nicholas I had been
indebted for early acquaintance with the news, and
the day was still young when I set out for the Royal
residence, to inscribe my name and congratulations
in the King's book. Ere I had yet accomplished
that agreeable duty, the door opened and the
King himself summoned me within. Then I saw

P

a monarch in threefold guise. Now the father glorying in the exploits of his son; again the ruler lauding the bravery of his people; but through it all the devout Christian praising God for the blessing that had been vouchsafed to his country. For half an hour the King unburdened his soul to me. Janina, the impregnable fortress, had been captured. The impossible of military critics had been accomplished.

"This," said His Majesty to me, "is the proudest moment of my life. You cannot think what this event means to me and to Greece. For fifty years I have striven to unite the dynasty to the people, and the taking of Janina has completed the work. Tied at last are those tongues which still dared wag of '97; silenced for ever are those lips which prattled on of a Greek promenade to Salonika. Who now can suggest that we have not the right to annex this Ægean town?"

King George, never old, became thenceforth rejuvenated, and he guarded that regained youth till he laid down his earthly sceptre and entered the Heavenly Kingdom.

George I. was an inveterate pedestrian. An enthusiastic lover of nature—of which, be it admitted, there are few enough examples in Salonika—he devoted every afternoon to a health-giving promenade. "On his walks to the forts at little Karaburun or the famous White Tower by the water-side, he was accompanied by a single equerry, except on such occasions as his fourth son, Prince Andrew, joined the little company. The unwisdom of this course was a source of considerable anxiety to his entourage, who were well aware of the dangers arising from this unguarded frequenting of crowded thoroughfares at a time when racial feeling ran high. But the King would have none of it. He had implicit confidence in the people he loved. In the main, he was justified, for during his short sojourn the entire population—Greeks, Jews and Turks—had learned to reciprocate his affection. Nevertheless, the risk from individual fanaticism was great. On one occasion four Cretan gendarmes were ordered to follow in his wake. Their characteristic tread, however, betrayed their presence to the Sovereign, who ordered their immediate retreat. Henceforth, he was followed only by two gendarmes at long distance.

On the fatal afternoon His Majesty had walked to the White Tower. There he rested a while and listened to the military band, finding time to accept a simple bouquet from a poor Mussulman, whereupon he remarked to his equerry:

"See what kindly hearts there are among these Turks."

Nearly half-way between the White Tower and the Palace there is a little side street which runs to the sea. At the corner is a large stone, and that afternoon there sat upon the stone one Alexander Shinas, a good-for-nothing Greek of feeble intellect whom sickness and want had made fruitful soil for the assimilation of anarchist doctrines. Shinas had determined to die, but before so doing had decided to kill the King of Greece. He had no reason other than that his world was out of joint. As King George passed this point Shinas rose, levelled a revolver and fired a ball which pierced the monarch's heart, thus cruelly ending a reign which had been one long story of goodness and well-doing. It was an act as cowardly as it was unjustifiable, for the assassin rendered a brutal act more dastardly by attacking his defenceless victim from behind. Like a flash the equerry, Colonel Frangoudis, swung round and seized the hand of the murderer already poised for the second shot. Bravely covering the weapon with his own body, he grabbed the felon by the throat and handed him, powerless, to the soldiers who ran to his assistance. But the first bullet had found its billet, and the King had sunk to earth. Quickly placed in a passing cab, His Majesty seemingly continued to breathe for a few minutes; but long ere the hospital could be reached the light had failed, and the first ruler of modern Greece had gone to his Maker. That night the Royal corpse was sorrowfully carried back to his Salonicien home, and a week later made its last promenade to the water-side, where the remains were embarked for the Greece he loved so well and served so faithfully.

King George had no premonition of death; but it is a strange coincidence that during the whole of his last day upon earth he talked unceasingly of the glorious incidents which had crowned his fifty years' reign. At luncheon, as during the fatal promenade, he referred repeatedly to the joy which the exploits of his army, and the recapture of Salonika and Janina, had given him; of the regeneration of Hellas; of the valour of his son and of his people. His last words were a reference to his satisfaction that on the morrow he was to pay an official visit to the German dreadnought *Goeben*, when the Greek flag was to have been saluted in Salonika by the battleship of a great Power.

In death, his face was illuminated by an expression of the happiness and contentment which pervaded his closing thoughts.

On the morning of 25th March, 1913, the remains of the late King were transferred to the Royal Yacht *Amphitrite*. A misty veil darkened the sun in the eastern sky, as if the heavens themselves mourned the loss of this beloved monarch who now set out upon his last earthly journey. It was a simple yet imposing cortège, International colour being lent by the presence of detachments of British, Russian and German bluejackets, in whose navies King George had held the rank of Admiral. Perhaps the most pathetic note of all was struck by a deputation of a hundred poor Mussulman refugees from the camp outside the town. The deceased ruler had manifested considerable interest in the lot of these unfortunate outcasts, paying frequent visits to their camp, and satisfying himself that everything possible was being done to improve their condition and lighten their sorrow. It was fitting, therefore, that they should have demanded permission to pay a last token of respect to him who had done so much for them.

The coffin and the Royal mourners once aboard, the International fleet weighed anchor, and the *Amphitrite* took her place between the two lines of battleships—British, Italian, and Russian to the left, German, French, and Austrian to the right. Few onlookers could fail to have been impressed with the spiritual fitness of Nature's tribute as the Royal yacht, with its sorrowful burden and imposing escort, rode out across the placid waters of the gulf and disappeared, phantom-like, into the mist.

So passed a good King, an adored ruler, a beloved parent, and a perfect gentleman.

# CHAPTER XXI

## THE SERBO-GRECIAN ALLIANCE

IT is unnecessary to repeat the various incidents which had come thick and fast to trouble Greco-Bulgarian relations, and which have received adequate attention in a preceding chapter. More disturbing than their deeds, however, were Bulgarian words. No opportunity was neglected of impressing upon the Greeks that their occupation of Salonika was but temporary, and that they would either voluntarily retire, or be forcibly thrown south of the Vistrica River. This information was conveyed in a manner often impolite, sometimes sarcastic, and generally arrogant. The Bulgars, who had everything to lose and nothing to gain by it, refused to entertain the idea of partition on the basis of priority of occupation. A newly arrived official from Sofia thus explained to me the point of view of his Government:

"Three things must govern any partition of the conquered territory, viz.,

    (*a*) Geographical considerations
    (*b*) Losses during the war
    (*c*) Ethnological considerations."

Thus Serres and Drama were to be annexed

because their geographical proximity to Bulgaria rendered any other suggestion illogical; Salonika was to be taken because Bulgaria had suffered the heaviest losses during the war; and the Kastoria region, being ethnologically Bulgarian, was destined to form, *ipso facto*, a part of greater Bulgaria.

The application of ethnological and geographical principles to the partition of Macedonia, or to its division into spheres of influence, can be used with telling effect both by Greek or Bulgar, if they are but permitted to decide where one and the other shall be applied. We have seen above how eloquently they were used to serve Bulgarian aims; but if the position is reversed, and Kastoria is adjudged on a geographical, and Serres and Drama upon an ethnological basis, both these districts must needs be accorded to Greece. The arguments which can be advanced are so conflicting, and yet, in their individual way, so just, that an accord based on their joint consideration would have been impossible. The ethnological principle not only inevitably opened up the thorny Macedonian question in its entirety, but, since some 350,000 Greeks in Thrace were destined to enter the Bulgarian fold, its introduction might well have been considered irrelevant.

While Greece and Bulgaria were busily realising their true sentiments towards one another, the relations between Servia and Bulgaria had likewise been undergoing considerable alteration. If the chief object of Bulgaria in entering the Balkan alliance was to secure control of Macedonia, the driving force behind all Servian action was a desire to gain an outlet to the sea, and secure a port on

H.R.H. PRINCE ALEXANDER OF SERVIA.

Though but twenty-four years of age, Alexander, Crown Prince of Servia, is
a brilliant soldier and possesses an intimate knowledge of European politics.
A charming personality he will make an ideal ruler of his gallant people.

the Adriatic. On the realisation of that ideal all the national hopes were founded. It meant freedom from the thrall of Austria, deliverance from isolation by neighbouring—and possibly hostile—states, and the end of commercial dependence upon Austria and Turkey. After a march over the Albanian Mountains, which constituted one of the most notable military feats of the whole war, the Servian tricolour was planted at Durazzo, and then Austria, the hereditary enemy of the Serbs, rose up and launched her demand for an independent Albania, which was to deprive Servia of her hardly won territory. The Serbo-Bulgarian Treaty had foreseen neither the creation of an Albanian state nor the conquest of Thrace. It dealt exclusively with Macedonia and the Austrian peril.

Servia then saw herself, despite the great sacrifices she had been called upon to make, destined to be the only one of the allies to reap an inadequate harvest from the war. True, according to the treaty with Bulgaria, she would have gained a slight increase of territory, but both her neighbours would have become proportionately stronger, and this, in the case of Bulgaria, might have entailed national annihilation—for the memories of Slivnitza had not been forgotten. Further, whereas she had previously been separated from the Ægean only by complacent and easy-going Turkey, both Bulgaria and Greece now blocked her road to Salonika.

Small wonder then that the Serbs began to feel that the conditions under which their alliance with Bulgaria was concluded had been radically altered, and upon subjecting to analysis the terms of the

treaty and the military convention annexed thereto
they found :

1. That at the moment when Servia was
threatened by Austria, Bulgaria was unable to
supply the 200,000 men whom she had promised
under the treaty.

2. That instead of an army of 100,000 Bulgaria
had sent but 20,000 to their aid against Turkey,
and that even this small force had abandoned the
Servian army after three days of warfare and
had then set off on its unchallenged march to
Salonika.

3. That, conversely, Servia had supplied an
army of 50,000 to assist the Bulgarians before
Adrianople, although such assistance was not called
for either by the treaty or the military convention.

4. That Bulgaria refused to sign a peace with
Turkey in December, 1912, solely in her own
interest, and had thereby obliged Servia to maintain nearly 400,000 men in the field.

5. That upon the recommencement of hostilities Servia had loaned to Bulgaria the siege guns
without which the capture of Adrianople would
have been impossible.

6. That owing to the creation of Albania, the
territory falling to them had been materially
lessened. On the other hand, the action of
Bulgaria in Thrace (a development not anticipated
when the treaty was signed), had considerably
increased the territorial expansion of their neighbour. Too great a disproportion of the forces of
the Balkan States was to be condemned. Before

the war, Servia comprised 48,000 square kilometres with 2,900,000 inhabitants, and Bulgaria 96,000 square kilometres with 4,300,000 inhabitants. After the war, and without territorial compensation, Servia would have had 68,000 square kilometres with 4,000,000 inhabitants, and Bulgaria 172,000 square kilometres with 6,500,000 inhabitants. Given the compensation claimed, Servia would have stood with 83,000 square kilometres and 4,500,000 inhabitants, against Bulgaria with 157,000 square kilometres and 6,000,000 inhabitants.

The Serbs therefore speedily decided that national prestige and their responsibilities towards their heirs imposed upon them the necessity of retaining those other territories which they had conquered at so great a cost. Faced with the loss of Albania, it was politically unthinkable that they should consent to be hemmed in by Austria, Albania, Bulgaria and Greece; deprived of their own port in the Adriatic, it became economically necessary that they should secure territorial proximity too, and commercial facilities at, Salonika. Once Bulgaria became a menace instead of a possible convenience to Servian national interests, the racial ties were automatically severed. Said a distinguished Balkan diplomat on one occasion: " La question de la race ne joue acun rôle lorsqu'il s'agit de l'intérêt d'un peuple." Therefore Servia demanded not the application but the revision of her treaty of alliance with Bulgaria, by reason of the changes wrought at the commence ment of and during the progress of the war.

While yet the Peace Conference was sitting in London and while toasts and protestations of friendship were being exchanged in banqueting halls, Prince Nicholas, Military Governor of Salonika, became speedily convinced of the grave danger which threatened his country.  He realised that both Greece and Servia had serious differences with Bulgaria, while as between themselves there were no points of dispute but what would speedily yield to diplomatic treatment.  There existed, moreover, no apparent causes of future friction, and it was self-evident that the Greek occupation of Salonika would, in view of the facilities which could be accorded without inconvenience, be commercially agreeable to Servia and would to some extent compensate for the loss of Albania.

It was in the course of a conversation with Prince Nicholas on 1st December, 1912, that the writer first learned that a consideration of the situation and its dangers had led His Royal Highness to the conclusion that a compact would be arrived at between the two states whereby Greece and Servia would agree to support their respective claims to Salonika and Monastir.  The approval of the late King George having been obtained, Prince Nicholas was next confronted with the necessity of "sounding" the Servians—a matter of no little difficulty, and one demanding the exercise of considerable caution.

While "ways and means" were still under discussion, an intimation was received of an impending visit by the Servian Crown Prince on 23rd January. Prince Alexander's ostensible object was a voyage of inspection to Monastir; his real mission was to investigate the truth of a rumour, current in Belgrade, that Greece had come to an understanding with Bulgaria whereby she should be left in unchallenged possession of Salonika in return for active assistance in forcing the Servians to evacuate Monastir. The opportunity presented would have been seized by a much less talented diplomat than the Greek Prince. Prince Alexander was speedily convinced of the inaccuracy of the disconcerting rumour, Prince Nicholas exposed his plan of a Greco-Servian understanding, and on that day the foundations of the alliance between Greece, Servia and Montenegro were laid.

It should be clearly understood that, at this time, the Governments took no part in the conversations. The Cabinets, both of Athens and Belgrade, were still under the spell of the projected Balkan Confederation. Mr Venezelos remained true to his ideal, and Mr Pasitch was, as is generally known, a partisan of a close understanding with Bulgaria. Prince Alexander, however, had the backing of the Servian military party, who were determined to hold what they had won, while Prince Nicholas received the support of his father the late King, his brother the Duke of Sparta (then commanding the Greek forces in Epirus) and a small circle of confidants. Both princes were, moreover, convinced of the justice of their policy, and optimistic as to its ultimate realisation.

Prince Alexander proceeded to Monastir, accompanied by Mr Baloukditch, the former Servian Consul-General at Salonika, and a sharp partisan of the projected alliance, and the Servian Minister of Commerce. The presence of the Servian Minister was fortunate. The visit to Monastir determined his policy, and upon his return to Salonika he declared that Servia was prepared to fight Bulgaria but would never give up Monastir. On this occasion Prince Nicholas held an important conversation with Mr Baloukditch, and, as a result of same, addressed a report to his Government which ultimately became the basis of negotiations.

It is interesting to note here that Mr Venezelos had on several occasions during the proceedings at the London Conference attempted to discuss the partition of the conquered territory with Dr Daneff. The Bulgarian statesman, however, avoided the subject as far as possible, and upon the Greek Premier explaining that his ideas led him to ask for all the littoral east to the Mesta River, pulled a wry face and insisted that Bulgaria required Vodena and Kastoria in addition to Monastir. Eventually Dr Daneff declined to enter into further discussion while in London, and voiced the opinion that peace should first be concluded with Turkey, the Balkan Confederation then formed, following which the spoils could be divided up. A knowledge of these conversations convinced Prince Nicholas that Bulgaria would attempt to negotiate first with one and then the other of her allies, and he accordingly impressed upon the Servians the necessity of a prior arrangement in order that they might subsequently present a united front to Bulgaria and demand that negotiations for partition should be conducted *à quatre*.

In due course the London Peace Conference

reached its unsuccessful conclusion, and the delegates departed for their respective capitals. The writer journeyed to Uskub to meet Mr Venezelos, and from thence to Salonika on 7th February had an excellent opportunity of discussing the project with the Greek Premier. The inferences to be drawn from this conversation were, in themselves, none too favourable to the idea of a Greco-Servian Alliance. Mr Venezelos had, while in London, been unable to realise the seriousness of the situation, and he was obviously prepared to jettison his ideal of a Confederation only under stern compulsion.

The result of three days' investigation in Salonika, however, came as a great shock to the Premier, and served to shake his optimism, if not to reduce his determination to work for the materialisation of his dream. Relations as between the allies thereafter rapidly worsened, and the Athenian Government was ultimately obliged to give its official countenance to the negotiations with Servia. At this stage considerable delay was manifested upon the Servian side, but just as fears were being freely expressed in the small circle at Salonika, which was aware of the *pourparlers*, that an impasse had been reached, the welcome announcement was received of a further excursion by Prince Alexander "to Monastir."

The Servian Heir Apparent spent the day of 10th March in Salonika, and during the discussion which then took place negotiations were considerably advanced. Ultimately, a pledge of secrecy having first been exchanged, Prince Nicholas outlined the Greek proposals, which were accepted in principle by Prince Alexander, and the two royal diplomats "shook hands" over their historic agreement.

The causes which had led up to the consideration of this new understanding in themselves rendered it essential that nothing should be left to chance, and in view of this, subsequent negotiations were of a somewhat protracted nature. The underlying principle followed by both Cabinets was that, if possible, war with Bulgaria was to be avoided. The idea of fratricidal strife between the former allies was repugnant to no one more than to Mr Venezelos, and it needed the goad of self-preservation to drive him into any *entente* directed against Bulgaria.

The alliance, in its conception, was of a purely defensive nature. It was, in effect, an understanding between Greece and Servia to mutually resist any attempt on the part of Bulgaria to take from them the territory which they had conquered. The first step, therefore, was to fix their minimum demands, and to come to an agreement concerning the new Serbo-Grecian frontier. On the whole, but little difficulty was encountered. Servia gave up her claim to Florina, and Greece yielded on Gievgeli. There was some bargaining over smaller townships —always, however, conducted in a most amicable spirit—and the existing frontier between the two nations up to its junction with the Vardar River below Gievgeli was finally agreed upon.

But the treaty went further. It provided both for the joint action of the Greek and Servian armies should either country be attacked by Bulgaria, and the division of the territory lying south of the eastern Roumelian frontier, in the event of a successful campaign. The "peace" frontier confined Servia to the right bank of the Vardar River, while Greece's minimum led her down the centre of Lakes Ardzan and Amatovo, leaving Kilkich, Doiran, etc., to Bulgaria. According to the treaty, however, war was to see the extension of Servia east, and Greece north, to Lake Doiran, the Serbs taking the town and the Hellenes the railway station. From the lake the divisional line was drawn along the Belesh planina, and thence approximately due east to the Mesta River. A clause was also included providing for the descent of Servia through a neutral belt down to Porto Largos, thus giving her an outlet to the Ægean Sea.

On 14th May, prior to the signature of the actual treaty, a military convention was concluded at Salonika. The presence of the Servian officers who were acting for the Belgrade Cabinet was carefully veiled from the Bulgarian authorities then in Salonika, and, as a matter of fact, they were conveyed by sea from their place of residence to the Palace of Prince Nicholas on that eventful morning when the convention, so full of import for the future of the Balkan Peninsula, was actually signed.

The formal treaty between the two Governments was signed in Salonika on 1st June by Mr Alexandropoulos, Greek Minister at Belgrade, and Mr Boschkovitch, then Servian Minister at Athens. Thenceforth, Greece and Servia endeavoured to ensure an amicable settlement of their differences with Bulgaria. Mr Venezelos put forward his arbitration proposal, and while Europe was awaiting the reunion of the projected *Conference à quatre*,

Bulgaria simultaneously attacked the Greek and Servian lines, and the dark clouds of internecine strife, which had been slowly gathering for nine months, burst and showered desolation and despair over an already half-ruined Macedonia!

# CHAPTER XXII

## THE WAR OF THE ALLIES

An Eventful Journey.—The Balkan League was, from its very inauguration, an inharmonious, unnatural thing, foredoomed to speedy disintegration, and the statesmen who had fondly awaited the formation of a powerful confederation, which would throw its weight into the scales of the side of the Triple Entente, built up their policy on a foundation of quicksand. They forgot the past, they ignored the present, and they sadly misjudged the future.

The removal of Turkey from the field of discussion was, perhaps, a necessary and justifiable preliminary, but the real strife in the Balkans was, is, and probably ever will be, one between Serb and Greek and Bulgar. Each of these peoples regards the peninsula as its heritage, and though the menace of a common enemy may again succeed in bringing about a temporary coalition of their forces, no leagues, alliances, or confederations can do more than delay the struggle for racial supremacy. Balkan wars are no mere combats over questions of amour-propre. Insult is not necessarily a *causus belli* in the Orient. These races are not tempted to fight for "Fashodas" or "Agadirs." They have more serious pigeon to pluck.

The " War of the Allies " was due to no wave of madness, but to a decision on the part of each of the combatants that its future should not be jeopardised.  Shorn of all previously signed treaties and agreements, and disentangled from the arguments deluged upon the world from Sofia, Athens, and Belgrade, the situation in June, 1913, was just this: Bulgaria, feeling herself the stronger power, had set her ambitions upon the re-establishment, to-day or to-morrow, of the old Bulgarian Empire which Boris and Simeon had founded.  She wished to-day to push her boundaries south to the Vistrica River and west to the frontiers of Albania, and to-morrow to drive the Greeks still farther south, pierce her way to the Adriatic, swallow up Servia, and create the long-dreamed-of " Empire of the Four Seas."

Greece and Servia, however, were not prepared to accept peace at any price.  Their terms covered a limitation of Bulgaria to the left bank of the Vardar River and north of Salonika, and the establishment of an approximate equilibrium in the Balkans which would enable them to effectually checkmate any attempt on the part of the Bulgars to overpower them in the future.  The right of priority of occupation as a basis for the division of the land conquered from Turkey was at first opposed by Sofia as firmly as it was insisted upon by Athens and Belgrade, and it was a subsequent desire to adopt the principle of her old allies, but on her own terms, that led the Bulgarians to their Waterloo.  The absence of any prior agreement with Greece, and an arrogant contempt for the military value of the

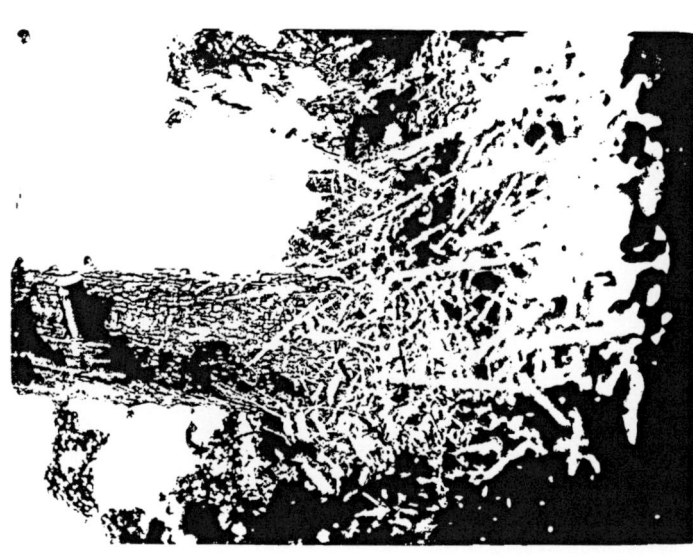

THE HELIOGRAPH AT WORK

A BULGARIAN SHELL.

Intercepted view at Hadji Bodli  some 80 metres from the town

Servian and Hellenic armies, drew Bulgaria into
the error of attempting, by force of arms, to share
the occupation of the disputed ground.

The frontier agreed upon under the Greco-Servian
Treaty could, and doubtless would have been eventually altered had the St Petersburg Conference
become a *fait accompli*, but in the meantime
military preparations were undertaken with common
accord, and the troops disposed in such a manner
as to counter the new concentration of the Bulgarian
army. The more chauvinistic sections of the Servian and Greek armies chafed at delay, and condemned the tactics which gave time to the Bulgarians
to bring their troops up from Tchataldja; but the
statesmen, striving always, even in spite of themselves, to secure a harmonious settlement of their
differences with their powerful neighbour, effectually
opposed any hasty action, and succeeded, often with
great difficulty, in keeping the military parties in
check.

It is significant that only from Sofia was the world
consistently advised of the apparent inevitability of
war, and one is forced to the conclusion that the
determination to embark upon a new military movement was then known to a privileged few outside
Government circles. On 26th June, following a
request made to Prince Alexander of Servia for certain information of a political nature which I desired,
I received a telegram from His Royal Highness
inviting me to visit him at Uskub. Fearing, however, that war might break out in my absence, I
called upon Colonel Dousmanis, Chief of the Greek
General Staff, who advised me of his firm conviction

that outstanding questions would receive a peaceful solution, and that all risk of war might safely be considered at an end.

.    .    .    .    .    .    .    .

Two things impressed me forcibly on my day-long journey to Uskub.  The first was the ingenuity with which the Serbs had succeeded in doubling the time occupied on the voyage; the second, the almost complete disappearance of the fez.  Various reasons were advanced for the tortoise crawl to Uskub.  The Servians said that the permanent way was in bad condition; the railway company's officials claimed that the engines were too heavy; unkind people suggested that slow travelling effects an enormous economy in fuel consumption.  Whatever may be the real cause, the fact remains that we never had anything quite so bad even in Turkey-in-Europe.

I arrived in Scoplja—to give it its new old name—to be there met by an officer of the Crown Prince's staff, who, to my surprise and delight, spoke English a good deal better, as I subsequently learned, than Servian.

"His Royal Highness regrets that he has been obliged to leave for Koumanovo to-day, but requests you to be good enough to take the train for that destination to-morrow afternoon, when an automobile will be in attendance to conduct you to the camp."

The waiter at the squalid little hotel where I passed the night spoke Servian and a little Italian—"Piccolo Italiano," he called it.

He had not underestimated his linguistic talent, for his knowledge proved to be limited to such comparatively familiar words as "macaroni," "spaghetti," and "salami," while he with difficulty squeaked out a "gratzia" in exchange for a tip. I well remember, on my first visit to Belgrade, being impressed with the incongruity of electric street cars running side by side with antiquated oxen wagons. There, in my Uskub hotel, I found electric light throwing into hideous prominence filthy floors and dirty, broken walls, which had not tasted whitewash since the day they were slapped up by Albanian masons—for the masons of Macedonia are mostly Albanians, who, when trade is bad, emigrate to America, and build up comparative fortunes by drawing four dollars a day, and living on bread and cheese. With the exercise of due precaution it is possible to pass the night in a Uskub hotel without entertaining too much company! By drawing the bed well away from the walls, and carefully examining the bedding, one can sleep with tolerable comfort.

The following morning I called upon Colonel Milovanovitch at the Servian headquarters.

"What is the latest news, Colonel?"

"Oh! it seems that the dispute will be arranged by the diplomats, and that we shall have no war. We sometimes think that, as a further conflict is inevitable in the near future, it would have been well to fight it out now, but perhaps it is better that the men get back home and resume their vocations."

Ere the Colonel could finish his statement, the door opened, an officer entered, saluted, and handed his superior a dispatch. Colonel Milovanovitch looked across at me and wagged his head.

"It has commenced," he said; "the Bulgarians have opened fire on our whole line from Gievgeli to Istib."

"The railway?" I gasped. "Is the line to Salonika cut?"

"Yes," he answered, "the Bulgars captured Gievgeli shortly after daybreak this morning."

"Then how on earth am I to get back?" I demanded.

At which the Colonel gave his shoulders one of those expressive little shrugs which speak volumes when an Oriental is the shrugger. One route after another was considered, only to be immediately rejected as impracticable, until I decided to make my way by train to Veles, thence in carriage over the mountains to Monastir, and so back to Salonika.

The Servian passenger service had been immediately suspended, but the authorities at once offered me the hospitality of a military train, which was to convey a battalion of Montenegrin warriors to Veles overnight. My instructions being to attend at the station at ten o'clock, I appeared at the appointed hour, only to find the time of departure no more precisely fixed than it had been earlier in the day. While we waited, the firstfruits of the new war arrived in the shape of two hundred and fifty badly wounded warriors from the fight at Krivolak, accompanied by an equal number of fugitive Turks, homeless, destitute, and possessing nothing more than the rags which hung around their trembling bodies.

"Where are you from?" I asked them.

"From Valandovo."

"Why have you run away?"

"Because people came in from the surrounding villages telling us that the Bulgars were advancing, and had massacred the entire male population."

"Where are your *hanoums?* "

"We had no time to save them, so we left them behind."

My ideas of Ottoman chivalry received a rude shock. That the Bulgarians should have massacred the Turks who lay in their path surprised me but little after my previous experience, but that Moslems should have left their women-folk to the mercy of the advancing hordes, was disconcerting to previously conceived notions of the Moslem character.

Our Montenegrins were packed into the emptied trucks, I took my appointed place among them, and we were off for the seat of war. The men from the black mountains are kindly fellows, who go into war light of heart and gay of soul. A delightful intimacy exists between officers and men, but, strange to say, discipline is not thereby weakened, for the orderly who has been cracking a joke with his captain does not fail to spring to attention and swiftly obey the order which he often receives ere the laughter has died away.

Sitting in the corner of our wagon, his arms round the neck of a youthful warrior, was an old wizen man in mufti, who must have seen well over sixty summers.

"What is the old grandfather doing with you?' I asked of an officer.

"Ah!" he replied, "that is common enough in our army. He is off to the war to watch over his boy. I remember when we were fighting the Turks at Tarabosh I observed just such another old man sitting a few yards from one of our guns."

"'What are you wanting here?' I queried.

"'That's my son over there,' he said. 'I am just following him round to see that he does his duty, and to attend to him if he should fall.'"

This striking instance of family affection, which could only occur when, as in Balkan struggles, whole nations go to war, recalls another story told me by a Servian officer. One of the transport wagons was observed to be systematically carrying less than the regulation load. Investigations made, it was found that the owner had fitted his vehicle with a false bottom, while in between the two floors lay the dead body of his brother. In this manner he had hoped ultimately to convey the corpse home for burial, attempting to preserve it from decomposition by daily covering up the face with wet cloths.

At 2.30 a.m. we eventually reached Veles, where one of the saddest sights in my experience of two wars met my gaze. From early morning fighting of a most determined nature had been proceeding a few miles away, and now the *enceinte* of the station was littered with the terrible results of the struggle. Lying motionless upon stretchers, crouched against walls, or huddled underneath trees, lay hundreds of wounded warriors. Their wounds had received primitive attention, but otherwise they bore a fearful testimony to the horrors of war. The night was bitterly cold. Clad in the lightest of garments, suitable only for my anticipated two days' travel in a sun-baked railway carriage, to remain

THE SERBO-BULGAR CAMPAIGN.

outside in the arctic temperature was unthinkable. So I demanded shelter.

"There is but the waiting-room," replied the stationmaster. "You are welcome to go in there, and a bench in the corner will, perhaps, permit you to rest a little."

I entered this mortuary. My first impulse was to beat a hasty retreat, but the bitter cold without forced me back again. Within, packed like sardines upon the floor, were the most seriously wounded of the day's engagement. The surroundings were hideous. The moans and groans of the stricken soldiers, the stench of stale blood and iodoform, would have sickened the stoutest heart, while, as if to complete the horror, every twenty minutes or so orderlies would enter with a stretcher to remove some poor soul who had given up the fight, and to fill his place with one of the more serious of the cases which had perforce been hitherto left outside. This was the rough end of the war; here was the reverse of the medal of martial glory; and I felt that could the nations have sat and gazed upon that sad, heart-rending spectacle, as did I, the cause of universal peace would have been thereby advanced more than by a thousand monster demonstrations in European capitals.

As the sun rose and dispelled the chilly night, I quitted the chamber of death and suffering, and joined the maimed warriors outside. I have said that their wounds had received primitive attention, yet it did not need the labels pinned on to their coats to tell the story. One man had his head half smothered in bandages, but his blackened eyes and swollen jaw told of a deadly missile that had nearly shot off half his face. Another lay still on the ground, while the small rent in his blood-splashed trousers declaimed that a murderous bullet had shattered the leg that now rested motionless by his side. Round the corner, just out of sight, was a row of fresh, warm corpses—death's harvest of the newly passed night. It was strange to see these Servians handle death. To them it seemed but an item in their daily life—to be awaited by all and feared by none. One man, who had died by the side of my doss, groaned for an hour, and then, when the end came, gave what sounded strangely like a grunt of satisfaction that all was over. Life has so little and patriotism so great a value among these nations in the making, that they count death but an added glory. And thus could I go on describing the mass of wrecked humanity which peopled a station that the day before had been gay and clamorous with the rushing of light-hearted travellers, and the cries of noisy water-sellers.

At daybreak the thunder of the cannon over the hills told of the renewal of the deadly struggle, and the wounded were brought up in their hundreds. As rapidly as possible the victims of this terrible carnage were refreshed with tea, packed into goods trucks, and evacuated to Uskub, the while I made inquiries for the carriage for which I had telegraphed the previous night.

"Carriage!" derisively repeated our friend the stationmaster. "Yes, I received your telegram, but you'll find no carriage here. The horses have all been commandeered by the military authorities."

My plight will easily be imagined.  To be hung up at Uskub was bad!  But to be stranded at Veles, with its speedy capture by the Bulgarians well within the realm of possibility, was infinitely more disconcerting.  My one hope lay in bringing home to the Préfect and the Town Commandant a correct appreciation of my predicament.  So away I trudged to the Préfecture.  The authorities fully realised my position, but——

"But!" I interrupted, "there must be no 'buts'; you have seen my papers, and you must find me horses, otherwise I shall be obliged to telegraph to Uskub."

The threat had the desired effect, and two gendarmes were sent out to scour the town for any horses that had been overlooked by the military.  An hour's search resulted in the discovery of two careworn, underfed animals owned by a Turk, who agreed to drive me to Monastir for a sum which was certainly calculated to include an assurance against capture by a Bulgarian band.  He further demanded a delay of two hours to prepare for the journey, a stipulation which rendered the prospect of my catching the Salonika train the following morning exceedingly hazardous.  But there are some occasions upon which one is forced to bow to the inevitable—and this was undoubtedly one of them.

"Very well," I concluded.  "You will be at the station at 11 o'clock, and you, monsieur," I added, addressing the Commandant, "will be good enough to provide me with a soldier."

"Quite unnecessary," he replied.  "There are no bands on the route."

"That may be," I rejoined; "and for myself, I should be sorry to oppose one solitary soldier to the attack of a Bulgarian band, but you will have patrols on the road who may not be able to read my papers, and as I shall have to drive all through the night if I am to catch the train to-morrow, I cannot risk any unnecessary delays."

"But we have no soldiers."

"Then I must ask you to be good enough to find one, even as you did the horses."

And so it was arranged that a corporal was to accompany the carriage to the station.

At 11.30 a.m. the carriage appeared—of course, without the soldier. One gets accustomed to such lapses in the Orient. I ordered the *cocher* to drive back to the Konak, where I re-found my Commandant.

"Where is my soldier?" I demanded.

"Ah! Yes! the corporal," quoth he: "is he not there? Dear me! how annoying!"

The gallant Colonel rang his bell, summoned the Captain of the Guard, and held a conversation with him, from which I easily divined that no soldier had been hitherto ordered. Half an hour more of precious time was wasted ere we at last got under way, and set out for Prilip.

The first item of interest we met was a Servian convoy of oxen wagons outspanned exactly in the centre of the road, so that each individual vehicle with its beasts had to be pushed into the ditch before we could pass. Henceforth, however, we encountered but little delay, and by walking up the hills in order to ease the burden of our horses, we made fair progress.

Kuprili to Monastir was the scene of the last trek of what remained of Zeki Pacha's Vardar army after the rout at Koumanovo, and it still bore evidence of the retreat. On the hill-side, blackened fields formed an appropriate link between a ruined village and one of those devastated Moslem cemeteries peopled with toppling tombstones which are an all too frequent feature of Macedonian scenery. Here and there a fresh earthen mound, surmounted by a crude wooden cross, marked the spot where some Christian warrior had been laid to rest as the Serbs sped along at the heels of their Mohammedan prey, and the very *hans* by the wayside, that minister to the needs of weary travellers, had been wrecked by fleeing Turks or pursuing Servians; until at last, tired and footsore, we reached the foot of the famous pass of Prilip. We halted there to rest before attacking the steep ascent which lay before us. As one stands in the valley, one sees the road wind nigh a score of times until it reaches the plateau at the summit of the mountain upon which the Turks had planted the guns which rained shrapnel on the advancing Servian army.

The sun had already sunk behind the tree-tipped hills, and storm clouds were sweeping up on a northerly wind as we set out to negotiate the most difficult phase of our journey. We had scarce entered the twisting roadway, but were already lost amid the giant undergrowth of the mountain-side, when an unseen voice broke upon the eerie silence of those everlasting tors and summoned us to stop. The Turkish coachman darted to my side. The Servian whispered " Bulgars," and took another swig at a bottle of Balkan fire-water with which he had armed himself; then he kissed his gun and waited. We were far from possible succour, in the centre of a district famous as a shelter for lawless bands, with whom my protector was now at war, unable to retreat, yet fearing to press onward. It was some minutes—they seemed like hours—before we discerned, on a bend in the road above us, the figures of four Servian soldiers. Thus reassured, we commenced to advance, but automatically the patrol—for such it was—covered us with their rifles. I sent the Servian ahead; his fellow warriors kept their guns levelled at him, only to lower them and present their bayonets at his abdominal regions, when at length he reached them. This display of caution, as I subsequently learned, had its origin in a well-merited fear that some Bulgarian "komit-adji" might without difficulty murder a stray Servian and commandeer his uniform. Explanations offered, and our papers examined, we were allowed to proceed on our way. This incident, now however robbed of much of its excitement, was repeated twice ere we neared the end of our climb, and entered into the rain clouds which clothed the top of the mountains.

My tropical clothing was speedily saturated, and the cold became almost unbearable. At length we halted on the summit and surveyed the country which lay between us and Prilip. We stood, as it were, at the head of a horseshoe of black, forbidding mountains, which had for years provided a secure hiding-place for some of the political bands which had plagued Macedonia, and defied the ineffective

Turkish attempts to restore peace and tranquillity. To the north, storm clouds were bursting on the rugged pinnacles, and lightning flashed as the noise of thunder rent the darkened heavens. Down in the valley, a two hours' drive away, and now almost invisible, lay the famous Bulgarian revolutionary centre of Prilip. Beyond, we knew the flat plains spread away to Monastir, so with a consciousness that we had now left the worst part of our journey behind us, we commenced the descent to our next resting-place.

By the time we reached the flat country below rain was falling, and the inky blackness of the night would have closed the road to any driver less experienced than was ours. He, willing soul, crouched down behind the dashboard for shelter, while I, taking our corporal beside me, sought to share the insufficient protection afforded by his service overcoat. Thus, cold and numb, we proceeded upon our way, fearing always that the clatter of our horses' hoofs might betray our presence to some stray band of Bulgarians, until once more a summons to halt rang out from the night. This proved to be nothing more disquieting than outposts outside Prilip. We were subjected to a minute examination before being permitted to go forward, but no further adventure befell us until we were brought to a stop without the walls of the town itself.

Once in the cobbled streets we felt safer, but at every corner a sentinel stayed our progress, and carefully scrutinised us before allowing us to proceed. At length we reached the bolted and barred door of the friendly *han*. Thrice we

R

knocked before a Servian voice within deigned to answer our summons. Our coachman explained our desire for shelter, food, and rest, and then the door was unbarred and—a hand grasping a villainous-looking revolver appeared, followed by its ever-suspicious owner. The driver's face proving familiar, and my indentity having been explained, we were admitted within. I called for brandy to heat our stiffened bodies, the while we discussed plans for our future progress. Conversàtion had, I should perhaps explain, been somewhat difficult throughout, as it was necessary for me to address my coachman in Turkish, he in turn translating my remarks to the others in broken Servian.

We had made satisfactory progress. It was then 10 o'clock, so that we had covered the first stage of our journey in little more than the regulation ten hours. A further eight hours lay between us and Monastir, whence the train for Salonika departed at 9 a.m.

" Which means," I explained to the assembled company of innkeeper, driver, soldier, and several small boys, " that we must leave here at 1 a.m."

My suggestion met with universal disapproval. The innkeeper hissed and chucked his head back in a manner which, in the Orient, means an emphatic negative, and explained that it was forbidden to leave the town before sunrise ; the coachman declared that his horses absolutely could not proceed until the morning ; the soldier murmured " Bulgars," and drew his finger across his throat with a significant gesture.

I knew that the coachman and soldier could be bribed to go, but the innkeeper's objection, smacking, as it did, of official obstacles, needed more serious attention.   So, at my request, we all set off along the winding alleys in search of the town Commandant.

As we turned a corner and saw in the distance a more than usually brilliant light, the sentry who stood beneath its glare summoned us to stop, and levelled his gun at our defenceless bodies.   Once more I sent the corporal in advance, and once more his companion covered him until, at some ten yards' distance, he brought him again to a halt.   The Commandant was away, he informed us, and anything we had to say should be communicated to the Préfect.   So we went in search of M. le Préfect. Here a similar reception awaited us, but by dint of much perseverance we eventually succeeded in gaining entrance to the courtyard, where a company of soldiers turned out and carefully surrounded us with fixed bayonets.   I hesitate to recall what manner of argument was necessary before a friendly noncom was prevailed upon to communicate our desire for a short interview with His Excellency.   There was much hammering and an altercation through the bolted door, until the barrier opened, and the Préfect appeared, hatless, but with his trusty rifle in his hand.   The authority examined my papers and agreed that, on account of same, I was at liberty to proceed at my will, but, in view of the general insecurity of the district, and the probable presence of Bulgarian bands, he strongly recommended me to delay my departure until daybreak.   My own soldier flatly refused to proceed, illuminating his refusal with another of those now annoying suggestions that he possessed a wholly unwarrantable objection to having his throat cut.   It was only when I succeeded in conveying to his dull intelligence that any disinclination to obey my orders would probably result in his being hanged, that he raised his hands in despair and resigned himself to the inevitable.

We had returned to the inn, and were discussing final arrangements for the morrow when shots rang out in a street near by.

" What's that? " exclaimed the company in chorus. The scared look on their unshaven faces would have automatically steadied the nerves of any Englishman.   The most appropriate remark I could make was to the effect that it sounded as though somebody had fired off a rifle.   As an antidote I ordered a round of drinks.

There was no immediate repetition of the shooting; nerves accordingly calmed down, and I was able to suggest that we retire to rest, and to leave orders that I was to be called at one o'clock.   I climbed to my room—unusually clean, by the way —and was in the act of removing my damp outer garments, when there was a renewal of the firing outside.   This proved to be the signal for a general invasion of my bedroom by the entire population of the *han*.   The situation certainly was unpleasant.   We were caged up in a Bulgarian revolutionary centre, the Servian garrison was small, and a band of two hundred Bulgarian irregulars would have experienced little difficulty in putting the town at

PRINCE ALEXANDER OF GREECE AND PRINCE AAGE OF DENMARK
DIG A DRAIN FROM THEIR TENT AT LIVOURNOVO.

THE BRIDGE OVER THE STRUMA RIVER AT DERBEND.
The centre span was blown up by the retreating Bulgarians.

their mercy, in which case there would have been very few of us drinking coffee in Prilip the following evening. It was a case, however, which called for sang-froid, so I pointed out to my panic-stricken guests that it would avail them little to lose their heads, advised them to arm themselves, and provide me also with a weapon, and await developments. As for me, I proposed to sleep.

Thus I was left in peace, but as I reclined upon the bed the silence of the night was broken by a prolonged rattle of musketry on the hills outside. It was evident that the fears of these poor wretches were not groundless, and our lives undoubtedly hung on the ability of the Servian soldiers to drive off the band with whom they were in combat. Tired and weary, I resigned myself to fate much as a sea-sick traveller looks with satisfaction on the possible disappearance of his ship beneath the waves, and dropped off to sleep. What happened away over the mountains I never learned, but I was still slumbering soundly when I was awakened by the innkeeper to find my bedroom bathed in the light of the rising sun. These unhappy people, determined not to leave Prilip in the darkness of the night, had allowed me to sleep on until daylight rendered the route to Monastir safe for travel.

Henceforth, events moved quickly. I rushed downstairs, roused everybody into activity, and after surprisingly little delay we set out upon the last stage of our voyage. We had but six hours in which to do a normal eight hours' journey. I surrendered my threadbare cushion to the soldier, sat myself upon the box next to the driver, and by dint of whipping our poor, unfortunate horses over the entire distance, eventually reached Monastir just in time to leap into the train as it moved out of the station. I had caught the last train for Salonika!

# CHAPTER XXIII

AT the moment when Russian diplomacy was congratulating itself upon its success in arranging for a meeting of Balkan premiers at St Petersburg, and when European statesmen had become convinced that all danger of the war between the allies had at length passed, the Bulgarians, on 29th June, suddenly overpowered the small Greek outposts at Leftera and Pravista. In the early hours of the following morning they attacked the Servian positions on the Rivers Bregalnitza and Zletovska and at Gievgeli. In other words, they delivered a simultaneous assault upon the entire front held by their allies. Gievgeli, which was the point of contact between the Greeks and Servians, and which was held by a few companies of Servian reservists of the 3rd ban—old men armed with antiquated rifles—speedily fell, and the Bulgarians cut the connection between the allied armies and obtained possession of the railway line over a length of several miles. Under the first military convention between Greece and Servia, Gievgeli had been counted a position of great strategic importance, and was to be defended by a Servian division under the command of the Greek Commander-in-Chief.

263

Subsequent consideration, however, led to a redistribution of the two armies, and the possibility of a temporary occupation of the town as a result of a Bulgarian raid was regarded as of little importance.

It is probable that the intention of the Bulgarians in thus suddenly violating the agreed-upon line of demarcation, was to fight their way into the disputed territory, depose the existing administrations, and then proceed to argue the matter out at St Petersburg. Exactly what resistance they expected to encounter we do not know, but that they held the military force of their neighbours in great contempt was common knowledge. The policy of despising one's enemies will, however, probably come into even greater disrepute than hitherto as a result of their experience. The Bulgarian attack touched the lever in the Greco-Servian Treaty which set the allied armies simultaneously in motion, and the demonstration, coming as it did after a plethora of threats from Sofia, and following upon great activity in Macedo-Bulgar circles, was accepted as a declaration of war. That even the Bulgarians were conscious that international honour had been outraged by their action, was evident from the persistent but ineffectual attempt made by them to lay the responsibility for the commencement of hostilities at the door of the Greeks and Servians.

My own experiences, related in a preceding chapter, render inevitable the deduction that the war was due to an anticipated and brutal attack by Bulgaria upon her erstwhile allies. It is not often, however, that a nation is prepared to itself produce documentary evidence of its own treachery. Yet, thanks to internal mud-slinging and a bitter combination of party politics and personal jealousy, Bulgaria to-day stands self-convicted of perhaps the greatest of national crimes. The circumstances are simple, almost childish. General Ivanoff, who was defeated by the Greeks, seeks to shift the responsibility for his unsuccess on to the shoulders of his Commander-in-Chief, who, resenting the accusations, publishes in the semi-official journal, the *Mir* of Sofia, the orders given for the Bulgarian attack of 29th-30th June, 1913. I preface them by extracts from a preceding Bulgarian order which demonstrates that the attack was due to no sudden inspiration, but was part and parcel of a determination to proceed to an armed occupation of the disputed territory. The diplomatic negotiations undertaken by the Bulgarian Cabinet, and the pretended acceptance of arbitration had, therefore, no other object than to humbug Greece and Servia, together with the European Powers, until such time as this new military concentration was completed.

On 17th June, 1913, General Kovatcheff, commanding the 4th Bulgarian Army, issued the following order (No. 29) to the troops under his command:

" In six or seven days at the latest, the last detachments of the army will arrive at the front of our concentration, and then the destiny of our relations with our neighbours—until now our allies—will be definitely settled. It is of supreme importance, in this matter, to take every possible step that will enable us to uplift and maintain at its highest level the *moral* of our soldiers, by the giving of lectures by the officers concerning the reasons which have forced us—after the conclusion of peace and instead of returning to our homes—to turn against this new perfide and infamous enemy.

.    .    .    .    .    .    .

" Our men must be informed that the Greek and Servian soldiers, who are so courageous when opposed to defenceless populations [*sic*] are merely cowards whom our simple approach has filled with fear. Upon the arrival of our first detachments their *moral* weakened; to-day it is reduced to nothingness. The confirmation of this fact is found in the enormous number of deserters from the Servian and Greek lines who daily surrender to us, and who declare that their comrades are resolved to lay down their arms upon the commencement of hostilities [*sic*].

.    .    .    .    .    .    .

" I repeat once more that the maintenance of the highest degree of martial spirit is of capital importance, in order that we may well and quickly settle this crisis which has been imposed upon us by our allies."

Following the issue of these bellicose instructions, the Balkan air was filled with arbitration proposals, and the Bulgarian Government played its double game with Oriental subtlety. When she expressed a fervid desire for an amicable settlement with her ex-allies, her military chiefs were elaborating a diabolical plan of campaign against them;[1] while the Sofia Press Bureau was announcing Dr Daneff's departure for St Petersburg, the Bulgarian headquarters' staff must have been drawing up the following incriminating order from General Savoff to the 4th Army, and which, embodied in coded telegram No. 5647, was dispatched from Sofia on 30th June at 3.55 p.m.   I give the text in full:

"To the Commander of the 4th Army at Radoritza.

"According to Order No. 24, I have ordered the 4th Army to continue to act on the *offensive*, and the 2nd Army (Ivanoff), after having completed its operations towards Tsaigesi, to immediately proceed to its concentration on the line indicated *in order to attack Salonika*.

"The Commandants of the army must take into consideration that our attack *against the Serbs and the Greeks* will be made *without a*

[1] On 19th May, 1913 (v.s.) General Savoff telegraphed the following dispatch (No. 4683) to M. Gueshoff, Premier of Bulgaria :

"It is indispensable that the situation shall be maintained in a condition of suspense until 10th June (23rd).  In any case, the critical period will have elapsed by 31st May (13th June).  On that date (31st May) we shall be in a position to undertake energetic action at certain points."

To which M. Gueshoff replied :

"Persuaded that, in order to ensure success, it is necessary to maintain the situation in suspense, I had a meeting with Pashitch (Servian Premier) yesterday, and we have agreed, in principle, to a conference between all the allied States."

*declaration of war*, and that they are dictated by the following important reasons:

" 1. To as far as possible uplift the *moral* of our troops and to make them consider our ex-allies as our enemies.

" 2. To confront Russian policy with the danger of war between the old allies, and oblige it to hasten the solution of the question instead of retarding it.

" 3. By our violent attack upon our allies, to render them more conciliatory.

" 4. As we claim the territory that our allies occupy for the moment, to attempt to seize it by armed force before the European Powers intervene to stop military operations, and, as this intervention may occur from one moment to the other, it is necessary to act quickly and energetically.

" The 4th Army will endeavour, at any cost, to occupy Veles (Kuprili) as soon as possible; that will have great political importance. It is obvious that it is necessary to solidly occupy the line Tsar Vrh-Kratovo-Klisseli.

" The 2nd Army, when it shall have completed its concentration, will, if the operations of the 4th Army permit, receive the order to attack Salonika. In this case, it will be reinforced by two or three brigades.

" If the railway line, section Krivolak-Gievgeli, is occupied by our troops, the bridge must be guarded by strong detachments. By this means we shall assure to ourselves the possession of the two banks of the Vardar River."

Let me quote again (omitting mere military details) from an order sent by the Commandant of the 2nd Brigade of the Bulgarian 4th Division to the "Commanders of troops and administrative sections." It is dated from Bonia village on 29th June, 1913, at 8 a.m.

"1. Military operations between Serbs and Bulgars begin to-morrow.

"2. To-morrow the 30th inst., at 3 a.m., the army will advance and attack the enemy.

"4. Components of both columns are to proceed to Zletovo to-morrow at 3 a.m., and *to advance in silence and destroy* the outposts of the enemy! Subsequently, they will proceed energetically towards their objectives as designated. *The enemy must be surprised!*"

Were any further confirmation necessary, it could be found among the important documents discovered by the Greeks after their capture of the Bulgarian fortress at Kilkich, and which indicate clearly that the attack against the Greeks was likewise premeditated. We find additional proof in dispatch No. 5590 of 28th June, from General Savoff to General Ivanoff at Serres:

"Even before the completion of the concentration, attack the 'enemy' at Leftera and Tsaigesi in the most energetic manner, and fortify yourself in their forts." [1]

[1] Yet another interesting official communication has been published by the Sofia Press since this book was written. It con-

It is indeed difficult to adequately express the natural repugnance which one feels in investigating

sists of a letter from General Savoff to the Bulgarian Prime Minister, dated 6th May, 1913, in which the General writes :

"War between us and the Serbs and Greeks is inevitable. The army will accept this war with enthusiasm and will fight with the utmost vigour against these disloyal adversaries. Any concessions made by us to these crafty allies will provoke profound discontent in the army—a discontent which, moreover, nothing will allay.    Apart from this, it is a matter which vitally affects the future of our country, for it concerns the settlement of the question of *preponderance in the Balkans*. The moment is a favourable one for *profiting by the pretexts* which our allies furnish, and to set in action all our forces with the object of assuring the hegemony of our country—a proceeding which will be no longer possible in a year or two because Europe will not permit it.

"Therefore *we must make use of all our cunning* to provoke an armed conflict with our allies without fail, and, by inflicting a serious defeat upon them, to deprive them for all time of any hope of placing an obstacle before the realisation of our national dreams. *It would be an unpardonable fault on our part to let slip this extremely propitious moment.* This war will not be of long duration.

"According to the military information which I have received bearing upon our future enterprise, the Greeks will be separated from the Serbs four days after the outbreak of hostilities, and they will find themselves in such a difficult situation that they will request the conclusion of an independent peace with us in order to save themselves. Thereafter the whole of our army will act against the Servian army, which will not be able to resist ours at any point."

According to General Savoff, therefore, the Bulgarian army, as far back as May, 1913, was determined to ensure national preponderance in the Balkans, and to pick a quarrel with Greece and Servia in order to ensure that preponderance which would apparently have been disconcerting even to Europe.

The war was *not* of long duration, but the General's further prophecy of an easy triumph over the Greeks went sadly agley.

the evidence of such ignoble treachery as that of
which the Bulgarians were guilty, and I cannot do
better than repeat the comments of that well-known
British journalist, Dr Dillon.    Writing in the
*Contemporary Review* of August, 1913, he says:

> " ' Success justifies itself ' was the maxim of
> these enterprising patriots, to whom all means
> that appeared efficacious were welcome.    Accord-
> ingly everything was arranged with care.    The
> Servian outposts, with whom the Bulgarians were,
> in many places, living on terms of intimacy, were
> to be surprised at dead of night, the others
> butchered in their sleep, the bulk of the army
> taken prisoner, and all knots of outstanding diffi-
> culties thus cut by the sword.    Truly one of the
> most revolting massacres in cold blood recorded
> in history.    In most parts of Europe people do
> not need to be told how to qualify a secret, sudden
> and deadly attack like this on an army which is
> spoken of and has claims to be treated as a friend
> by the would-be assailants.    To murder in their
> sleep unsuspecting soldiers with whom you smoked
> and chatted and played cards a short while before,
> is a crime which most cultured peoples would
> recoil from in horror.    The Bulgarians perpetrated
> it for their country's sake. . . . History will draw
> a veil over these abominations, and contemporaries
> will forget them soon.    But there are times when
> it is well to realise how near to the surface the
> human beast lies vigilant in some nations hastily
> set down as civilised."

It is pleasant, after the recapitulation of such

revolting details, to turn to a development which, if it reflects no greater credit upon Bulgarian diplomacy, nevertheless is invested with a certain comic relief. It might have been anticipated that the Bulgars, immediately they found that the *moral* of the Serbs and Greeks was not such a minus quantity as they had arrogantly estimated, would have blamed the incident upon some unfortunate staff officer and presented a complete apology to Greece and Servia. Instead of adopting some such subterfuge as a cloak to their treachery, however, they, with magnificent audacity, actually delivered a note to the Great Powers on 1st July, 1913, protesting against an alleged Greco-Servian attack. The reader, now *au courant* with the real course of events, will readily appreciate the unintentional humour of the Bulgarian *communiqué*, which read as follows:

"According to the reports of the chief of our Macedonian army, the Greeks, in the environs of Leftera, and the Serbs, around Zletovo, near Istib, yesterday attacked our outposts without any apparent cause or any provocation on our part.

"Behind the Servian front a notable movement of troops was then observed, and at Krivolak, on the line from Uskub to Salonika, artillery and numerous troops were concentrated.

"This simultaneous attack by the Greeks and Serbs appears to have been premeditated and effected with the intention of provoking our troops, who, having exercised prolonged patience, were finally obliged to reply.

"We infinitely regret that at the very moment
when we were about to come to a decision relative
to the partition of the conquered territory, the
Greeks and Servians should have provoked us by
sanguinary incidents which may have very serious
consequences. Under these circumstances, we
decline all responsibility for the situation thus
created and for all consequences which may result
therefrom."

Finally, apparently with the idea that the policy
of "bluff" could be continued indefinitely, General
Savoff, convinced of the failure of his manœuvre,
and realising that he had let loose the dogs of war,
telegraphed an order to terminate hostilities—following which the journalists of Sofia advised the world
that Bulgaria had protested against the unjustifiable
attacks of Greece and Servia, which were (or would
have been) especially reprehensible at a moment
when a pacific settlement of the territorial dispute
was impending. It was further announced, through
the same medium, that strict orders had been issued
to the Bulgarian troops to desist from hostile operations, and only to retaliate in case they were *again*
attacked by the Servians or Greeks.

This wilful misrepresentation of facts triumphed
for twenty-four hours only; until, in effect, the
Greek and Servian Governments submitted their
respective versions of the Bulgarian aggression.

The responsibility for the commencement of this
cruel war, this repugnant outrage against civilisation
and humanity, which drew a bloody toll of 40,000
lives, lies then at the door of King Ferdinand's

s

statesmen.   If any shadow of justification ever existed, it was surely destroyed by the treachery of the attack and the premeditated, cowardly attempt of the culprit, with an utter disregard for elementary truth, to enshroud the innocent with the mantle of his own guilt.

# CHAPTER XXIV

## THE OPENING MOVES

THE FIGHT IN SALONIKA.—In view of the seriousness of the enemy's attack, and the fact that, despite
the incredulity of Europe, war, real war, had actually
been begun without the customary formal declaration, the Greeks cannot be accused of harsh action
in deciding to remove the Bulgarian garrison in
Salonika, and to thus free their II Division for
service at the front. The temptation to offer the
enemy no option to unconditional surrender, and
thus to weaken King Ferdinand's forces by over 1300
picked men, must have been great. It was, however, decided to allow the troops to leave the town
—of course, unarmed—and, at 4.40 p.m. on the 30th
June, the Greek General commanding addressed the
following ultimatum to the Colonel of the Bulgarian
battalion:

> " SALONIKA,
> " *30th June*, 1913,
> " 4.40 *p.m.*

" The Bulgarian army having commenced
hostilities against our troops, I have the honour
to request you to leave the town of Salonika
within one hour from the receipt of this letter.
The arms of your troops must be delivered to

officers who will be designated for that purpose; your officers may retain their swords. A special train will transport your troops to our outposts, and measures will be taken to ensure their security.

"After expiration of the delay herewith indicated, I shall, to my great regret, be obliged to give the order that your troops are to be considered and treated as a hostile force.

"GENERAL CONSTANTINE KALARIS."

The delay accorded was subsequently extended to two hours at the instance of the French Consul, who hoped to be able to induce the Bulgarian Commander to leave the town. Mr Jousselin's efforts, however, availed nothing, for though every hour was precious to the garrison, they had no intention of accepting the Greek offer of a safe conduct to their own lines. Their action had been carefully planned, and they had cheerfully accepted the risk of defending their citadels until a few hours later when their comrades should arrive with the scalps of the Greek army hanging from their belts.

It is affirmed on excellent authority that, during the course of the previous week, General Hassapdjieff, the representative of the Bulgarian Government, had called together his officers, and having informed them that war was inevitable, and having exposed the plan of action so far as it concerned Salonika, added, that if they wished to proceed to headquarters he was ready to issue their *feuilles de route*. He promised them, however, that if they decided to resist, the Bulgarian army would enter Salonika in nine hours.

HOUSES OCCUPIED BY THE BULGARIAN SOLDIERS DURING
THE FIGHT IN SALONIKA.

With such a triumph in view, the invitation to fight could not be refused.

Documentary evidence, subsequently discovered in the Bulgarian quarters, shows that the Bulgarians had prepared a general attack against Salonika for Wednesday, 2nd July. For that reason, General Hassapdjieff left the town on Monday, 30th June. It was anticipated that the garrison would be given a delay of twenty hours in which to leave, and it would thus have been necessary to offer a resistance of several hours only before the general commencement of hostilities.

The Bulgars had installed themselves in half a dozen quarters of the town, and around each the Greeks had placed strong detachments of troops, thus rendering escape impossible. Against the principal Bulgarian stronghold, situated in the Boulevard Hamidié, the Greeks showered bullets from the houses opposite, while from quick-firing guns posted on top of the famous White Tower, a murderous leaden hail swept up the street at given intervals. A Bulgarian sentry stood rigid at his post until a well-directed shot flung him to the dust, and, little by little, the defenders were forced to seek refuge in the basements. At the post office the men fought with Cretans attacking them from below, and bombs bursting among them from above, until resistance became hopeless suicide. In the houses near the old mosque of St Sophia, they withstood the attack till the plaster was riddled with bullets, and the walls had been opened from roof to pavement by shell fire. At the mosque itself treachery stained the Bulgarian record, for there four defenders hoisted a white flag, and subsequently fired upon the approaching Cretans, killing three of the brave islanders. Then the gendarmes rushed the building, and the twenty Bulgarians who remained inside paid the penalty. Through the long night, bullets, shells, and bombs played their several parts in ending the resistance; one by one the citadels surrendered, and the Bulgarians, leaving their dead to the care of the ruined houses, were marched off to their prison transports. The men, deserted by general and officers, had stood tenaciously at their posts, displaying a bravery all the more commendable because they were fighting a losing battle. The total casualties were 31 Bulgarians and 33 Greeks killed and wounded.

The fight in Salonika had attained two desirable military objects. It had cleared the town of Bulgarians, and it had freed the Greek II Division for service at the front. In addition, the incident served another purpose: it justified the arrest of Bulgarian "komitadji," and the perquisition in the local Bulgarian houses, concerning which a tremendous howl of indignation had been sent up from Sofia. There had, from the very commencement, been little reason in this. The seizure of arms, ammunition, gun-cotton, and bombs should have been amply sufficient to silence criticism, but it apparently necessitated an open demonstration of hostile intent to convince Europe that the measures adopted by the Greeks to suppress the unfriendly preparations, which were being made under their very noses, were something other than spiteful measures of repression directed against a subject population, which presumably desired but the right to live in peace and tranquillity under the flag of an allied state.

Looking back on the incident, it must be said that the Greek authorities did their work very well. Public tranquillity was untroubled, and every effort was made to induce the enemy to surrender. Time and again, at the risk of their lives, Bulgar-speaking Hellenes approached the besieged troops and begged them not to uselessly sacrifice themselves, only to be met with the answer, " What can we do ? Our officers have deserted us after giving us orders to resist to the end, and we must fight on."

The officers, less confident than the men in the ability of their General to return in the promised nine hours, all collected in a house, from whence some, disguised as women, effected their escape ; the others surrendered. No officers figure among the killed and wounded !

THE GREEK CONCENTRATION.—With the liberation of the II Division, the Greek forces completed their concentration, and the eight divisions occupied the positions hereunder stated, and which are more clearly indicated on the detailed map of the battle of Kilkich :

| | |
|---|---|
| VII. East end of Lake Beshik. | IV. Dautbali. |
| I. Langavuk. | V. Topsin. |
| VI. Laina. | III. Doyandzi. |
| II. Salonika. | X. Bohemitza. |

The strength of the Bulgarian army massed against the Greeks has been the subject of much discussion, and while their actual numbers will never be made known to the general public, there can be little doubt that the several estimates which emanated from Bulgarian sources after the initial Greek victories were grossly misleading. Defeats must of necessity be explained, and while it is but natural that the Bulgarians should claim to have been outnumbered by their victors, it is obvious that statements issued from their side, even if subsequently backed by soi-disant official documents, must be accepted with great reserve. The first official Bulgarian estimate that they had but 26,000 men under arms, like the information I subsequently obtained from private Bulgarian sources, that General Ivanoff's army numbered 40,000 bayonets, may be at once dismissed as incorrect. The last Bulgarian version fixes the force at fifty-seven battalions, thirty-five batteries of artillery, and ten squadrons of cavalry.

Though the methods adopted by King Constantine's staff to ascertain the strength of their enemy do not permit one to speak with more than an approximate degree of certainty, they are, nevertheless, the most trustworthy available, and give us figures which are in any case more worthy of credence than any *chiffre* put forward as part of a scheme designed with the object of explaining the subsequent Bulgarian rout. After the battle of Kilkich, I was informed by the Greek General Staff that on the basis of the information obtained from an examination of the clothing of the dead and wounded, and a verbal examination of prisoners, they considered that the Bulgarian force opposed to them on the entire front numbered between eighty and eighty-eight battalions. This estimate, it is interesting to note, was supported at a later date by official documents seized after the Bulgarian evacuation at Serres. Amongst these was found a confidential report drawn up by Lieutenant-Colonel Popoff of the Bulgarian General Staff, and it shows that on 4th June, 1913, the 2nd Bulgarian Army was composed of eighty-three battalions, one battalion of sappers, one regiment and seven squadrons of cavalry with two hundred and sixteen pieces of cannon. Part of this force (one brigade of Thracian Infantry) was subsequently moved up against the Serbs, but as we know that right up to the outbreak of war troops were continually passing westward through Serres, it is quite possible that the losses were made good.

While, therefore, I consider it not improbable that the Bulgarians massed against the Greeks on 1st July actually numbered eighty battalions, it is naturally impossible to obtain conclusive evidence of this. I consequently prefer to confine my estimate to the forces whose presence I feel able to attest, and I thus arrive at the following minimum figures:

INFANTRY                                        Battalions

| | | |
|---|---|---:|
| July 1-4. | The army of operation (General Ivanoff) . | 66 |
| ,, 5. | Reinforcements—One Brigade of VI Division . | 8 |
| ,, 18. | Reinforcements—At least one Brigade of IV Army | 8 |
| ,, 22. | Reinforcements—One Brigade of IX Division . | 8 |
| ,, 22. | Reinforcements—At least one Brigade of XII Division . . . . . . . . | 8 |

| | |
|---|---:|
| TOTAL BULGARIAN FORCE DURING WAR . . . . | 98 [1] |
| GREEK ARMY OF OPERATION . . . . . . | 73 [2] |

[1] The Greek battalions were at full strength, viz. 1000 bayonets. There is reason to believe that in many instances Bulgarian battalions were under strength.
[2] After the advance from Menlik, the VIII Division commenced

### ARTILLERY

|                                                                                              | Batteries |
| -------------------------------------------------------------------------------------------- | --------- |
| ACKNOWLEDGED STRENGTH OF BULGARIAN ARTILLERY AT THE BATTLE OF KILKICH-LAHANA . . . .         | 35        |
| GREEK CANNON IN ACTION AT KILKICH-LAHANA . . .                                               | 36 [1]    |

In these figures I have included mountain batteries.

*Note.*—The brigades by which the Bulgarian Army was reinforced doubtless brought their cannon with them, and we know, in fact, that the whole of the artillery of the IV Army, which had been opposed to the Servians at Istib, was attached to General Ivanoff after the fall of Strumnitza. This fact is worthy only of passing notice, for so many of the enemy's guns fell into the hands of the Hellenes as the result of their sequence of victories, that the reinforcements did little more than replace the losses.

### CAVALRY

|                                   | Squadrons |
| --------------------------------- | --------- |
| THE BULGARIAN CAVALRY COUNTED .   | 10        |
| THAT OF THE GREEKS . . .          | 8         |

I trust that I have succeeded in dealing fairly with a much debated question. So overwhelming were the Greek victories that I am convinced that the addition of one or two hostile brigades would have affected their ultimate success but little.

There can be no doubt in the mind of anyone who was thrown into constant contact with the Bulgarian officers in Salonika that their chief object was the speedy capture of the Macedonian seaport. General Hassapdjieff, who was well aware of even the secret dispositions of the Greek army, must have known

to arrive, but it was dispatched into Thrace to act as an army of occupation, and took no part in the fighting.

[1] Six Greek batteries remained at Tsaigesi and did not participate in the engagement.

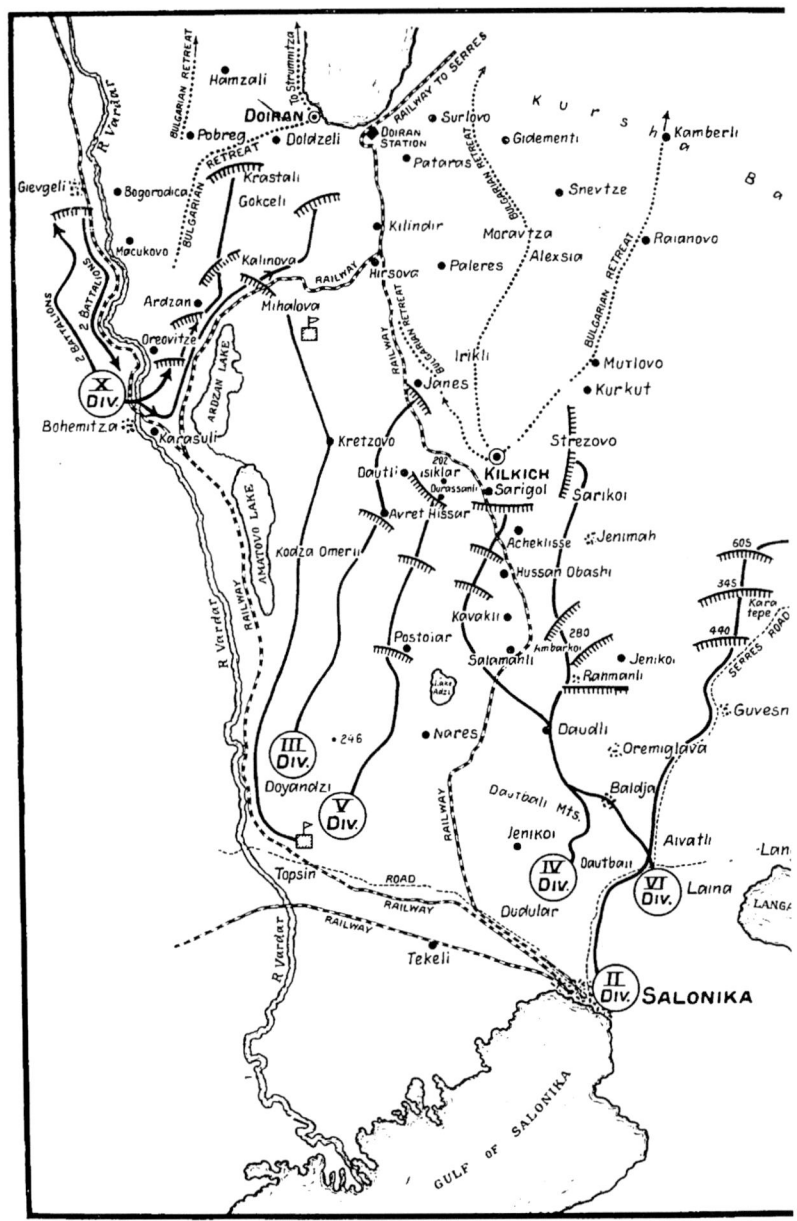

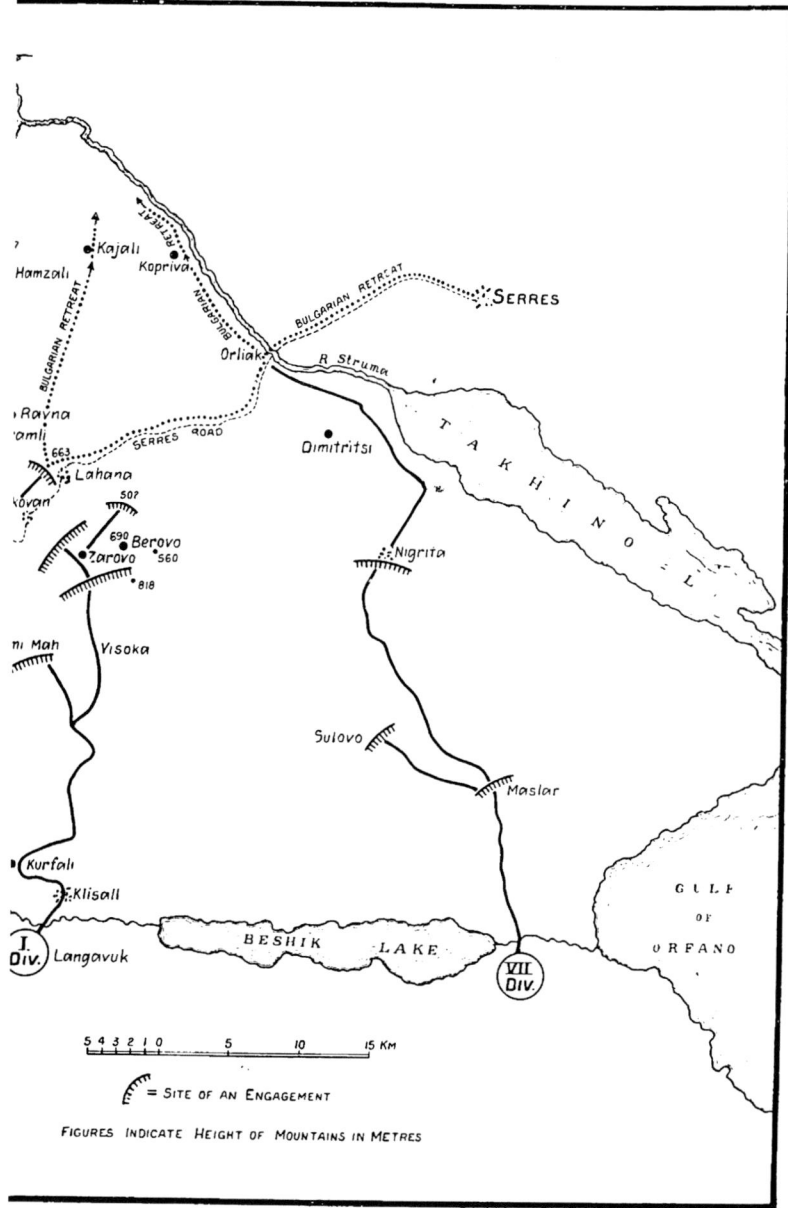

Kajalı
Hamzalı
Koprivai
SERRES
Orliak
R. Struma
T A K H I N O L
Ravna
amli
663
SERRES ROAD
Dimitritsi
Lahana
Kovan
507
690 Berovo
Zarovo 560
818
Nigrita
nı Mah
Yisoka
Sulovo
Maslar
Kurfalı
Klisall
I. DIV. Langavuk
BESHIK LAKE
VII DIV.
GULF OF ORFANO

BULGARIAN RETREAT
BULGARIAN RETREAT
BULGARIAN RETREAT

5 4 3 2 1 0    5    10    15 Km

= SITE OF AN ENGAGEMENT

FIGURES INDICATE HEIGHT OF MOUNTAINS IN METRES

that Salonika was defended by an elaborate system of fortifications (upon which a considerable number of cannon were mounted) and by a steel ring of 70,000 bayonets. To have contemplated a speedy conquest of this force with even eighty battalions demanded the exercise of no little optimism; to have attempted it with less would have been sheer folly.

Though the secret of the Greco-Servian treaty alliance was well kept, the Bulgarians were, towards the end of June, quite aware that they would have to reckon with the united strength of both armies. Indeed, exactly one week before the outbreak of hostilities General Hassapdjieff discussed the possibilities very frankly with me in Salonika. He then maintained that his Government had an army of 500,000 men in the field, and that they could easily overwhelm the combined Servian and Greek forces. Upon that occasion I insisted that I found myself unable to credit the Bulgars with more than 400,000 bayonets, and that I was firmly convinced that any attempt to seize the disputed territory by force would inevitably result in a Bulgarian catastrophe. The General smiled.

# CHAPTER XXV

## THE BATTLE OF KILKICH

IF Nature has designed to facilitate the defence of Salonika, she has at the same time provided admirable points of vantage from which an attack on the seaport can be directed. Between the Gulf of Orfano on the right and the Vardar River on the left, the lakes of Beshik and Langazar with their surrounding marshland stretch for a distance of nearly 50 kilometres until the main road running north-east to Serres is reached. To the west of the road rise the heights of Baldja and Dautbali, which command not only the trough of the Vardar River, but also the low-lying land which descends to the Gulf of Salonika. North of the lakes rises another range of mountains culminating at Lahana, a point 663 metres above sea level, and at the foot of which passes the Serres road. To the east the railway to Serres runs along a plain between the mountains to Kilkich (from whence an advance across the plain is commanded), and thence to Doiran. It was, therefore, natural that Kilkich with its strategical advantages and its railway communications with Doiran and Serres—the headquarters of the Bulgarian civil and military administration of Macedonia—should have been chosen as a centre of concentration. For nine months the Bulgars had been feverishly engaged in supplementing its natural defences by the construction of elaborate fortifications, and the work was accomplished with fitting thoroughness.

They had likewise thrown up entrenchments and placed guns in position on the heights of Lahana, and thus not only provided themselves with admirable bases for their projected attack upon Salonika, but held the two routes along which an opposing army could advance.

When hostilities broke out the Serbs and Bulgars were already at close quarters and the battle royal commenced immediately. The Greeks and Bulgarians were, however, at some distance from one another, and the Hellenes advanced a day's march northwards before they encountered their enemy. The proximity of the armies of Prince Alexander and General Kovatcheff was due to the great strategic value of the Bregalnitza River, and both the combatants had planned to secure possession of it at the earliest possible moment. There was no such inducement in the southern theatre. Kilkich and Lahana were the obvious fortresses for the Bulgarians, and the Greeks kept their entire army well back on Salonika. The first shock was therefore felt on the Serbo-Bulgarian front, and while General Putnik decided to attempt to throw his enemy back on Kotchana, he telegraphed to Salonika requesting the Greek staff to rush the three divisions of their left wing up to Gievgeli in order that they might attack the Bulgars in the direction of Strumnitza and co-operate with the Servian right on Istib.

It is difficult for the layman to see how the

adoption of such strategy would have been other than fatal for the Greeks. Their extreme right was well able to take care of itself, but it is highly probable that the complete subtraction of three divisions from the operations in the centre would have permitted the Bulgarians to have advanced from Kilkich and Lahana. Moreover, the enemy would have been able to move down along the railway line towards Salonika. So far from splitting the Bulgarian forces in two, the manœuvre might easily have resulted in a fatal division of the Greek forces.

If, on the other hand, the movements of the Servian army are left out of consideration, the most satisfactory plan for the Greeks would seem to have called for the concentration of the bulk of their army farther east, from whence they could have conducted a general attack on Kilkich and Lahana. This theory becomes still more feasible when it is remembered that the unique routes for the transport of Bulgarian reinforcements or supplies lay along the railway from Demir Hissar to Doiran, or the roadway along the Strumnitza Valley to the town of that name. It was therefore of vital importance to the allies that possession of these roads should be threatened at the earliest possible moment. That fact alone would have led to the immediate retreat of the Bulgarian armies in both theatres. Indeed, as events subsequently demonstrated, immediately the Greeks bore down upon the Strumnitza Valley, to the north of Doiran, the Bulgars commenced their retreat from Istib.

Between these two extremes—the one the desire of the Servian staff and the other his own ideal—

GEORGE, DUKE OF SPARTA.
Crown Prince of Greece.

King Constantine chose what proved to be the happy medium. Instead of making his chief objective Kilkich and Demir Hissar and Petritch on the right, he advanced towards Kilkich and Doiran on the left, leaving to the three divisions (I, VI and VII), which formed his right wing, the duty of driving his foe from Lahana and checking a subsequent retreat along the railway. His object, therefore, was to seize the Bulgarian fortress at Kilkich, capture their base of supplies at Doiran, and forthwith threaten the rear of Kovatcheff's army, which was fighting the Serbs at Istib, by taking Strumnitza and cutting off their retreat along the valley.

Thus, when His Majesty arrived at Salonika from Athens on 1st July, he immediately issued the following *ordre de jour*:

HEADQUARTERS,
SALONIKA,
*1st July*, 1913,
8 *p.m.*

Orders for 2nd July, addressed to:

I, II, III, IV, V, VI, VII, and X Divisions, the Brigade of Cavalry, and the Army Services.

1. Following yesterday's attack upon our feeble outposts, the enemy has to-day remained inactive. The prisoners taken at Salonika number 17 officers and 1300 men.

2. Our army will to-morrow continue the forward movement which it commenced to-day, and will proceed to attack the enemy.

3. The VII Division will advance to Nigrita. The initiative is left to its Commander, who, if he

thinks it necessary, will proceed farther north towards the bridge of Orliak.

4. The I Division will recommence its march at 5 a.m. via Visoka and Zarovo, and advance towards the line Lahana-Likovan. I give to the Commanding Officer permission to turn towards the left in order to assist the right flank of the VI Division, with which he must keep in constant communication.

5. The VI Division will commence its march at 5 a.m. from Ajvatli, and advance by Guvesne towards the summit 605.

6. The II Division will commence its march at 5 a.m. from Baldja, and advance by Dautbali and Jemi Mah. On encountering the enemy it is to attack in deploying its left flank in the direction of the heights which lie to the west of Sarikoi.

7. The IV Division will march from Dautbali at 7 a.m., but must so govern its movements that the road from Baldja to Dautbali is left free for the passage of the II Division as from 5 a.m. The IV Division will march by Salamanli and Akceklise to encounter the enemy, when it will attack in deploying its right in contact with the left of the II Division, and its left towards the heights Sarikoi and Sarigol.

8. The V Division will march from Nares at 7 a.m., and advance by the west of Lake Adzigol, and by the summit 250 towards Kilkich Lake. On encountering the enemy it will attack in deploying its right in contact with the left of the IV, and its left towards Kilkich.

9. The III Division will march from the height 246

at 5 a.m., and will advance by Avret Hissar towards Kilkich.   On encountering the enemy it will attack in deploying with its right towards Kilkich.

10. The X Division will cross the Vardar and march from Karasuli at 8 a.m. to attack the enemy lying near Kalinova and to the north of that position.   It will drive the enemy back and, according to the tactical necessities of the moment, will attempt to advance towards Kilkich.   The Commanding Officer of this division will estimate the situation and act on his own initiative in consequence.

11. The Cavalry Brigade will work towards Kodza, Omerli and Kretzovo, in regulating its march by the advance of the III Division.   It will maintain communication between the III and X Divisions.   The Brigade must ascertain by reconnaissance if the enemy's force lies towards Kilkich-Kilindir and Kilindir-Kalinova, or if this force is in march from Doiran towards Kilkich.

12. Each Division (and also the Cavalry Brigade) having driven back the enemy from their positions, will follow up the retirement with the utmost vigour.

13. My headquarters will be at Baldja at 8.30 a.m. to-morrow, when the officers of communication, excepting those of the I, VII, and X Divisions and the Cavalry Brigade, must be in attendance.

Constantine R.

These orders are exceptionally clear, and plainly

T

indicate the Greek plan of operations over a front extending from the Gulf of Orfano to the Vardar River—a distance of over sixty miles. I exclude the Panghaion, because, after a line of demarcation was agreed upon between the two countries, the Greeks were there represented only by small outposts, and retired the division west of the Struma. Throughout the campaign the action spread over a very wide front, and made it impossible for one to pay more than spasmodic visits to any part of the field, and at the same time keep in touch with the general movements of the troops.

By their surprise attack on 30th June the Bulgarians drove the Hellenic outposts west of the Struma, and occupied the port of Leftera. There were no developments on 1st July, but on the morning of 2nd July the Greek divisions left their concentrations and marched north in accordance with the orders of their Commander-in-Chief.

The VI Division came in touch with the Bulgarians who were entrenched on summits 440 and 395, and after a short engagement occupied the heights of Kara Tepe. The II Division found the enemy at the village of Amberkoi, and on summit 280. They attacked about midday. The battle raged for some hours, but the Greeks eventually stormed the positions and took them at the point of the bayonet. The success was dearly bought, however, for the casualties were heavy, and included the Colonel of the VII Regiment. The Bulgarians retired towards their entrenchments south of Kilkich, while the Greek division halted between Jeni-Mah and Dzurna.

The IV Division encountered nothing more than a desultory artillery fire directed from the heights of Hassan Obasi, but the V Division had a running fight with the Bulgarians the whole day, and after a succession of combats arrived west of Hassan Obasi.

Similarly the III Division was opposed during the whole of its northward march by a strong, hostile force, and its progress was thereby slightly—though not materially—delayed.

The X Division, which was made up of eight battalions of Evzones, had the busiest time of all. Having crossed the Vardar River, they attacked and defeated a Bulgarian force in position at Orevitza and Ardzan, and then turned towards the enemy entrenched between Kalinovo and Mihalovo.

If the first day's fighting had largely consisted in the driving in of the Bulgarian advance guard, the combats were nevertheless severe. The Bulgars held entrenched positions, mostly upon commanding heights, from which they raked the advancing Greeks with shot and shell. Despite the tropical weather, the Greeks had, with almost unhoped-for success, moved forward with truly remarkable speed, and everything pointed to the morrow as a critical day. The army orders for the next day were simply that all divisions should continue their advance.

The initial movements of the VII Division were marked by a piece of successful strategy. The Bulgarian XI Division was concentrated on the left bank of the Struma, and it was considered desirable that it should not be allowed to cross the river.

With a view, therefore, to masking his advance, Colonel Sautilis left a regiment and the whole of his wheeled artillery (six batteries) at the extreme mouth of the river, where it was joined by the fleet, the while he advanced with his remaining two regiments and mountain batteries on Nigrita. The manœuvre attained its object, for the Bulgars, in the belief that the whole of the VII Division was before them, guarded their positions. Ere they discovered their mistake, it was too late, and they were obliged to retreat towards Nevrekop. The men of this division, who had taken part in the combats of Nigrita and the Panghaion, were full of confidence in their ability to emerge victorious from the struggle, and not only succeeded in driving off their enemy, but cleverly carried out a bold flanking movement, and captured an entire Bulgarian regiment together with its colonel and officers. It was a telling stroke, as disconcerting to the one side as it was encouraging to the other. The Bulgars had, however, drawn compensation after their own manner, for the Hellenes entered Nigrita to find the town a smoking shambles, among which lay the inanimate bodies of its massacred Greek and Turkish inhabitants.

On the morning of 3rd July the I and VI Divisions were steadily bearing down upon the strong Bulgarian positions at Lahana. The VI had found the enemy strongly entrenched on the summits 605 and 534, and, in order to join in the attack, the I deployed in to the left west of Djami-Mah. The two divisions succeeded, after a sanguinary combat in which the bayonet was freely used, in driving the Bulgarians from the heights, and at nightfall the

Greeks occupied the line Likovan (VI) -Berovo (I).
The ultimate result of these operations was to force
the enemy back on to their last line (663-502)
commanding the stronghold of Lahana.

In the principal theatre the other divisions continued their attack on the fortified Bulgarian positions
at Sarikoi-Sarigol-Durassanli, the outlying defences
of Kilkich.   The Greek II, III, IV, and V Divisions were engaged on this front, and the fight
waged all day with ever-increasing intensity.   The
enemy was well placed in deep, narrow trenches,
and as the ranges had obviously been measured in
advance, the Hellenes were not only unable to
bring their own artillery into action, but the infantry
were compelled to advance across the parched, sun-
baked plain, exposed to a terrific and well-directed
fire from the hostile guns.   Towards evening the
Greek infantry were ordered to take the trenches by
storm, and, singing patriotic songs, the men rushed
across the open ground, and were soon fighting
*corps-à-corps* with their foe.   The combat waxed
furious, and many are the tales of heroism which
are told by the survivors.   By sunset, the Greeks
were in contact with the line Sarigol-Isiklar-Dautli,
which was subsequently occupied during a night
attack.

That evening, King Constantine telegraphed to
Admiral Condouriotis:

" The enemy has been beaten all along the
line.   We have captured many cannon and quick-
firing guns, and a great quantity of rifles. At many
places the enemy was attacked at the point of

the bayonet. The capture of Kilkich is imminent."

The royal message admirably summed up the
situation. The King, aided by the wonderful
enthusiasm of his army, had advanced with remarkable speed, and had given his adversary no time to
recover, and he was swiftly investing their fortress
of Kilkich. Any doubt as to the ferocity of the
fighting was set at rest by the enormous casualties.
By the end of the second day no less than 4000
wounded had arrived at Salonika, to which must
be necessarily added the dead who lay on the field
of battle, and the patients retained in the field
hospitals.

Up to this time the Hellenes had been sadly
handicapped by the inaction of their artillery. So
intimate was the enemy's acquaintance with the
terrain that the appearance of a Greek gun on
the plain proved sufficient to bring down a shower
of shrapnel from the Bulgarian cannon. Thanks,
however, to a reconnaissance made by the Cavalry
Division—then to the west of the III Division—the
II Division was, during the night 3rd-4th July, able
to advance its artillery, place it in position against
the enemy's line Sarikoi-Strezovo, and thus threaten
the left of their forces defending Kilkich. The
division itself deployed in the same direction, and
at daybreak attacked Kilkich from Darizo and
Kalikos. Towards 10 a.m. on 4th July, the infantry
advanced under cover of the guns, and having captured the heights of Strezovo and Sarikoey, they
proceeded to attack the Bulgarians who were in the

town itself and in positions to the north on height
197. Their fortifications once captured, the enemy
commenced to retire, and after an attack on the
front, the retreat northward became general. The
town of Kilkich was already in flames as the result of
artillery fire when the Greeks entered—a fact worthy
of attention, since it was afterwards alleged to have
been burned in its entirety by the victorious army.
In their retreat from Kilkich the enemy first formed
into two columns, one of which concentrated to the
north-west of the town towards Janos, and the other
behind height 197. At this juncture the Greek
cavalry, effecting a reconnaissance, observed a mass
of retiring Bulgarians moving towards Janos, and
communicated this information to the III Division,
whose Commander immediately sent his artillery
across the plain at the gallop, and occupied a position
north of summit 202. From this vantage-point the
guns shelled the Bulgars at a distance of only fifteen
hundred yards, inflicting a heavy loss upon them.
At the same time the cavalry charged the fugitives,
who were dispersed in the direction of Kilindir.

The other Bulgarian column again split into two
fractions, one of which retreated in the direction of
of Irikli and Moravtza, and the other via Mutlovo,
Raianovo and Kamberli, both having as their destination the valley of the Struma.

Simultaneously with the assault on Kilkich, the
two divisions of the right centre (I and VI) on 4th
July prepared their attack upon the position 663 and
502 defending Lahana. Advancing in battle formation, they arrived at a distance of six hundred
yards from the Bulgarian trenches, which, like those

of Kilkich, were well prepared and strengthened by numerous field guns and maxims, and occupied by a force approximately numerically equal to that of the Greeks. At Lahana itself the Serres road enters a pass overshadowed by high mountains, the summits of which (663) were held by the defending force. Summit 502 is situated about three miles to the south-west, and not only protected Lahana against a flanking movement, but controlled the road north from that village. Therefore, had Lahana been forced, troops advancing along the highway could have been freely shelled from 502. As a preliminary manœuvre, the Greeks threatened this position, with the result that the enemy, refusing battle, evacuated the mountain and retired to a hill about a mile to the north, from whence they could both render more effective aid to Lahana, and exercise a better control over the road.

The final assault was timed for 3 p.m. The altitude of the Bulgarian positions, and the broken nature of the ground, materially detracted from the value of the Greek artillery, and finding that reliance must again be placed almost entirely upon the infantry, the Hellenes fixed bayonets and proceeded to work up the hill. Much of the fiercest fighting of the whole battle here occurred. Men fell in their hundreds under the murderous fire from the heights,[1] but advancing with supreme courage and a total disregard for life, the troops, taking advantage of what cover they could find, got right up to the Bulgarian works. Still the defenders held fast, and

---

[1] The losses of the VI Division alone amounted to 19 officers and 805 men.

a hand-to-hand tussle took place in the trenches. From the trenches on they went to the guns, where the same fierce determination was manifested on both sides. In several cases after the battle the soldiers of the two armies were found dead, transfixed on one another's bayonets. Greek élan carried the day, however, and the Bulgarians retired, leaving behind them 21 cannon, of which 11 were quick-firers, and 3 machine guns, and an immense quantity of stores.

In the meantime the Hellenes had hauled artillery up to the summit 502, from whence they commenced to shell the retiring Bulgars. The retreat was thus turned into an utter rout, one column making for the bridge over the Struma at Orliak, and another via Kadjali, whence they reached the same waterway. A regiment of the II Division pursued the fugitives for a couple of hours, and the Greek divisions halted for the night between Lahana and Orliak (I) and Lahana and Ravna (VI). During the Bulgarian retreat the Greek VII Division, following an engagement north of Nigrita, approached the Bridge of Orliak, with the result that part of the hostile column, which retired along the Serres road, found their retreat cut off, and were obliged to turn north and follow the valley of the Struma towards Kopriva.

On the extreme left the X Division continued its operations against the Bulgars, who were at once opposing an advance on Strumnitza round the east of Lake Doiran, and protecting the retreat of their main force from Kilkich. The enemy held a very strong position at Kalinovo, and it was to this that the Evzones turned their attention on 3rd July. They attacked the trenches of their adversary in force, and succeeded, after a prolonged combat, during which they suffered enormous losses, in driving him back on Gökseli. But the Bulgarians, who had at the outbreak of hostilities occupied Gievgeli, now re-crossed the river, and descended in the rear of the division. The Greeks were thus prevented from following up their victory at Kalinovo, and turned to meet the new-comers, whom they eventually succeeded in driving towards Pobreg.

The following morning (4th July) the X Division turned once more towards the Bulgars at Gökseli, who had in the meantime been reinforced by a brigade (eight battalions) of the Bulgarian VI Division from Doiran.

But the Greek army, after its four days' continuous marching and fighting under the broiling July sun, was in need of repose, and there was a slight *attente*. The II Division was ordered to rest at Kurkut, the IV in Kilkich, the V towards Irikli, and the III at Janos. Only a brigade of cavalry and the artillery of the III Division were sent in pursuit of the enemy. The cavalry eventually reached Hirsova, south of Kilindir, where it was checked by further fractions of the VI Division, which had descended from Doiran.

Although the Greek army almost immediately continued its advance—indeed, the forward movement never actually ceased—we cannot do better than take advantage of this lull in the operations to consider some of the aspects of the great battle of Kilkich-Lahana. The task which had been set the Greeks was worthy the metal of any army. All through the engagement the Bulgarians had occupied strongly fortified heights. Their deep, narrow trenches were practically invisible and well protected by artillery fire, and but for the repeated bayonet charges of the Hellenes the fortress would undoubtedly have resisted attack for a prolonged period. Moreover, from their positions, the enemy had been able to control the entire plain, and, knowing every inch of the ground, their fire was throughout very effective, and regimental commanders, as they mounted hillocks in order to direct the advance of their troops, were at once made the object of personal attack. No less than six Greek regimental commanders were put out of action, several having been hit by live shell.

The natural disposition of the country and the excellence of the defence works more than counterbalanced any numerical superiority which the Hellenes may have possessed, and the crushing nature of the defeat inflicted upon the enemy without doubt characterises this battle as one of the most important in the long history of Balkan wars. The Bulgarians abandoned a large number of guns and an enormous quantity of rifles, ammunition and stores. The Greek losses themselves bear eloquent testimony to the severity of the combat. During the three days of battle they lost over 10,000 men, or 14 per cent of their fighting force. The casualties were occasioned, for the most part, by the effective fire of the Bulgarian artillery over previously measured ranges, while a goodly number were placed *hors de combat* as the result of hand-to-hand bayonet fights in the trenches.    A comparatively small proportion of the wounds were serious.

If it took those of us, who virtually lived in the Greek camp some little time to realise the overwhelming nature of the Hellenic victory, despite the confirmatory evidence offered by the capture of strongly fortified citadels after a determined resistance, we may perhaps pardon the incredulity with which the news was at first received in Europe. While assisting in the work of attending to the most pressing requirements of the wounded, it was possible for me to converse with a large number of them, many of whom, thanks to a more or less prolonged residence in the United States, possessed an adequate knowledge of the English language.    There was a convincing sameness about the testimony of these men which went much further than official reports to prove the completeness of the Bulgarian rout.    They were soldiers who had seen with their own eyes the enemy flying panic-stricken from the battle-field, and who had, in many cases, received their wounds as a result of the almost foolhardy impetuosity with which they had rushed forward into the Bulgarian trenches.

Since the Greeks surprised everybody (and not least the Bulgarians themselves), it is not uninteresting to note the causes which contributed to the precipitated flight of an army which had not ceased to belittle, in the most arrogant manner, the military qualities of its opponents.    The genesis of the Greek success was the very high order of generalship exhibited by King Constantine and his staff, and the lead given to the troops by their Royal

Commander-in-Chief. All evidences go to show that the attack from Gievgeli to Nigrita had been carefully worked out in the minutest detail, and the movements were executed with manœuvre-like precision. All the cleverness of the General Staff, however, would have been of little avail had the King's battalions failed him. But they did not fail, and His Majesty himself must have been amazed at the manner in which his peasant soldiers seconded his efforts.

The officers, too, were splendid. I well remember, some few weeks after the great combat, sitting in a Salonika tramcar opposite to a Greek soldier with a bandaged foot.

" You English feller? " he twanged out with a thick American accent as he glanced at the copy of the *Times* which I was reading.

I pleaded guilty.

" What you doin' here? " was his next effort.

" Looking for trouble," I replied carelessly, with a due sense of my journalistic responsibilities. And then I took up the cross-examination.

" What do you do in America? "

" Pea-nuts," he jerked out.

" Where did you get hurt? "

" Lahana," he responded, and then, finding I was interested, he brightened up considerably.

" Say, you fellah," he continued, " know anything about fightin'? "

" I've seen a little during the last eighteen months," I said.

" Wall, say feller! that was a great fight, Lahana. Yes, sir! Search me! Yer see them dem Bulgars was up on the top of the hill in trenches with cannon and all the rest of it. Our guns couldn't get at 'em, so we had to scramble up the mountain. Our officer was great. Yes, sir, he was the real thing. 'You stay right here, boys,' he says, and then he goes crawling along until he finds shelter. 'Now come on here, one after the other,' he shouts, and when he'd got us all under cover, off he goes again hisself ter find another hole. So we got up near the Bulgars' trenches, and then we gave a shout and rushed at 'em with our bayonets, and cleaned 'em right out, 'cos they had to go, yer know—'twern't no good their waitin'."

"And your officer?" I asked.

"Ah!" he replied, "pore feller, he got a bit o' lead in his head half-way up the hill; but he was great, I tell yer, real great!"

The artillery, always excellent, surpassed itself, spreading fear and panic into the Bulgarian camp. But the most surprising feature of the battle was the magnificent élan of the Greek infantry, which, despite a well-nourished fire from the Bulgarian guns, led them into the enemy's trenches right on to the hostile bayonets of their stubborn, determined, and gallant foe. The spirit of the Greek rank and file was magnificent. Patriotically possessed of a total disregard for danger, they rushed forward to victory or death; and if laid low by bullet or bayonet, they bore suffering with cheerful grace, for these men, after long hours of exposure on the field, jolting in crude ambulance wagons, and tiresome journeys in goods trucks, drew into Salonika sending up resounding cheers for King and country. In short, the battle of Kilkich was a story of a general who knew how to command and an army which knew how to obey.

The Bulgarians themselves, however, had laid the foundation of their defeat. The contempt in which they held their former allies led them into a fatal miscalculation of the military value of the forces opposed to them. They expected to cut through the Servians like cheese and scatter the Greeks as sheep on the mountain-side. They anticipated a few hours' resistance on the outskirts of Salonika, to be followed by a glorious entry into the Macedonian capital. They certainly never imagined that King Constantine would immediately throw his battalions against their magnificently fortified positions at Kilkich and Lahana; still less did they dream of the possibility of defeat. As to the Greek soldier of Kilkich, he may be said to have been a creation of Bulgarian arrogance.

One interesting effect of the peace-time attempts at aggression on the part of the Bulgars now became universally apparent in military and political circles. Whereas in the early days of their association the Greeks were obsessed by a respect, almost amounting to fear, of the Bulgarian soldier, the combats of the Panghaion and Nigrita—where their unaided infantry had repulsed an attack by a superior Bulgarian force assisted by artillery and cavalry—served to familiarise them with their future enemy, and gave birth to a spirit of confidence. While these incidents set many a Salonicien wiseacre wagging his head in wonderment, the *moral* of the Greeks received a noticeable uplifting, and when they ultimately went into action before Kilkich there was not a single Hellene, from Commander-in-Chief to drummer-boy, but was convinced that the campaign could have only one ending—the triumph of Hellas over its hereditary foe.

PART OF THE STORES ABANDONED BY THE BULGARIANS AT DOIRAN.

BULGARIAN PRISONERS OF WAR.

# CHAPTER XXVI

## THE CAPTURE OF DOIRAN

THE track of a retreating army is a death-besprinkled tragedy. Just as that road of suffering and despair which marked the Turkish flight from Yenidje-Vardar will ever rest a vivid picture in the mind, so the trail of the Bulgars from Kilkich to Doiran will remain deeply imprinted in a memory already crowded with the kaleidoscopic events of the past year in Macedonia.

It was a tableau drawn on a vaster scale, in which a background of highways and hedges gave place to mountains and valleys, and it spoke with yet stronger voice of the pathos of defeat. To stand amid the blackened ruins of that once flourishing township of Kilkich, and scan the serried trenches, the formidable redoubts and the gun-decked vantage-points which command the approaches from the rolling southern plain, and then to think of all we have heard and read and seen of the Bulgarian soldier, was to wonder what unseen hand had helped the Greeks to victory.

The whole scene, when I saw it, was littered with the emblems of disordered flight. Knapsacks, water-bottles, hats, clothes—all bespoke a hurried exit. And these evidences of Greek victory continued along the tracks which serve for roads as we crossed the blackened fields (for the Bulgars had fired the crops to cover their retreat) and passed by hill and dale until we approached the rising slopes south of Doiran. The journey was full of the shady side of warfare.

The thought of retiring from Kilkich had obviously entered little into Bulgarian calculations, for thereafter there were few preparations for defence visible. Doiran, however, offers natural disadvantages to a defending army, of which the enemy did not fail to avail themselves, and the earthworks which had been more or less hurriedly thrown up transformed the position into one of considerable strength. Strategically, the point was of the utmost importance to the Bulgarians, and they accordingly defended it stubbornly. That they failed to make still more complete preparations for the reception of their adversary must be attributed to the rapidity of the Greek advance. If the Bulgars had expected King Constantine to repeat their own tactics after their Thracian victories, and to allow his quarry to burrow a new hole the while his army recovered from the fatigue of the three days' attack on Kilkich, they misjudged their man, for the Royal Commander-in-Chief kept his troops on the march and set them at the Doiran heights with scant repose.

It will have been already noted, in the preceding chapter, that the Bulgarians were retreating in three directions: their right and part of their centre in the general direction of Doiran, their centre towards Lake Butkova, and their left over the Struma towards Demir Hissar. The information at the disposal of

Greek headquarters was that their enemy had fortified the mountain range of Kursha-Balkan, together
with the naturally strong position of Dova-Tepé,
which commands the railway line from Doiran. The
next objective of the Hellenes was Doiran, and they,
therefore, continued their advance on 5th July, as
follows:

II Division via Alexsia and Snevtze to
Gidementi.

IV Division via Irikli to Moravtza.

V Division from Irikli towards Pateros and
Surlovo.

III Division by Janos and Kilindir on Doiran.

X Division via Krastali and Doldzeli towards
Hamzali with the object of outflanking Doiran.

I Division via Kopriva along the valley of the
Struma.

VI Division via Kajali and along the valley of
the Struma.

VII Division was held in reserve at the bridge
of Orliak, it being uncertain in which direction the
Bulgarian XI Division would retreat.

The last three divisions (I, VI, VII), then formed
the Greek right wing and were placed under the
command of General Manoussoyannakis.

The strategic movement in three columns designed
to envelop Doiran commenced on 6th July. The
III Division met the Bulgarians at Kilindir and
opened a vigorous attack. For some time the
enemy's artillery, very favourably placed on the
heights south of Doiran, succeeded in staying
the Hellenic advance, but the advantage was soon

neutralised, and when the V Division arrived on the same line, the invaders swept forward, and bayonets completed the work commenced by shrapnel. The X Division likewise forged ahead resolutely, until, finding themselves steadily driven back and with Pateros in danger, the Bulgars, after several hours of heavy fighting, evacuated Doiran, with the result that the Greek III Division occupied the town on the evening of 6th July. Many prisoners, an enormous quantity of stores and twelve cannon were captured. It is interesting to note that the latter were all charged ready to fire—a fact which testifies to the hurried flight of the enemy.

The Bulgarian losses were great. A captured sergeant told me that of his company the captain was killed, the other officers wounded; he and six privates who surrendered being all that remained unscathed. At another point in the field, an entire machine gun company, with its officer, was taken prisoner.

.    .    .    .    .    .    .

When I arrived at Doiran an hour or so after King Constantine had there installed his headquarters, the scene bore eloquent testimony to the thoroughness of the Bulgarian rout. The approaches were littered with discarded impedimenta of every description. The hills and fields, their smooth brown monotony unbroken save by the newly evacuated trenches, were peopled with the still unburied bodies of the dead Bulgars which lay motionless in the summer sun. Along the railway line were strewn thousands of empty cartridges telling of the fierce resistance which had been offered to the advancing Hellenes, while at the station itself the Bulgarians had left hundreds of tons of provisions—boxes of sugar, bags of galettes, sacks of flour, cases of tea—booty which meant hungry stomachs for the battalions of beaten warriors who had just disappeared over the western hills.[1]

Doiran is an ugly picture in a beautiful frame. The great placid lake lies snugly nestled in an amphitheatre of hills, dotted on their lower slopes by villages—then, alas, nothing but a heap of smoking ruins. At the southern apex is Doiran itself—a hideous contrast to the alpine scenery it disgraces. With tender consideration for artistic feeling, the railway leaves the town away to the left, and the train draws in at the lake-side station on the eastern shore. We descended as a passing battery clouded the air with sandy dust. There remained many signs of the recently terminated Bulgarian occupation. The Slavic name on the station-house still peeped through its first coat of obliterating whitewash, the immense walls of Bulgar stores shut out the lake view, scores of Bulgarian prisoners awaited transport to Salonika, and stacks of hostile rifles that had ceased their murderous cackle lay piled in the sun.

I passed the stern sentries—Greek sentries are not immobile—under cover of Prince Nicholas, and entered the Royal presence. This was Greek headquarters. The Court was held in open air. For carpet, the cartridge-littered earth; for furniture, two

[1] The inventory of the stores left by the Bulgarians at Doiran was as follows : Flour, 162 tons; cheese, 16½ tons; rice, 3¾ tons; beans, 37½ tons; biscuits, 51 tons; sugar, 45 tons; wheat, 3¾ tons; barley, 450 tons; bran, 37½ tons; hay, 450 tons; 60,000 tins of conserves; 50 sacks of lard; 25 cases of tea.

rickety, black-painted deal kitchen tables and half a dozen locally made chairs whose broken joints had been crudely bandaged with steel wire. The throne, or more correctly, the only chair upon which His Majesty considered it safe to sit, was an old threadbare fauteuil which creaked incessantly under the unaccustomed strain. There were no purple panoplies, but instead improvised awnings of Willesden canvas which shaded the seriously wounded who lay at the feet of their General. Beyond the cordon of sentries who kept intruders at a respectable distance from the King, were war correspondents sitting on ammunition boxes scribbling gory tales of fierce bayonet charges that they had been just too late to see; Turks, who on their own initiative, were bringing water to the thirsty troops; and all the usual panorama of camp life. On the shady shore of the lake, some twenty yards in front of the rickety table and uncertain chairs, the heliograph was flashing orders to the rearguard eyes of the divisions perched on the heights of the mountains opposite.

There was a short, brotherly meeting between King and Prince, following which His Majesty turned to me with a friendly greeting.

Constantine XII looks every inch a king. Tall, and of massive build, he towers well above the average man. The square-set jaw tells of unusual determination; the eyes bespeak merriment; the whole countenance denotes a strong, clean, straightforward character. When the King talks his words come fast, strong and pointed.

" Well! What do you think of my soldiers?

Splendid? Yes, they are wonderful—fought like lions. Do you remember telling me in Salonika that my men couldn't stand up to the Bulgars?" (His Majesty's memory is unfortunately long.) "They didn't think I'd have the courage to attack them, what? Much less that we'd clear them out of their fortifications. Seen Kilkich? Wonderful place. Should have been held for weeks. The truth is that there was no stopping my troops. Their blood was up, and they were determined to hurl the Bulgarian taunts back in their teeth."

"I think, sir," I replied, "that you have astonished everybody—most of all the Bulgarians. But your losses must have been very heavy?"

"Unfortunately yes; we've lost a lot of men—10,000 out of action up till now, including 200 officers and 7 regimental commanders. But it was worth it," reflected the King. "Just imagine, it's only a week since the Bulgarians attacked our outposts, and here we are already at Doiran with the enemy in open retreat. Their resistance here was all in vain. Our artillery has inflicted enormous losses upon them, and they cannot withstand the shock of our bayonet charges. Where are they now? Just over yonder hills; the cannon ceased shortly before your arrival."

I mentioned Nigrita, and the King stiffened as he told me of the horrors committed by the Bulgarian troops in their retreat. But it would serve no useful purpose to record here this part of our conversation. There are journalists who have ventured to criticise King Constantine for the manner in which he lent his name to protests against these atrocities.

I would that His Majesty's critics could have talked with him personally. They would have remarked, even as I did, the pathos with which the royal words were permeated as he told of the crimes committed against civilisation and humanity, the results of some of which he had been a horrified witness. Is it unkingly that a monarch, whose soldier's heart is rent by the sufferings of his people, should appeal to the judgment of Europe? Is it a grievous fault that a ruler should plead the cause of massacred innocents, of butchered babes, of outraged maidens, and of mutilated men before the tribunal of public opinion? We rob kingship of much of its sanctity when we deny it the right to advocate the cause of defenceless humanity. Had there been less criticism and a wider acceptance of King Constantine's first appeals to Christian Europe, the probability is that the subsequent horrors of Demir Hissar, Serres and Doxato would not have further blackened the already too sordid pages of Balkan history.

In the baggage-room of Doiran station, around rough, map-covered tables, sat the General Staff—in their shirt-sleeves. Colonel Dousmanis, as became the "Chief," reclined at the head in a dilapidated deck-chair, while officers with compass in hand measured distances and planned the future movements of the divisions. The General Staff of the Greek army was composed of young men who had passed with distinction through the military academies of Paris and Berlin. They brought to bear upon the problems which confronted them minds highly trained in the science of war, and moved huge masses of men with a facility which is not possessed, if we may judge from the results, by other Balkan armies. A great deal of absurd rubbish has been written concerning the relative fighting value of Servians, Greeks and Bulgarians. Bulgaria produces a warrior who is, physically, probably without a superior in the whole of Europe ; but it must, I think, be admitted by the most violent Hellenophobe that during the two campaigns with which we deal in this book, the palm for organisation and strategy must be awarded to the Greeks. The men were magnificently directed and led, and the writer, who confesses to neither "phils" nor "phobes" where Balkan States are concerned, and whose whole bias, if bias there be, is the result of the humanitarian conduct of the Greek soldier and the administrative ability of the Greek officials, in direct contrast to that demonstrated by the Bulgarians, gives it as his opinion that the most noteworthy generalship displayed during the two wars was forthcoming from the Greek General Staff.

But we have digressed, and must return to Doiran.

The staff very considerately let me into the secrets of their strategy, but as the subsequent movements of the Greek divisions will be unfolded as our story continues, little advantage can accrue from an immediate exposure. Suffice it to say that so well calculated was the Greek advance, that we knew not only where the troops would be at any given hour, but also the probable military history of the morrow. The plot to trap the retreating Bulgarians in the Strumnitza Valley was carefully laid, and had the Servians succeeded in following up their quarry

more quickly, there would have been little left of
the Bulgarian armies from Kilkich and Istib. The
Servians, however, were unable to work round in
time, and the mass of fugitives were thus enabled to
set their course for Pechevo.

.    .    .    .    .    .    .

It was dusk. The sun had just set behind the
western hills in a blaze of glory, and night was
closing in—for there is little twilight in the Near
East. The King stood beside the heliograph on
the lake-side and beckoned me to him. Suddenly
and simultaneously, there flashed from half a dozen
hill-tops on the far side of the lake the messages
from the divisions to the General Staff. It was but
an example of the excellent organisation which then
distinguished the Greek army, and I was expressing
my natural admiration at the incident when " Boom!
Boom! Boom! " there echoed the report of a great
explosion, and before the sounds had died away
there curled up a great cloud of smoke from the road
which skirts the lake. Out came the staff, binoculars
in hand.

" ' Komitadjis,' " said everyone.

" They've blown up some rocks and blocked the
road for the artillery," observed a more thoughtful
mind.

Then a message was flashed from the heights:

" We see our own troops below; probably the
artillery are widening the road to allow the guns
to pass."

Four times were the explosions repeated, when a
cavalryman dashed up and reported that a shell in
an ammunition wagon discarded by the Bulgarians

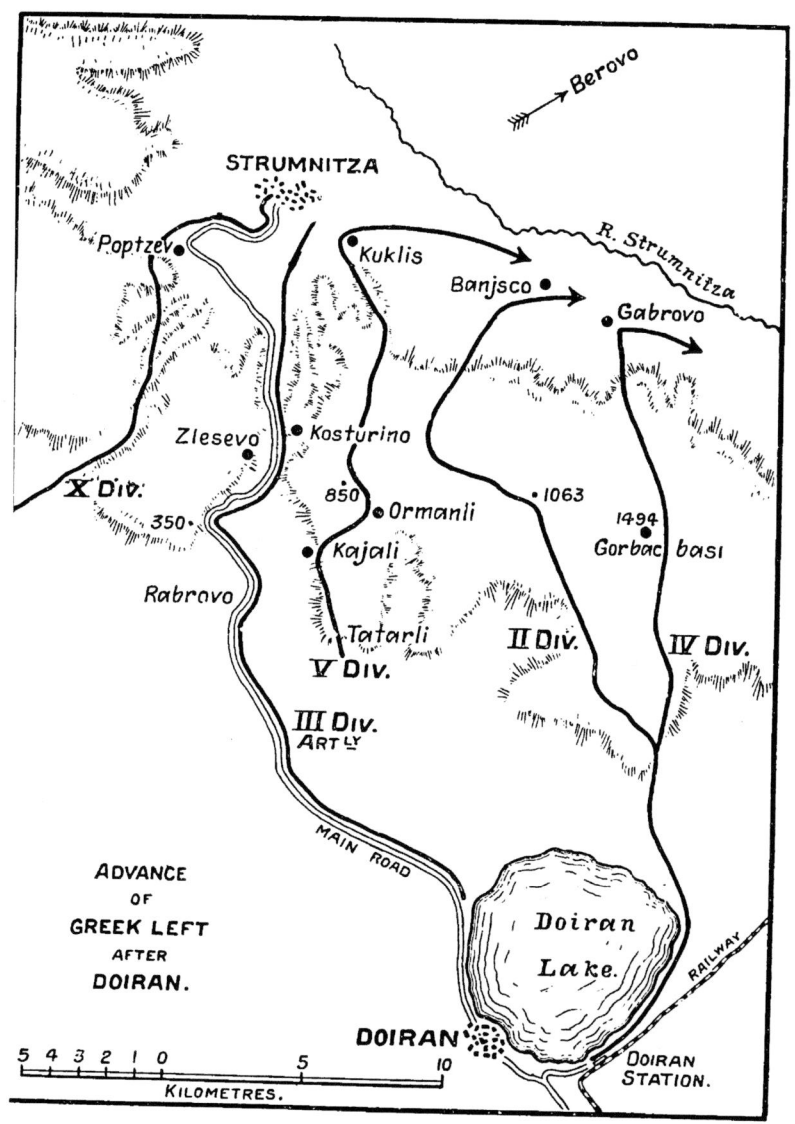

ADVANCE
OF
GREEK LEFT
AFTER
DOIRAN.

having exploded, the wagon was on fire and nobody would approach until it was ascertained that no live shells remained. What the object of this outrage was we shall probably never learn, but the charred body of a Bulgarian irregular was subsequently found among the debris.

Ere the excitement had subsided, night fell and displayed as entrancing a panorama as ever man beheld. All round the lake, nestled on the sides of the mountains and away across the country-side to the south and east, the long columns of smoke which had curled heavenwards the day long, vanished into invisibility and disclosed in their stead the outlines of blazing villages. It was magnificent but awe-inspiring. This, then, was the story of those blackened townships which dotted the land on the Bulgars' trail from Kilkich. Greek villages burned in the thirst for vengeance; Bulgarian hamlets, deserted by their populations and fired lest the Greeks should find a haven there; others burned in revenge by the Hellenes. This was the toll of war. Ruins, ruins everywhere, and the unhappy victims of years of Macedonian strife were now to return to crumbling walls and the remains of what were once their homes. Poor, luckless Macedonians, helpless sufferers from the blight of ages.

# CHAPTER XXVII

It would be difficult to over-exaggerate the military importance of the capture of Doiran. It was, in point of fact, the base of supplies for the two Bulgarian armies operating in Southern Macedonia. To this centre huge quantities of stores were transported from Dedeagatch in preparation for the war, for it was obvious that one of the first operations of the Greek fleet would be to blockade that Ægean port, and it was doubtless with the object of protecting these supplies that Kilkich had been so elaborately fortified.

As I have already insisted, both the Bulgarian II and IV Armies were dependent upon the railway along the Struma Valley on the south of the Belesh Planina, and the roadway in the Strumnitza Valley on the north of that formidable mountain range. The Greek possession of Doiran, therefore, not only threatened the rear of the left wing of Kovatcheff's IV army which was opposed to the Servians at Istib, but also faced the Bulgarian Commander with a probable loss of his only line of retreat, for, though the infantry might disappear over mountain tracks, the retirement of the wheeled transport and artillery would necessarily have to be effected along the Strumnitza Valley to Petritch.

316

Simultaneously with his advance on the town of Strumnitza, whither the Bulgarians from Doiran had retired, King Constantine laid plans to trap both his own enemy and that opposed to the Servians, in the valley. He therefore enlarged upon the strategy which had won for him Sarandaporon, and while ordering his mobile division of Light Infantry (X) to carry out a wide flanking movement on Strumnitza via Terzseli, Cepelli and Poptzevo, he advanced the III Division, together with all his field artillery, along the Doiran-Strumnitza road, and sent the remaining three divisions, with their mountain batteries, over the mountain-tops; the V with the town, and the II and IV with the valley as their destination. It is naturally difficult for anyone unfamiliar with Macedonia to appreciate the enormous difficulty of the task imposed upon these three divisions. Not only is the Belesh a range of imposing altitude, but the only routes over it consist of stony bridle paths which skirt its precipitous mountain-sides. The men were obliged to march up hill and down dale in single file, handicapped by a torrid heat, blinding dust and a weighty equipment.

Incidentally, it now became obvious that the Greeks had succeeded in rendering the desired service to their allies, for immediately they commenced their march on Strumnitza, General Kovatcheff, realising the difficult nature of his position, was obliged (7th July) to commence his retreat from Istib via Radovishte and Strumnitza to Petritch.

The Bulgarians in retreat from Doiran threw up earthworks at Rabrovo, where they doubtless intended to check the Greek advance, and solidly entrenched themselves farther north on the line Zlesovo-Kosturino—850, where the terrain offers many natural advantages to a defending army. The III Division, as we have already noted, advanced along the main road with the massed artillery in its wake, and had on its right the V Division, marching via Tartarli, Kajali and Ormanli, *en route* for Strumnitza; the II was ordered to cross the range by summit 1063, and the IV by summit 1494, towards the Strumnitza Valley.

On 7th July the III and V Divisions operated against the Bulgarian advanced positions at Rabrovo and Ormanli respectively. They were not yet in touch with the main forces of the enemy, but the fact that they were unable to place more than three batteries of artillery in position against Rabrovo, coupled with the stiff inclines which had to be negotiated, and the stifling midsummer heat, rendered the forward movement somewhat difficult. Yet by nightfall they had arrived at a distance of a few hundred metres from the Bulgarian trenches, and several bayonet charges took place, as a result of which the III Division arrived at the summit 350 on the main road, while the V Division bivouacked at Kajali.

Simultaneously, the II Division had arrived at summit 1063, and the IV at Gorbac-basi. In view of the important positions held by the Bulgarians at Zlesovo—850, the II Division received orders to deploy to the left with the object of rendering assistance to the V Division, and advantage was taken of the obscurity of the night to move up the artillery into position. The next day (8th July) the Greek infantry, now assisted by the guns, attacked the Bulgarian trenches; but only to find that the enemy had already begun their retreat towards Strumnitza. Little remained then for the Hellenes but to follow up their victory, and, after capturing nine cannon and a quantity of provisions, they entered the town on 9th July.

On 8th July, the IV Division had been ordered to hold its position at Gorbac-basi, but during the day, a cavalry patrol, having made a reconnaissance towards Gabrovo, reported that the enemy was developing a retreating movement in the valley below. Upon receipt of this information, the Divisional Commander advanced a column of infantry with a battery of mountain artillery, and, having engaged the convoy, succeeded in capturing 24 guns and 400 transport wagons—practically the whole of the artillery and transport of a division. This attack had the further effect of obliging the Bulgarian infantry to retire over the mountains towards Berovo. The same evening (8th July) the II Division descended to Banjsco and joined the IV in the pursuit of the enemy, while the V entered the valley, east of Strumnitza, at Kuklis. The X Division at this time was at Poptzevo, and although the infantry of the III Division entered Strumnitza on 9th July, great difficulty was encountered in advancing the artillery, for the Bulgarians had destroyed a small bridge near Poptzevo and the guns were thus delayed for two days until the necessary repairs were effected by the engineers.

The attempt to trap the enemy in the Strumnitza

Valley had, then, been only partially successful. Thirty-three guns and four hundred transport wagons was indeed a substantial haul, but the principal mass escaped, and great must have been the chagrin of the Greek outposts as they saw the long columns of Bulgarians—soldiers, peasants and transport—making their way eastward. The destruction of the Poptzevo Bridge served the fugitives in good stead, for without the assistance of their field guns the Hellenes were unable to make any effective attack on their enemy, who, it may be added, covered their retreat in an admirable manner.

The situation now called for a new distribution of the Greek left wing. The Servians were at Tzarevo Selo, and the general plan suggested an advance by the two armies on Dubnitza and Kuestendil in two columns. King Constantine therefore decided to detach his III and X Divisions and to send them over the mountains from Strumnitza, via Hamzali and Berovo, to Pechevo, their mission being to serve as a liaison between the Servian and Greek armies. The rest of the divisions of the left (II, IV, V) were ordered to proceed along the valley of the Strumnitza and march on Petritch, which town they ultimately occupied. Between Doiran and Petritch the Greeks captured 37 cannon, 50 officers and 2500 men.

While the left wing of the Hellenic army had been driving the enemy from Doiran and Strumnitza, the centre (I and VI) continued its pursuit of the Bulgarians who had retreated from Kilkich and Lahana north and north-east to the Struma Valley. The fugitives did not attempt to hold Dovatepe, but retired to their fortified position at the entrance to

## KING CONSTANTINE AT HADJI BEJLIK.

King Constantine is no more titular Commander-in-Chief. He is the actual, living head of the Greek army. During the two Balkan wars he displayed great military genius, and it was due to his tremendous personal energy that his troops swept forward with never slackening speed, and gave the enemy no opportunity to re-form their shattered forces.

Derbend Pass. The possession of this pass was
a matter of first importance to the enemy, for not
only did it command the entrance to the roadway
running north to Bulgaria through the famous
Kresna Pass, but it also covered the town of Demir
Hissar.

On the plateau which crowns a high precipitous
rock, rising sheer up from the roadway on the eastern
shore of the Struma River, the Bulgarians had placed
their artillery, including four siege guns, in position.
Before them ran the river, some four hundred feet
wide, spanned only by the railway bridge; to right
and left of the river-bed lay the plain of Serres,
offering neither protection nor points of vantage to
an advancing army. The western side of the stream
is again flanked by mountains—the termination of
the Belesh Planina—but there are here no roads, and
the employment of field artillery is accordingly impracticable. On this occasion the Bulgarians were
probably at least numerically equal to the Greeks;
they possessed a great advantage in cannon, for not
only were the Hellenes unable to bring their field
artillery into action, but they were outranged by the
siege guns; they had, further, thrown up extensive
earthworks on all the commanding heights, and, in
short, held a well-nigh impregnable position. The
odds, therefore, were all in favour of the Bulgarians.

The two Greek divisions (I and VI) advanced
eastward along the railway line, to the north and
south respectively. On approaching the pass the
VI deployed to the south, and crossing the river at
Obaja, engaged the enemy's principal position. The
real object of this strategy was to facilitate the

x

advance of the I Division along the north of the railway line, and on 9th July it arrived at Hadji Bejlik, from whence the troops were able to drive the Bulgarian advance guard out of the village of Kesislik. Further progress was found to be impossible, for the Greek guns were outranged and the troops were unable to reply to the sustained fire of their adversary. During the night, however, the Hellenes moved up their cannon into effective range, and at daybreak the battle recommenced. As the result of an artillery duel of two hours' duration and a decisive attack by the infantry, the enemy was dislodged from the village of Vetrina, following which a regiment of Evzones, with a mountain battery, worked round a small valley and came out upon a height well north of the Bulgarian position at the entrance to the pass, where they unmasked their guns and opened a spirited artillery and rifle fire. Thereupon the Bulgarians, finding their rear once again threatened, commenced to retreat northward, leaving behind them the four siege guns, four *canon-a-tir-rapide* and a large quantity of ammunition. This victory also rendered the Greeks masters of Demir Hissar, where, in addition to the massacred bodies of 140 of their fellow-countrymen, they found enormous stores [1] and 150 Bulgarian state railway wagons.

---

[1] The inventory of the stores abandoned by the Bulgarians at Demir Hissar was as follows : Rye, 1000 tons; rice, 411 tons; salt, 131 tons; flour, 206 tons; bran, 192 tons; barley, 25 tons; wheat, 12½ tons; maize, 160 tons; pepper, 1½ tons; beans, 3½ tons; sugar, 125 cases; tea, 200 cases; cheese, 30 cases; with 40 sacks of horseshoes, 1200 pairs of boots and 70 ambulance wagons

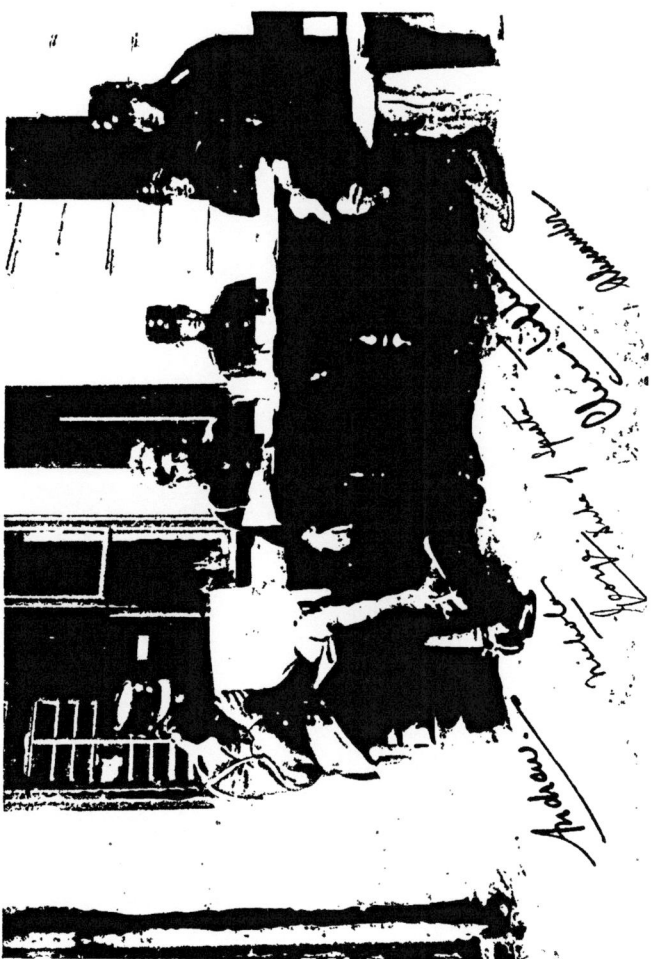

THE GREEK PRINCES IN THE FIELD.
Breakfast at Hadji Bejli.

Prior to their departure from Derbend, the Bulgars dynamited a span of the railway bridge which crosses the Struma, and thus effectively delayed the Greek advance. This was, strangely enough, the first occasion upon which any destruction of the communications had been attempted, and it is somewhat surprising that the Bulgarians for so long neglected so primitive a method of retarding their enemy.

After the capture of Demir Hissar, King Constantine ordered the VI Division to continue the pursuit along the carriage road on the eastern bank of the Struma, and the I Division to advance as rapidly as possible over the mountains in the same direction. At the same time he moved his headquarters up to Hadji Bejlik.

On 13th July, Mr Venezelos arrived at headquarters on a visit to his sovereign. Russia, seeing the catastrophe towards which Bulgaria was inevitably drifting, had proposed that the allies should sign an armistice and enter into conference at St Petersburg. Neither King nor Premier, however, found the Russian proposition acceptable. They were willing enough to negotiate with Bulgaria, but felt themselves unable to enter into interminable discussions. Mr Venezelos was determined to insist upon the creation of three approximately equal states, and thus assure a balance of power; and, already wearied of the never-ending bickering at the London Conference, his motto was now: " Peace on the battle-field."

When I descended from the train at Hadji Bejlik there was much commotion and several white patches on the platform. One answer explained both

phenomena.  The Bulgarians had left us a legacy,
and the surroundings of the station were polluted
with cholera.  The white patches marked the spots
where men had fallen stricken by the fell disease.
Very stringent measures were immediately taken to
prevent a spread of the plague, with most satisfactory results.  This is, perhaps, a suitable occasion
upon which to testify to the efficacy of the anti-
cholera serum with which most of the troops were
promptly vaccinated.  There was a markedly small
percentage of deaths among the men who had been
so treated, despite the fact that the whole of the
ground over which the Bulgarians had passed was
found to be infected.  During the entire campaign
the Greeks only lost a total of 540 men from all
descriptions of sickness, whereas the Serbs found
their ranks decimated by cholera.  Moreover, the
only staff officer who died of the disease was one
who had refused to be vaccinated.  He, a gallant
soldier, passed away at Hadji Bejlik after only
seven hours of acute suffering.

Here, as at Doiran, King Constantine was accompanied by all the male members of the Royal family
save his brother, Prince George.  On the whole,
comparatively little hardship was suffered until headquarters left the railway line, and I bear willing and
thankful testimony to the excellence of the Royal
kitchen.  The conditions of life at Hadji Bejlik
were very similar to those which I have already
described at Doiran, but an added interest was
furnished by the visit of Mr Venezelos.  It was here
that we received news of the horrors perpetrated by
the Bulgarians at Demir Hissar and Serres; here

also that the Moslem Hodja of the village came in and reported that the "Duchman" (enemy), as he called them, had massacred 200 of the inhabitants ere they departed. Anxious to test the truth of this statement, I set off across the fields, and, encountering many peasants, received confirmation from one and all.

It was not until 17th July that the bridge over the Struma River was repaired and the Greeks were thus able to continue their general advance northward. In due course the divisions arrived at the following positions :

| | |
|---|---|
| X III. | On the extreme left in close contact with the Servians. |
| VI. | Menelik. |
| I. | Livournovo. |
| II. | Startzovo. |
| IV. | Giurgievo. |
| V | Mare Kostinovo. |
| VII. | Nevrekop. |

The last to arrive on this new concentration, which stretched almost in a straight line across the country over which the Bulgarians were being swept northward, was Colonel Sautilis, with the VII Division.

After having captured Nigrita, this division hastened north to the bridge over the Struma at Orliak, with the two-fold object of following up the units of the Bulgarian XI Division which it had defeated, and cutting off that means of retreat for the enemy flying from Lahana. On their arrival, however, they found that the Bulgars, having effected their own crossing to the Serres side of the river,

had destroyed the bridge.   In operating their retreat
they left a strong rearguard in position on the left
bank; but under cover of their own guns, the Greeks
collected all the boats available in the vicinity, and,
having succeeded in landing troops on the other
side, delivered a spirited attack on the hostile
batteries the while their engineers repaired the
damaged bridge.

Thus by the evening of 4th July the Hellenes
were in possession of both shores of the river, and
the Bulgarians continued their retirement towards
Serres.   The VII Division was now charged with
the duty of following up the retreat, and, at the same
time, warding off a possible attack on the flank of
the I and VI Divisions advancing towards Demir
Hissar.   While Sautilis was bringing up the balance
of his artillery from Tsaigesi, and making preparations for a renewal of his forward march, the Bulgarians, finding the position of the troops composing
their XI Division precarious in view of the rapidity
of the general Greek advance, decided to withdraw
in the direction of Nevrekop.[1]   On 5th July their
main army abandoned Serres and retired on Porna.
Six days later an irregular force, armed with cannon
and led by regular officers, reappeared and reduced

[1] The appearance of the Greek fleet under Admiral Condouriotis, accompanied by five empty transports, off the town of
Kavala, coupled with the bombardment of the Bulgarian garrison at Leftera, caused the enemy to hasten their evacuation
which, there is reason to believe, had already been decided upon.
Kavala was taken during the night of 9th-10th July.  In their
retreat, the Bulgarian garrison exacted their now customary
revenge on the population of Doxato.  Aided by the local Turks,
they slaughtered men, women and children with an utter disregard for either age or sex, and completed their dastardly
enterprise by destroying the town.

three-quarters of this most flourishing of Macedonian townships to cinders, adding pillage, extortion and massacre to their other abominations. The sacking of Serres casts a lurid light upon the Bulgarian character, and, if it has a parallel in modern times, the same is exclusively provided by the destruction of Kniazhevats by their army operating against the Servians.

Sautilis entered Serres on 11th July. In the meantime the Bulgars began to concentrate around Zernova, a position which controlled the advance on Nevrekop, and against which the Greeks were ordered to march in two columns. Two regiments and one group of artillery were directed via Brodi, and one regiment with the remaining artillery was charged with the capture of Drama, from whence they were to proceed against Zernova. The first column encountered considerable opposition on its march, and there was a running fight for three days (15th, 16th and 17th July) at Brodi and Starchista before, upon the arrival of the second column from Drama, the Bulgars were attacked in force, dislodged from their positions, and driven towards Nevrekop. During these combats the Hellenes captured eighteen cannon, and pressing home their advance, succeeded in taking Nevrekop as the result of an unimportant encounter on 18th July.

# CHAPTER XXVIII

## MOUNTAIN WARFARE

THE Greek army now entered the most difficult phase of the war. The men, it is true, were possessed of that confidence which is born of victory, and the Bulgarians were already a beaten enemy, but the very nature of the country over which they were to pass, abounding as it does in points of vantage where a few irregulars have often held vastly superior and trained forces at bay, must have given the stoutest heart cause for serious thought. Before the Greeks lay tier upon tier of alpine mountains, often towering up to summits over 5000 feet in height. The ways were but stony, winding, and precipitous mule tracks, save the solitary road along the Struma Valley, and that again was commanded by the famous Kresna Pass. Moreover, the country is ethnologically Bulgar; the enemy was constantly nearing home and reinforcements, and there was a constant danger of flank attack from the IV Army, which had retired over the Plaskavitsa Planina.

In his movements, after the capture of Derbend, King Constantine determined to make use of the three natural lines of advance towards the Bulgarian frontier, viz., the valleys of the Bregalnitza, Struma, and Mesta Rivers. The main advance was necessarily fixed along the Struma road—the only road suitable for the transport of wheeled artillery—while the divisions in the Bregalnitza and Mesta Valleys were to act as flanking columns. We have here, therefore, an example of advance in three columns in which each section could, and at times did, carry assistance to its neighbours. Military students who are concerned as to whether, in an advance by parallel columns, each should rely for its own protection upon its own advance guard, or whether the provision of a general advance guard under a single commander is preferable, will accordingly find interesting subject for study. In the operations under discussion, the former system was adopted, but it remains to be ascertained to what extent this was due to the free choice of the Commander-in-Chief, or how far it was enjoined by the excessively mountainous nature of the country.

The Greek general advance coincided with the capture of Nevrekop (18th July). In the centre the I Division took the road; the other divisions, II, IV, and VI, crossed the mountain tracks, the IV and II to the left, and the VI to the right. These three divisions were accompanied only by their mountain batteries; half their field artillery followed in the wake of the I Division, and the rest remained behind with the V Division, which was held in reserve. Their object was the capture of the impregnable Kresna Pass.

Despite the defeats which they had suffered, the Bulgarians, aided by the mountainous nature of the country, were now able to resist the Greek advance, and fought an almost uninterrupted series of rearguard actions. Though the single road which winds along the left bank of the Struma had been destroyed in many places by the retreating enemy, the I Division made satisfactory progress northward. To the left of the river the IV Division, marching over the mountains, encountered three Bulgarian regiments strongly entrenched on Rosalin. During the night of 19th July they delivered an unsuccessful attack on the Greeks, who, the next morning, vigorously assaulted the hostile positions and, after a day-long battle, carried the heights at the point of the bayonet, and secured possession of the mountain. The Bulgars then retired to the high ground around Halilcesme-Dolencesme.

Simultaneously (20th July) the Greek left (III and X Divisions) advanced against the positions held by three brigades under General Teneff, who had previously been driven back on to his entrenched position on heights 1450—Bukovik.

It is important to note that here, upon their own showing, the Bulgarians possessed superiority in numbers as well as position; for Teneff with 24 battalions was opposed to 18 battalions of Greeks.

On 18th July the Bulgarians had had a more or less successful encounter with the Servians between Tsarevo Selo and Kotchana, and Teneff now requested the Commander of the IV Army to send his nearest brigade to make a flank attack on the Greeks holding the line Ratovo-Vladimirovo. He thus brought his forces up to 32 battalions. The battle began at 4.25 a.m., and continued until nightfall with ever-increasing intensity. The greatest obstinacy was displayed on both sides, and the

IN THE KRESNA PASS.
Greek Sappers make a road for the passage of Artillery.

IN THE KRESNA PASS.
A Pontoon Bridge built by Greek Engineers.

losses were unusually heavy, but, having developed an attack on the plateau south of Kaditza, the Hellenes occupied that position, from whence they stormed and carried the hill (1750) itself, after dislodging their enemy from five successive lines of trenches at the bayonet's point. Following this victorious and creditable exploit, they rapidly gained ground to the east along the valley of the Bregalnitza, and ultimately stormed and took the summit of Bejaztepe (1235), which they held against repeated counter attacks. The whole movement, it cannot be other than admitted, reflects the greatest credit upon the Greeks. It was a triumph of which any army might be proud.

On the right, the VII Division, advancing from Nevrekop, encountered the enemy at Kremen, where a stubborn battle was fought, resulting in the now familiar retreat of the Bulgarians.

After the capture of Rosalin the Greek IV Division advanced to Dolencesme; the II moved up to Bresnitza, and the I to Jenikoi. The Bulgarians, having destroyed the bridge over the Struma near Jenikoi, again withdrew, and their centre was, by 21st July, in positions of defence on a line stretching across the entrance to the Kresna Pass.

The Greek staff now determined to outflank Kresna, and the II Division was therefore ordered to advance over the mountain to the east of the defile towards Susitsa. It was this turning movement which determined General Sarafoff, commanding the Bulgarian centre, to abandon the entrance to the pass, and to organise the defence of the great line of formidable mountain ridges—Rugen (summit

850), Orehovo, Uranovo, Ognar Mah—thus effectively covering the exit from Kresna, and protecting the advance on Djumia.

On the Greek left the X Division followed the mountain ridges, while the III Division followed the Bregalnitza Valley, both working in the direction of Tsarevo Selo. General Teneff's forces fell back and entrenched the line Isternik-Hassan Pacha-Rugen, thus giving the Bulgarians fortified possession of a long line of mountain summits stretching from Isternik to Ognar Mah. The whereabouts of the brigade which had been detached from the IV Division to proceed to the assistance of General Teneff against Berovo are somewhat uncertain, but since we know that Teneff himself had been placed under the orders of the Commander of the Bulgarian IV Army, it may be assumed that it continued to operate against the Greek left.

In the Mesta Valley, General Deloff continued to retire before the VII Division of Sautilis, and was eventually ordered to base himself on the head of the valley, and to leave a strong covering detachment in the Pass of Predel Han.

The Greeks now disposed their forces for a concerted attack on the Bulgarian front. The enemy had destroyed the roads, and had placed their batteries in position to bear on the descents into the plain from the mountains. Siege guns commanded the northern extremity of Kresna, through which must necessarily pass the Greek field artillery, and at all points the enemy possessed a superiority in cannon, which had been mounted on the heights. The climatic conditions were of the most trying description, for the Greeks, clothed only in summer khaki, had steadily mounted from the scorching plains of Macedonia on to the high mountain ranges, where they suffered intensely from cold.

The Hellenes deployed as follows: The IV Division attacked Rugen; the II was sent against summit 850 metres; the I followed the main road to Simitli and Uranovo; the VI had as its destination the left wing of the Bulgarian centre at Gradevo and Ognar Mah.

In addition to the battery of siege guns to which we have already referred, the Bulgarians had eleven batteries of field guns mounted in the vicinity of Simitli. On 24th July the I Division began to filter out of the pass into the fire zone. The operation was slow and costly, for the Greek cannon dared not leave the shelter of Kresna, and the infantry made their exit in small groups in order to escape the attention of the Bulgarian guns. Little progress was made during the day, but under cover of darkness the Hellenes rushed some of the hostile outposts, and the next day an attack was delivered in force. When the Greek artillery ultimately came into action the movement was developed, and an heroic assault by a battalion of the I Division delivered the siege guns into the hands of King Constantine's soldiers.

Simultaneously the IV Division, at the cost of appalling losses, stormed and captured the height of Rugen, the II Division drove its opposition north and took Susitsa, and the persistent offensive of the VI Division forced General Sarafoff to retire from the line Uranovo-Ognar Mah. On 26th July the II and IV Divisions delivered a combined attack on Vidren. A terrible and sanguinary combat for possession of this height proceeded all day, and it was only at 9 p.m. that the Greek efforts were crowned with success, and the entire position of Trescovo passed into their hands. The VI Division captured Ognar Mah, and drove the enemy back on summit 1378. Roughly speaking, this great effort cost the Greeks about 3000 casualties.

On the right the VII Division, now greatly reduced in numbers as a result of its incessant but victorious combats, continued its advance, seized the Pass of Predel Han, and established itself at Marova. The III and X Divisions guarded their old positions.

The respective lines occupied by the rival armies at this stage in the operations (the night of 26th July) were as follows:

Bulgarians—Cuka Golek (1551); Golek (1120); Hassan Pacha (1495); Dubostiza-Mostance-Deljanovo (east of Djumia)-Arisvanitza range.

Greeks—Bejaztepe (III); Pantzarovo (X); Rugen (IV); Trescovo (II); Uranovo (I); Summit 1378 and Ognar Mah (II); Marova and Predel Han (VII).

At this time, as a consequence of the failures of the Servian attacks on Banja Cuka and Pobijen (N.E. Kotchana) the Bulgarians were able to dispatch heavy reinforcements to the assistance of their army opposed to the Greeks. Nine battalions and three batteries of field artillery of the I Army came up to strengthen General Sarafoff's left flank (Arisvanitza), and a part of the IX Division was descending on the Greek right via Jakuruda.

The subsequent temporary inactivity of the Servian army now led the Bulgarians, for the first time in the history of the campaign since their initial attack, to take the offensive. The plan of their headquarters' staff was to trap the Hellenes in the Struma Valley. They, therefore, planned to march their divisions from Cuka Golek and Golek (part of the IV Army which had hitherto been opposed to the Serbs) along the Bregalnitza Valley via Trabotiviste and Razloviche, and to accompany the movement by a descent of General Teneff's brigades from Isternik and Pancharevo. This continued attack had for its object the defeat of the III and X Divisions, following which the Bulgars would have marched due east through Bukovik, Djamitepe, and the road to its junction with the Struma at Jenikoi. In the eastern theatre the battalions of the IV Division were to unite with General Deloff's division, recapture Mehomia and Dobrinista, and close in on the Greeks from that point. The plot was carefully laid, and, had it been successfully carried out, would have bottled up the Greek I, II, IV, V, VI, and VII Divisions in the Struma Valley. What happened is as follows:

The divisions of the IV Army concentrated towards Trabotiviste and Razloviche, and part of General Teneff's division advanced by Isternik and Pancharevo, where they likewise concentrated. On neither hand, however, was any offensive undertaken.

On the same day (27th July) General Deloff, employing the 1st and 9th Regiments of the Bulgarian I Division, attacked the summit 1378, and, having driven out the Greek advance guard, turned against the VI Division at Ognar Mah and Asagimah. A terrific struggle raged all day, but thanks to the timely arrival of the VII Division, which had marched from Predel Han via Osenovo, the fight went to the Hellenes. In the evening the stronghold of 1378 was assaulted, and during the night fell to the VII Division. The left of the Bulgarian centre then retired in disorder towards Djumia, and on the evening of 28th July the Greeks held the approaches to Djumia, and on that evening they occupied the following line: VI and VII on height 1378; V, Papasbasi (1079); I, Trescovo; II and IV advancing against the Bulgarians at Hassan Pacha; on the left both sides held their positions without attack.

The defeat administered on the Bulgarian centre had obviously been severe, for the enemy retired north towards Dubnitza, setting fire to a quarter of Djumia in their retreat. They left behind them simple detachments of infantry, who watched the plain south of Djumia.

On the same day the III and X Divisions were attacked by the concentrated Bulgarian forces—greatly superior in number—on both their left and right flanks, which were then to the south of Bejaztepe (1235). One attack was delivered from the valley of the Bregalnitza, and the other from Pancharevo-Cervnik. The Greek position speedily became critical, and the General commanding the two divisions was obliged to withdraw towards Pechevo, and to occupy anew the line Bukovik—

1450. The retreat was carried out in good order, and nothing was lost, despite the fact that the Bulgars were often as close as 35 yards to the guns which had been left to cover the retirement. At Bukovik —1405 the Hellenes offered a further resistance, but in the face of a determined attack by the Bulgarian right, they were obliged to continue their retreat, and in the evening held the positions Bukovik (X) and Pechevo (III). The enemy halted at Umliano.

The Greek IV Division was at Rugen, and the II to the west of Trescovo. They had taken no previous part in the encounter, but in view of the new development, headquarters issued the following orders:

1. The (Greek) right, consisting of the I, V, VI and VII Divisions, is to maintain its positions, keeping watch on Bulgarian movements to the north.

2. The II and IV Divisions are, on the morning of the 29th, to attack the enemy's positions at Leska and Hassan Pacha, in order to cut off the retreat of the Bulgarians who are operating against the III Division.

3. The field batteries of the III and IV Divisions, which are posted on the main road south of the Kresna Pass at Jenikoi, are to cross the river and mount the road via Bresnitza to the heights of Djamitepe. Simultaneously the engineers of these divisions are to prepare the said road for the passage of the artillery.

4. General Damianos (commanding the III and X Divisions) is to resist the Bulgarian attack at

Y

all costs, and, on the first possible opportunity, to counter-attack.

These orders, which are certainly not those of a defeated general, were also communicated to Servian headquarters.

During the night 28th-29th, the Bulgarians delivered a night attack on the heights of Kaditza-Bukovik, held by the Greek X Division. They had evidently been assured that the turning-point in a hitherto disastrous campaign had at length been reached, for they advanced singing patriotic songs, and giving vent to loud hurrahs. The Hellenes, however, held their ground. Next morning, the battle was continued against the two divisions, and during the whole day the Bulgars repeated their determined effort to obtain possession of the coveted heights. The battle finished with a slight advantage to the left wing of the Greek III Division as the result of a counter attack.

A determined combat was meantime raging round Hassan Pacha. The importance of the occupation of paramount heights in the universally mountainous country over which the second half of the campaign was fought, will have become obvious to the layman, and it may be said that the possessors of Hassan Pacha held the key to the existing position. Neither side, therefore, spared any effort to emerge victorious from the struggle, and as a result of the fighting on the 29th, the Greeks succeeded in capturing the advance lines on the foothills.

Headquarters now received the somewhat disconcerting information that several battalions of Bulgarians, descending from Jakuruda, had re-occupied Mehomia, and that the Greek garrison of one battalion of infantry, with three mountain batteries, had been obliged to retreat to Predel Han with a loss of two batteries. The VII Division, which had remained in action to the west of height 1378, was then ordered to return to Mehomia, re-take the town, and restore communications with Nevrekop. The troops made a night march south, and on the morning of 30th July attacked the enemy vigorously, repulsed them, re-took the guns, and restored the *status quo ante.*

To return now to the Greek left. On the morning of 30th July the II and IV Divisions continued their attack on Hassan Pacha. The fight raged without interruption, for it was considered absolutely essential that all the hostile positions on Hassan Pacha and Leska should be captured. The Greek attack was rendered increasingly difficult owing to the presence of Bulgarian batteries in position north of Leska, who shelled the troops vigorously, and subjected them to a cross fire. This development forced the Greek Commander to detach a column from his left flank and deliver a counter attack. The Hellenes now succeeded in driving their enemy from line after line of trenches until, at 9 p.m., they arrived at a distance of only fifty yards from the last Bulgarian positions.

The same day, the III and X Divisions, after having repulsed the Bulgarian attacks of the morning, counter-attacked the enemy with such effect that by evening they had forced them back beyond the line Bukovik—1450. The six Greek batteries had by this time arrived on the heights of Djamitepe, ready for the attack of the morrow.

The orders issued by King Constantine for the operations of 31st July were for the III and X Divisions to push their attack towards the north, and for the II and IV to complete the capture of the heights Hassan Pacha-Leska and to proceed thence to attack the rear of the Bulgarian troops opposing the III and X Divisions. The VII Division was ordered to attack and take Mehomia at all costs. Complete tranquillity prevailed over the centre.

These orders were issued at midnight, and no sooner had they been communicated to the divisions than the telegraph began to tick out the news of the signature of the armistice at Bukarest.

It would appear, therefore, that it was in reality the Bulgars who were saved from a decisive defeat. Their attempt to reach Jenikoi had failed, the capture of Hassan Pacha and Leska was imminent, and their five or more brigades in the south would thereupon have been surrounded by the Servians on the west, two Greek divisions plus six batteries on the south and five divisions on the north. So had the tables been turned, and with this position, and the consequent failure of their strategy before them, it is difficult to see how the Bulgarians can claim to have been robbed of the fruits of their victories by the signature of the armistice. That the Greek troops were tired after their thirty days' continuous marching and fighting against a stubborn and courageous foe is necessarily obvious, and it demands the exercise of little imagination to assume

AT SALONIKA.

The Turkish Mavro constantinos kaga trianti ammah
Greek city...

AT LIVOURNOVO.

King Constantine in meditation.

that the armistice was agreeable to them.  But they were not a beaten, but a victorious army, and I am officially authorised to contradict an oft-repeated falsehood which asserts that King Constantine telegraphed to the King of Roumania beseeching him to impose an armistice as quickly as possible in order to ward off a catastrophy to the Greek army.

The entrance of Roumania into the ring was a disconcerting development for the Bulgarians, and to that extent do they deserve our sympathy; but to suggest that it contributed to the defeat of the Bulgarian army by the Greeks and Servians is to impose too greatly upon our credulity.  The Roumanians crossed the Danube on 10th July.  Their march, in accordance with a previous decision of the Bulgarian Government, was absolutely unopposed, and it did not prevent the Bulgars from planning the great *coup* which, twenty days later, was expected to deliver King Constantine and his army into their hands.

Throughout the campaign the strategy employed by the Greek staff was of a high military order.  It was realised that the most inexpensive method of driving an enemy from a strong position is to combine a determined attack on the front with a flank attack on the rear, and thus threaten the lines of communication.  The Bulgarians always held defensive positions of so great a value that their possession was equal to many battalions, but the frontal assaults were distinguished by such tenacity and bravery (and herein lies the secret of the appalling losses), and the turning movements were executed with such admirable precision, that the tactics were almost universally successful. During their victorious advance the Greeks captured:

| | |
|---|---:|
| Prisoners of war (including 71 officers) . . | 5,330 |
| Cannon . . . . . . . . | 84 |
| Ammunition wagons . . . . . | 215 |
| Maxims . . . . . . . . | 9 |
| Magazine rifles (older models uncounted) . | 7,900 |
| Transport carts; a number exceeding . . | 500 |
| Shells . . . . . . . . | 7,910 |
| Smokeless charges. . . . . . | 589 |
| Cartridges . . . . . . . | 1,200,000 |

At the outset of the war, a greater measure of co-operation between the allied armies was looked for. Indeed, it was fortunate for the Bulgarians that the Servians were unable to press more vigorously upon the heels of their retreat from Istib while the Greeks were forcing the passage of the Belesh Planina and the Derbend Pass. Had this been done, the Bulgarian II and IV Armies might have been taken on the flank and in the rear in the narrow Strumnitza Valley, to their almost certain destruction.

The " War of the Allies " will ever be distinguished by the great part played by the bayonet in the various combats. It is well known that, throughout both wars, the Bulgarians freely manifested their national love of cold steel both in attack and defence. In this, contrary to preconceived impression—for the Hellene was not usually regarded as a bayonet-fighter—they met their masters in the Greeks. The explanation of this phenomenon must be found in the wonderful élan of the Greek infantry, to which attention has already been drawn, and in the fact that the Hellenes were roused to the highest pitch of patriotic endeavour by the treachery of the Bulgarian attack and the atrocities committed *en route* by the defeated army.   It is, however, probable that King Constantine would have found his advance somewhat delayed had his enemy made more effica-cious use of the fire effect of modern weapons when defending fortified positions.

The author's account of the second campaign will be found almost ungarnished with pen pictures of actual fighting.   The reason is not difficult to find. The first business of the correspondent is to get home news of the progress of the armies, and modern warfare is fought over such an extended front that the only safe place for the journalist is at head-quarters (if he can get there), which, nowadays, keeps well in the rear.   Opportunity is some-times presented for a journey to the front, but the visit is of necessarily short duration.   To have followed General Damianos on the Greek left would have permitted the production of much picturesque detail, but the public would thereby have been left in entire ignorance of the doings of the centre and right.   As has been so often repeated of late, the war correspondent of olden days, with his glowing accounts of deeds of prowess on the battle-field, is a thing of the past, and it is only when the journalist can get in "at the death," as was my fortune with the Turks, that he is able to obtain a first-hand story from the firing line.

Yet the correspondent sees enough of the shady side of warfare to pray for its abolition.   It has been mine to laud the grand élan of the Hellene, to admire the wonderful bravery of the soldiers who rushed on regardless of self to almost certain death, to exalt their fortitude in suffering, and to vaunt the sanctity of their sacrifice; and yet, at its best (and in the " War of the Allies " we saw it at its best), war is a hideous, abominable thing. To listen to the never-ending, moaning thunder of the cannon, and to realise that away over the mountains humanity is butchering and being butchered, that life is ebbing out, that women are being widowed, that children are being orphaned, that sweethearts are being sorrowed—all this is the superlative of sadness. And then to watch that long procession of suffering as it wends its way from the battle-field. First, the lightly wounded, on whom fortune has surely shone and who walk with heads in bandage or arms in sling; then those with shattered limbs which must be severed ere the journey ends; then stretcher-loads of ruined bodies which will ever suffer from leaden ball in chest or stomach; then carts piled with dead warriors who will return no more to the fields or shops or offices which they left at their country's call. These are sights to sicken the stoutest heart; these are pæans of universal peace. See what a price Hellas paid for her glory:

| | |
|---|---:|
| Officers killed in action . . . . | 140 |
| Officers wounded in action . . . . | 429 |
| Soldiers killed in action . . . . . | 1,857 |
| Soldiers wounded in action . . . . | 18,888 |
| Officers dead from disease . . . . | 26 |
| Soldiers dead from disease . . . . | 540 |
| A total penalty of . . . . . . | 21,880 |

souls *hors de combat* in thirty days.

# CHAPTER XXIX

## BULGARIAN ATROCITIES

THE title of this chapter will conjure up memories of bygone days in many minds. It was, in fact, nearly forty years ago that Gladstone made all Europe ring with his denunciation of the massacres at Batak. The great statesman coined the phrase " Bulgarian Atrocities " to symbolise the massacre of Bulgars by Turks. In such sense did it continue in use until 1912-1913, when the words were invested with another meaning, and " Bulgarian Atrocities " now stands for the butchery of Turks and Greeks by Bulgars. After the Turkish massacres of 1876, Turkey lost Bulgaria; after the Bulgarian atrocities of 1912-1913 Bulgaria lost a huge tract of rich territory which for eight months she had counted and administered as her own.

This is a part of my narrative which I would fain have left untouched, but with which it is incumbent upon me to deal, because silence on my part might be taken as a tacit acceptance of the lies which have been so freely circulated with the two-fold object of covering up Bulgaria's guilt and rendering Greece responsible for disgraceful crimes of which she is innocent. I have seen some of the horrors of which it will be my painful duty to write. I have personally investigated the truth of others, and I am certainly better fitted to discourse upon them than gentlemen who were never within hundreds of miles of the incidents of which they profess so intimate and incontrovertible an acquaintance.

No part of my information has been culled from refugees. I have had, during my sojourn in Macedonia, an extensive acquaintance with this class of tale-bearer—Greek, Bulgarian and Turkish—and my experience leads me to place little reliance upon their stories. The average refugee assumes that the measure of relief he is likely to obtain will be in proportion to the pathos of his narrative, and, to these imaginative beings, it is ridiculously easy to sandwich in details of a heartrending nature. The reports which I intend to submit are bare, prosaic facts, unillumined by the impressions which are yet vivid in my mind. They are based either upon personal investigation or upon the testimony of European friends who enjoy my unrestricted confidence.

With the Bulgarian massacre of Turks during the first war I have already dealt—inadequately enough it is true—in a preceding chapter. The second war was but a few hours old before they began to exact a bloody revenge for their defeats upon the unhappy Greek populations in the territories from which they were driven. The quarrel between Greek and Bulgar is of old standing. It raged from the invasion of Europe by the Bulgarians (for this race is of Mongol-Tartar origin) until the coming of the Osmanli. Then the race feud comparatively slumbered for centuries, to be revived with the establishment of the Exarchate. It broke out in all its intensity with the introduction of the Austro-Russian reforms into Macedonia. Then began the attempt to Bulgarise the province by coercion and murder, and Macedonia was overrun by Bulgarian "komitadji," following which Greek bands were formed who sought to counteract the new propaganda along similar lines. On the *voivode* Sfetkoff, who was killed in 1905, was found a document which ordered that "any Christian who refuses assistance must be killed in such a manner that the blame may be thrown upon the forest guard, Imam or Déré Bey, and two witnesses must be forthcoming who will persuade the Court that the murder has been committed by some such tyrant." Schopoff (Secretary to the Exarchate) wrote in 1885: "The one enemy of Bulgarism is the Greek," and, at a later date, Sarafoff added that "the destruction of Hellenism must become an article of faith for the Bulgarians." In 1906 the already lurid pages of Balkan history were reddened by accounts of the *pogroms* of Varna, Pyrgos and Anchialos, where unthinkable crimes were committed against the Greeks. When, then, these two nations at length got to grips, this long-nourished hatred found expression in the massacres of Nigrita, Serres, Doxato and Demir Hissar, to speak not of the hundred and one smaller settlements which were devastated during the Bulgarian retirement.

NIGRITA.—Nigrita, under the Ottoman regime was a notable outpost of Hellenism. Its population was exclusively Turkish and Greek, and it is of interest to note that the old traditions of the

Olympic games there survived through the centuries. It will also be remembered that it was the scene of a sanguinary conflict between Greeks and Bulgars in the spring of 1913. When Colonel Sautilis entered Nigrita after a successful encounter with his enemy, he found the hitherto prosperous township transformed into a smoking charnel-house. Of 1450 houses but 49 remained standing. On all hands there were butchered and charred bodies of its massacred inhabitants. At a minimum estimate over 400 people had perished by fire or bayonet, and the town had been utterly destroyed by the Bulgarians prior to their retreat.

SERRES.—Serres is the centre of the tobacco culture and was the richest town in Eastern Macedonia. Prior to the Bulgarian occupation its population consisted of 16,000 Greeks, 12,000 Mussulmans and 1300 Jews. Following its unopposed capture by a handful of irregulars, it became the centre of the Bulgarian Macedonian administration and the seat of General Vulkoff.

One hot July evening prior to my return to headquarters at Hadji Beylik, I met two dishevelled, travel-stained individuals whom I subsequently recognised as American residents of Serres. From thence they had fled afoot to Salonika, and they told me the story of their terrifying experience in that unhappy town. To this I have added details of which their precipitated flight had left them ignorant.

It was on 5th July that the Bulgarian troops, by order of the General Staff, evacuated Serres. Sundry bands of soldiers who attempted to enter

THE TOWN OF SERRES.
Destroyed by the Bulgarians.

the town were driven off by the locally improvised gendarmery, but during the night of the 10th-11th a mixed force of Bulgarian infantry, cavalry and irregulars appeared and placed cannon in position on the hill of Dutli. Early the following morning they opened a cannonade directed against the four corners of the town, after which the troops arrived armed with bombs and crowbars wherewith to force an entry into houses and stores. Civil and military authority was fittingly represented, for, in addition to the officers, there were present Dr Yankoff, Secretary to General Vulkoff, Karagiosoff, ex-chief of police, and Orphanieff, chief of the gendarmery of Serres.

While bloodshed and rape did not come amiss to these disciplined soldiers, loot and destruction were their chief objectives. Houses and stores were ransacked, and then every third building was soused with petroleum and fire applied. Of the frenzied population some rushed out of the town, many being shot down *en route*, while the rest foregathered in the larger houses or sought refuge in water cisterns, gardens and such like places. The number massacred was subsequently ascertained to have been fifty-seven.

The Austrian Consular Agent thus reported to his Consul-General at Salonika:

"A Bulgarian detachment of cavalry and infantry bombarded the town of Serres on Friday morning. After several shells had fallen at various points the infantry entered the town, massacring some of the inhabitants and setting fire to houses and warehouses. The town has been almost totally destroyed; the victims of massacre and fire are numerous; about 20,000 persons are without shelter or clothes, and food is entirely lacking. On Friday, about midday, soldiers of the regular army attacked my house, driving me into the street, together with my family and a great number of persons who, flying from massacre and fire, had taken refuge with me. Immediately afterwards we were led on to the mountain. All the women and children with me were threatened with death, and we only secured our release upon the payment of a heavy ransom. I am safe, but my house having been burned down, I, together with my wife and family, am without shelter or clothes."

Immediately upon receipt of this information, Consul-General Kral left for Serres in company with his Italian colleague, Commander Macchiori Vivalba. After a detailed investigation into the catastrophe, Mr Kral telegraphed the following official dispatch to the Austro-Hungarian Government:

"I have visited Serres in company with my Italian colleague. This once rich, flourishing town is to-day three parts a mass of smoking cinders.

"The Bulgarians abandoned Serres on 5th July; on the 11th troops and 'komitadjis' appeared, conducted by officers and functionaries. They bombarded the defenceless town with four cannon, then pillaged and burned the most beautiful quarters from top to bottom, including our Consulate and many houses belonging to Austrian subjects. The damages are estimated at £1,800,000.

"Fifty of the citizens were massacred, included among them being a Hungarian subject, Albert Biro. Many persons perished in the flames. Five new tobacco warehouses belonging to Herzog & Co. (an Austrian Company) have been destroyed and are still burning; the losses amount to £100,000.

"Our flag was not respected. Our Vice-Consul Zlatko, holding our flag in his hand, was conducted to the mountain with 150 persons, who took refuge at the Consulate, and was only released after payment of a ransom."

When General Ivanoff's army retired from Serres on 5th July, they, after their custom, carried off with them a number of hostages. Seven of these unfortunates were subsequently discovered in a maize field on the bank of the Struma, north of Livournovo, by Mr Georges Bourdon, the brilliant French journalist and author (and with him several correspondents) who gave the following vivid account of the episode:

"An acrid odour assailed our nostrils—that hot, penetrating, persistent, ignoble odour of fermenting flesh. It led us to one body, then another—and what bodies! We found seven. The second was three hundred metres from the first, and three hundred metres separated the second from four others; the last was perched on a bank fifteen metres away. One had, without doubt, stumbled. Another, struck on the back, had fallen on his face, and his body was already half covered by mud carried by the rains. The third had received a terrible blow on the skull from a rifle; the butt, broken off by the force of the blow, lay a few feet away. One body lay on its back with outstretched arms, the fingers clutching the soil; the open mouth still seemed to utter a cry of terror. These victims were not peasants. They were well dressed in fine cloth or serge, with new boots and hats, the garb of an ordinary well-to-do citizen. They were certainly from Serres, for three out of the seven were recognised. They were Dr Papapavlos, Director of the Gymnasium; Dr Chrysafis, the principal physician of Serres; and Mr Stamoulis, the Manager of the Banque d'Orient."

The American manager of the American Tobacco Company told me the story of the butchery of the Greeks who were confined in the prison, and which he himself learned from one of his employees who had been left for dead but who survived for a few days after the incident. The victims were repeatedly beaten by their tormentors, and then, having been ordered to lie down on the floor, were bayoneted to death. The marks where the points had pierced the floor after passing through the bodies were plainly visible.

I have endeavoured to draw a pen picture of some of the incidents which have illumined my life in

Macedonia; but this sinister tableau of the Bulgarian reign of terror beggars description. It is difficult to conceive that it was the work of human beings. The whole of the Greek quarter, together with parts of the Jewish and Turkish quarters adjacent to it, was utterly destroyed. Of twenty-three churches only three remained standing. If it be true that the order, "If it becomes evident that Serres is lost to Bulgaria, the town is to be destroyed," really arrived from headquarters, it must be admitted that the Bulgars obeyed their instructions with characteristic thoroughness.

DOXATO.—It is a short ride from Serres to Drama, and from thence the carriage road to Kavala runs through the once flourishing township of Doxato. The most reliable account of the enormities there committed by Bulgarians in retreat from Kavala was furnished by two French residents, M. and Mme Valette, to M. René Puaux of the *Temps*. This is their story:

"The Bulgars based their decision to punish Doxato on the fact that some of the villagers fired on a few stragglers retiring from Kavala (four cavalrymen and three infantrymen during the morning, and two infantrymen during the afternoon), without, however, hitting any of them. At 6 a.m. on Sunday, 13th July, they surrounded our farm, desiring to arrest my dragoman, my guard and an employee—all three Greeks. I hoisted the French flag, and approaching the Commandant, then some two hundred yards away, protested against these arrests. Finally my point

z

of view was admitted, and two sentries were placed at my door. The order to attack the town was then given, and the infantry, together with four cannon, opened fire on Doxato. One hour and a half later the houses began to burn, and towards midday the fusillade ceased. At that moment two Bulgarian cavalrymen arrived, and, ordering the sentries away, addressed my farm hands (Moslem gipsies to the number of a hundred, who had sought refuge at my house) crying : ' Go to Doxato; there is excellent loot there.' The sentinels and cavalrymen then informed me that they had orders to take my Greek employees to Drama. I got two carriages and went with them. At Drama I found Mr Dobreff white with emotion. ' Ah! Mr Valette,' he said, ' it is a great misfortune. I am going to Doxato to assist the victims and bury the dead. It is a terrible misfortune.' Mr Dobreff left at 3.30 with Mr Bachivakoff, the *sous-préfet*, the *caimakam* of Doxato and the Mayor of Drama. They buried the bodies most in evidence and then returned to Drama."

It was not difficult to glean the truth of what happened within Doxato itself. There were many maimed survivors to tell the story, including one youth (who, despite ten bayonet wounds, was still alive), and several little children in hospital with scalp wounds inflicted by the swords of Bulgarian cavalry as they chased their infant victims across the fields. One girl of tender years saw her father and mother murdered and thrown on to a heap of corpses, and then, with extraordinary intuition, flung herself on to the bloody mass and was left for dead.

The while two detachments of cavalry, commanded by Majors Syneonoff and Birneff, pursued the fugitives, the infantry robbed and then killed their victims. The butchery lasted until 5 p.m. The Europeans who were the first on the scene agree that the total number massacred was not less than 400 (most estimates put it at 600). Many of the bodies had already been buried, some had been burned, but the rest lay yet exposed, and some but thinly covered with a sprinkling of sand. The visitors saw dogs feasting off human remains; courtyards reeking with blood, where batches of the unfortunates had been done to death; large stones covered with the blood-matted hair of the victims whose heads they had battered in; rooms, the floors, rugs, mats and cushions of which were thick with the life's blood of the slaughtered; and walls showing the nail prints where a woman and child had been crucified.

Some of the Turks, to their everlasting shame let it be said, aided the Bulgarians in this devilry, which was carried out in the presence of the Bulgarian officials, Athanese Pristeff (Chief of Police), Vakel (judge), Jean Boroff and Karakoff. The slaughter ended, the perpetrators completed their work by burning down the Greek quarter of the township.

DEMIR HISSAR.—Demir Hissar is a picturesque little Turkish town nestling at the foot of a rocky steep crowned by a ruined castle—the Demir Hissar (or iron fortress) of Ottoman days. They had a sad story to tell us, the inhabitants of this Greco-

Turkish town that basked so peacefully in the Levantine sun. The Bulgars had passed by there and had left their trail of bloody savagery. We received vivid accounts of the butchery from eye-witnesses—still too terrified to exaggerate, if perchance there be in the realms of fiction details more sickening than the facts of Demir Hissar. There were over twenty victims who, left for dead, yet survived the bayonet to tell the tale. Prior to the Bulgarian evacuation, over one hundred non-combatant Greeks, including the bishop and three priests, were arrested by the order of an officer of gendarmery, and imprisoned in an unfinished Bulgarian school. In the yard of the school the murderers caused a circular trench to be dug, and, having grouped their prisoners around this, they poked out the eyes of some, smashed in the heads of others, and bayoneted the remainder. They then flung the corpses into the trench and covered them up. One victim at least was buried alive but miraculously lived to recount the narrative, which was confirmed by a subsequent examination of the martyred bodies. These unthinkable acts, my readers, were committed by soldiers, who coupled with this unparalleled barbarism rape and robbery.

Nigrita, Serres, Doxato and Demir Hissar are the landmarks of the Bulgarian retreat. They can be dealt with individually, because in these cases the savagery found expression on a large scale. It is, however, impossible to tabulate the many instances where similar vengeance was exacted from smaller hamlets or isolated farmsteads, and we have passed unmarked the ravages committed around Kilkich, the tragedies of Xanthie and Dedeagatch, the mutilation of wounded soldiers, and the massacre of the hostages taken from Kavala and Doiran.

Correspondents with the Servian army have a similar tale to tell. Townships destroyed with a ferocity unparalleled by the Turks at their worst, maimed warriors massacred on the field of battle, Moslem peasants slaughtered the while their homes were razed to the ground, old women and young maidens violated by a frenzied soldiery—all these horrors are testified to by a commission composed of one French, one German, and one Norwegian doctor, a French journalist and a cinematograph operator. And the guilt-proving photographs are before me as I write.

Could we have altogether blamed the Greek and Servian soldiers if, maddened by this unthinkable savagery, they had turned with like fury upon the perpetrators? It is necessary to go back over fifty years—to the dark days of the Mutiny—to find a parallel in English history. Then English women were outraged and slaughtered by heathen blacks, and we are told that when British soldiers caught the fiends who committed the foul deeds, they blew them alive from the cannon's mouth. British infantry, at least, gave no quarter, and the world justified their action.

The Greeks returned good for evil. They cared for Bulgarian wounded as for their own, and they respected and fed their prisoners. These things I saw. Yet I do not wish to assert that the record of their army is stainless. I consider it possible, nay probable, that in the case of this conscript army, where almost the entire male population of a country was under arms, and where all sorts and conditions of men were herded together, there may have been some instances where more violent spirits, unnerved by the scenes they witnessed, ran amuck; but I can assert without fear of contradiction that such cases, if they occurred, were isolated, and were perpetrated in flagrant, if excusable, disobedience to the orders issued by the superior officers. The wonder is not that there may have been individual excesses, but that a single Bulgarian escaped the vengeance of the victors. No instance of any atrocity committed by a Hellene came to my knowledge, or to that of either of my colleagues of the Press, although we were free to roam where we willed within the region where the alleged misdeeds must necessarily have been committed.

Let it not be thought that I have delivered myself to the task of stating a case against the Bulgarians. I have merely recorded a page in history. I have passed unheeded the hideous details of the massacres, the systematic spoilation of the rich Greek villages during the Bulgarian occupation, the kidnapping of civilians for ransom, the expulsion of citizens that their property might be seized, and the tender of worthless *raspitchas* (receipts) in lieu of cash. All these outrages against what we are accustomed to term civilisation were perpetrated on the unfortunate subject populations, and were attested and deplored even in the columns of Bulgarian newspapers.

The effect of this conduct on Moslem thought

will be gathered from the following extract from the Constantinople *Ikdam*:

> "We see before us the savage Bulgarians, a race without humanity, without honour, without civilisation. Compare their deeds with those of the Mongolians. You will find them more monstrous. The Bulgarians have walked roughshod over every principle of mercy and humanity—the fundamental pretensions of their pretended Christianity."

[*The numerous " unpleasant " photographs of massacred bodies, etc., in the Author's possession have been omitted from this volume for obvious reasons.*]

# APPENDIX

## THE SECOND SERVIAN CAMPAIGN

[At Greek headquarters we were out of touch with the operations of the Servian army against the Bulgarians, and the information which reached us was limited to the bare facts necessary for the guidance of King Constantine's staff. The object of this chapter, therefore, is but to complete the reader's knowledge of the Macedonian campaigns by a brief recapitulation of the most important details of the Servian victories—AUTHOR.]

THROUGHOUT the long dreary months of armed occupation by the four Bulgarian armies under the supreme command of General Savoff, the fourth, and strongest, was concentrated in face of the contested territory held by the Servians. It comprised a total of 104 battalions and 6 squadrons of cavalry. This force was deployed in an angular formation, having the town of Istib as its summit and running thence along the River Zletovska to the north-east, and to Radovishte to the south-east; the front occupied a total length of about 75 miles. Against this concentration the Serbs placed their I and III Armies, the former (60 battalions, 26 squadrons, 145 cannon and 92 machine guns) stretching from Gievgeli to Veles, and the latter (44 battalions, 8 squadrons, 96 cannon, and 64 machine guns) on the line Veles-Kriva (Egri) Palanka and Gradatz-Golemi vis-Gradishte.

The Bulgarian IV Army on the one hand and the

Servian I and III Armies on the other, were, therefore, practically equal in strength.

An atmosphere of admirable good-fellowship pervaded the rival lines. The outposts exchanged visits, passed the dreary, monotonous hours in card-playing, and, on the day for which the treacherous attack was ordered, the Bulgarians invited the Servian officers of the outposts of Yejevo Polje to a banquet. The Serbs accepted the invitation; the revellers ate, made merry, and were photographed together; but shortly after the return to their respective camps the Bulgarian hosts fell upon their erstwhile guests and butchered them in their sleep. Under such circumstances, without parallel in the annals of organised warfare, commenced the Serbo-Bulgarian War of 1913.

Thereafter events moved quickly. Before the Serbs recovered from their surprise a hostile brigade from Doiran had captured Gievgeli; another from Strumnitza had thrown the Slavs across on to the right bank of the river at Gradsko; Krivolak was in imminent danger; Retke Boukvé was lost; near Istib disaster was averted only by the timely arrival of reinforcements; and the III Army, finding its left in danger of envelopment, was forced to evacuate the height 605.

During the day (30th June) General Putnik and his staff carefully examined the situation, when, far from showing the white feather, it was decided to assume the offensive the following morning. The critical battle for the possession of the Bregalnitza River then commenced.

THE BATTLE OF THE BREGALNITZA.—On 1st July,

hostilities were resumed, and in the early hours the Serbs attacked the position of Drenek, which had been strongly fortified with artillery during the night. The forces engaged were approximately equal in number, and it was realised that success in this first important engagement of the new war would exert a vital influence upon the ultimate result. Thus the battle raged with ever-increasing energy, and rapidly spread towards the summits 550 and 650. Little by little the Servian artillery demonstrated its superiority, until the Bulgars, under a hail of lead and shell, were forced out of their trenches. Then the Servian bayonets rushed across the open, Prince Arsene led his cavalry to the charge, and the Bulgarians fled across to the left bank of the Zletovska River, having abandoned many cannon and machine guns.

At the same time a violent combat was proceeding farther north towards Retke-Boukvé where, after a characteristic struggle between the two armies, the Serbs were again victorious and regained possession of the position. By nightfall, the Servian I Army (under command of the Crown Prince Alexander) occupied the line Lesovo-Ratavitza-Drenek-Tsar Vrh-Golemi vis.

The morning of 2nd July was heralded by the thunder of cannon, and the battle recommenced over the whole line. For some time the advantage swayed from side to side. Attack was followed by counter attack, until at length the Bulgarian front wavered, the white flag of surrender fluttered out along the line, and *parliamentaires* approached the Servian advance guard. This was apparently but a Bulgarian ruse to gain time in which to stave off disaster and to get their artillery up on to the positions of Raitchanski Rid; but the Serbs nevertheless succeeded in capturing 15 field guns, 36 ammunition wagons, 9 mountain guns, 4 machine guns, 100 officers, and 2720 non-commissioned officers and men.

General Putnik now ordered the I Army to take Kotchana, the Choumadia I Division to march on Raitchanski Rid, the Morava II Division to proceed to Toursko Roudovo in order to envelop the left wing of the Bulgarian army, the cavalry division to maintain communications between the I and III Armies, and the Danube I and II Divisions to cover Kuestendil-Kriva-Palanka.

During the day, the operations of the III Army successfully drove back the Bulgarians on to the left bank of the Bregalnitza. The position of the Timok II Division had, however, become increasingly critical, with the result that headquarters found it necessary to send one brigade of volunteers and one of Montenegrins to its assistance. On the evening of 2nd July, the line held by the III Army was Balsan-Ribnik-Dragovo-Chedba.

The 3rd July passed unmarked by any great event. The Servians continued to drive out the remnants of the Bulgarian forces who had remained, and the great battle of Bregalnitza, of the importance of which our brief narrative necessarily conveys no adequate idea, ended with the complete triumph of King Peter's soldiers. The heroism demonstrated by both sides, the countless examples of self-sacrifice, must be left to the reader's imagination. As to the

Serbs, they took little count of the cost, for Slivnitza had been avenged.

RAITCHANSKI RID.—It was to Raitchanski Rid, a veritable natural fortress, that the Bulgars retreated after their defeat on the Bregalnitza. There they assembled their weakened IV Army, with 80 cannon.

The Servians opened the attack on this new position at 11 a.m. on 4th July. For some hours a fiercely contested artillery duel proceeded without any decisive result, but towards the afternoon the Servian guns commenced to gain ground. The Bulgarian fire consistently weakened, until, at 4 p.m., the combined Servian and Montenegrin infantry rushed across the open and took the hostile trenches at the point of the bayonet. Once masters of Raitchanski Rid, the Serbs marched on Kotchana, which town, after a short combat, fell into their hands at 10 a.m. on 5th July.

KRIVOLAK-ISTIB.—While the right wing of the Bulgarian army had suffered the pangs of defeat, the battle had been more favourable to their arms at Krivolak and Istib. For four days a fierce and sanguinary engagement raged at Krivolak. The Servian Timok II Division defended resolutely, but was driven back step by step until, exhausted and decimated, it was forced to retire, and concentrated at the village of Kaslare on 5th July. Here, strengthened by its reinforcements, it succeeded in holding its own in the face of the persistent attack of two Bulgarian divisions.

In the meantime the Greeks were approaching Strumnitza, thus forcing the Bulgarians, their line of retreat threatened, to deliver a final and desperate attack on the Servian forces. The onslaught was subsequently repulsed, and General Kovatcheff was obliged to operate the retreat of his artillery and transport towards the Strumnitza Valley.

Around Istib the battle raged with murderous intensity without any definite advantage to either side. The precarious situation of the Timok II Division at Krivolak, moreover, obliged the Servian III Army to hold its position on the right bank of the Bregalnitza River. After the capture of Raitchanski, however, General Putnik was able to dispatch the Choumadia I Division to the assistance of the III Army. This division arrived after a forced march of 24 hours at Hadrifakeik at 8 o'clock on the evening of 5th July; but despite this reinforcement of his troops the Commander hesitated to take the offensive. On 8th July, Servian headquarters ordered him to capture Istib at all costs, and instructed the I Army to detach the Morava II Division, which was to cross the Bregalnitza between Tsernovtsi and Koutchitchino, to operate against the rear of the Bulgarian army.

The Bulgarians then became convinced of the uselessness of further resistance, and hastily abandoned Istib—the capture of which completed the Servian victory over the whole front. They retreated from Kotchana towards Tzarevo-Selo, and from Istib through Radovishte, which town was entered by the Servian cavalry on 9th July.

GOVEDARNIK.—July 17th to 22nd.—After the occupation of Istib, Radovishte and Kotchana, the Servian III Army concentrated around the latter town. They were stoutly opposed, and incessant fighting proceeded, but the country was of so mountainous a nature that the use of field artillery was impracticable save along the road Kotchana-Tzarevo-Selo. No decisive result was registered until the 19th when, after a severe engagement, the Serbs captured Tserni Kamen (825) and advanced towards Grlen. During the night and the morning of 20th July the Montenegrins continued the assault and succeeded in occupying several Bulgarian positions, but were subsequently counter-attacked and forced back on to the line Presseka-Bezikovo. Following up their victory the Bulgars continued to drive the mountaineers before them, and some sections of their army actually succeeded in recrossing the Bregalnitza. A heavy fog now settled like a pall over the battle-field, and, profiting by the cover thus produced, the Bulgars turned the Montenegrin right, occupied Veliki, and attacked Little Govedarnik.

The situation then became critical, and so continued until the Commandant of the I Army, in the nick of time, ordered his right to operate a demonstration on the Bulgarian flank. The movement was successful and the Serbs regained the offensive, following which there was a hand-to-hand fight in the trenches at Little Govedarnik, resulting in the retreat of the Bulgarians.

At Great Govedarnik, however, the Bulgars withstood all the Montenegrin efforts to drive them out. Next day a division of reinforcements arrived from Stratsin to the the assistance of the allies, and when the Bulgarian troops recommenced their offensive from Grlen, they were met by the fire of the Servian artillery.

The 21st July was marked by a hotly contested artillery duel at Koutchevnitza, on the right bank of the Kamenitsa, and the following day the Serbs delivered a general attack on the front and flank of Great Govedarnik. For some time heavy fighting proceeded. The Bulgarians now made a determined effort to reverse the fortunes of war, but at length, and undeterred by the appalling casualties of the day, the Serbs delivered a final assault, and captured the position at a cost of 3000 men *hors de combat.*

The object of the Servian army was to advance their I Army towards Kuestendil, and their III Army towards Doubnitza; but the Bulgarians were in great force, and strongly fortified in almost inaccessible positions. The country over which the fighting now proceeded is exceedingly mountainous in nature—the average height of the tors being 3500 feet above sea level. Progress was, therefore, but slow, and though the combats continued unceasingly, the Serbs hesitated to pay the toll which the capture of the Bulgarian positions would have entailed. It is probable that, had the Servians proceeded with the determination which characterised their operations on the Bregalnitza, they would have succeeded in driving the Bulgarians over their old frontier. But their military object had been gained, and though their subsequent comparative inactivity permitted the enemy to detach large forces from this front and send them over against the Greeks in the Struma Valley, it is but little wonder that, after the sacrifice of manhood which had been occasioned during the two wars, the Serbs should have been content with the successes already gained.

Once Servia realised the disadvantage to which the sacrifice of manhood had been occasioning the Greek army, the Servian III Army was ordered to renew a vigorous offensive and to get into contact with the Hellenic forces. A determined attack was then delivered against the hostile positions at Grlen, and, despite the desperate resistance offered by the Bulgarians, the first line of trenches was taken when the news arrived of the impending conclusion of the armistice at Bukarest.

THE NORTHUMBERLAND PRESS, THORNTON STREET, NEWCASTLE-UPON-TYNE

Lightning Source UK Ltd.
Milton Keynes UK
UKOW03f1919090514

231432UK00001B/32/P